Writing Centers

Writing Centers

Theory and Administration

Edited by

Gary A. Olson
University of North Carolina, Wilmington

National Council of Teachers of English
1111 Kenyon Road, Urbana, Illinois 61801

NCTE Editorial Board: Thomas L. Clark, Julie Jensen, John S. Mayher, Elisabeth McPherson, Zora Rashkis, John C. Maxwell, *ex officio,* Paul O'Dea, *ex officio*

Book Design: Tom Kovacs for TGK Design

NCTE Stock Number 58781

Library of Congress Cataloging in Publication Data
Main entry under title:

Writing centers.

   Bibliography: p.
   1. English language—Rhetoric—Study and teaching—
Addresses, essays, lectures.   2. English language—
Composition and exercises—Study and teaching—
Addresses, essays, lectures.   3. Resource programs
(Education)—Management—Addresses, essays, lectures.
4. Tutors and tutoring—Addresses, essays, lectures.
I. Olson, Gary A., 1954–
PE1404.W695   1984   808'.042'071   84-16518
ISBN 0-8141-5878-1

Contents

III. Special Concerns

Preface

The writing center is an indispensable adjunct to many college and university writing programs, and it is growing in importance on the secondary school level as well. Tutorial writing services have always been diverse in their pedagogies, philosophies, and physical makeups. But the writing center's period of chaotic adolescence is nearly over. Center directors are slowly articulating common goals, objectives, and methodologies; and writing centers are beginning to take on a common form, to evolve into a recognizable species.

Now that the field of writing center operation is about to enter adulthood, directors are beginning to examine the concepts underlying their work. Hence, one of the principal objectives of this book is to provide a forum for center directors to speculate formally on theoretical and administrative matters germane to the writing center. *Writing Centers: Theory and Administration* is in fact the first book to examine the pedagogical theories of tutorial services and to relate them to actual center practices.

Part I, Writing Center Theory, is comprised of seven essays discussing purely theoretical and pedagogical issues. Kenneth Bruffee, an influential pioneer of "collaborative learning," begins the section with a discussion of the nature of knowledge and the manner in which students "acquire" it; this discussion leads to a cogently articulated rationale for peer tutoring. John and Tilly Warnock attempt in Chapter 2 to establish a working theory of the writing center. In Chapter 3 Stephen North, coeditor of the *Writing Center Journal,* reviews the major research on writing centers and suggests directions this research should take in the future.

North's coeditor, Lil Brannon, and C. H. Knoblauch provide in the fourth chapter a philosophical perspective on writing centers, urging directors to constantly reexamine their professional assumptions about center pedagogy. Following Brannon and Knoblauch's advice, Patrick Hartwell scrutinizes in the fifth chapter some commonly held assumptions about composition pedagogy and writing center practices. In Chapter 6 Karen Spear applies principles of cognitive theory to writing center methodology, discussing specifically how to promote the cognitive development of tutees. The final essay in Part I is a Delphi study conducted by Bené Scanlon Cox; this research report attempts to establish clearly defined priorities and guidelines for future development of the writing center.

Part I is concerned exclusively with theoretical issues. Most of the essays deal with establishing a conceptual basis for writing centers and peer tutoring. In addition, most of the essays in this section, particularly the chapters by Bruffee, Hartwell, and Brannon and Knoblauch, are of direct interest not only to writing center directors but to all teachers of writing.

Part II, Writing Center Administration, emphasizes the practical concerns of writing center administrators. This section is very much a "how to" manual for both novice and experienced directors. The first essay in Part II deals with how to establish a writing center at a two-year institution, but it is relevant also to administrators in four-year colleges and even to directors of existing centers. In the second essay, Chapter 9, Peggy Jolly uses her expertise as a grant writer to explain how directors can secure funds from a variety of sources. And in Chapter 10, C. Michael Smith discusses how to streamline a center's paperwork and filing system.

The last three essays of Part II deal with center staffing. Loretta Cobb and Elaine Elledge discuss staffing a center with peer tutors. Going one step further, Linda Bannister-Wills illustrates an effective tutor training program. And Jeanette Harris completes the discussion by explaining how to devise an in-house tutor training manual.

Part III, Special Concerns, deals with topics of interest to individual directors. These essays often mix theoretical concerns with practical methodology, both pedagogical and administrative. The first essay in this section (Chapter 14) addresses a key concern of many centers: attitudinal problems of faculty, tutors, and tutees. In Chapter 15, Mary Croft deals with one category of the attitude question: how to cope with the tutee who resists writing center assistance. Thomas Nash then examines the subject of teaching invention in the writing center and provides a clever analysis of the theoretical links between the invention process and the tutorial. Rodney Simard discusses in Chapter 17 the "professional role" of the tutor—a unique essay from the perspective of a skilled tutor.

The final two essays in this collection are companion pieces in that both discuss expanding center services. Alexander Friedlander explains how to integrate an ESL program into a writing center, while W. Keats Sparrow and Bertie Fearing discuss how to incorporate the tutoring of technical and business writing into a center. In light of the influx of foreign students and technical-business writers into colleges and universities, both essays are of particular interest to center directors who must meet the needs of these students.

The final section of the book is an extensive bibliography of articles, books, and dissertations about writing centers, tutoring, and issues relevant to center directors.

The publisher and editor wish to acknowledge their gratitude to Thom Hawkins—a leader in the field of writing center administration—for the Introduction which he has contributed to this book. It is hoped that this book will provide center directors with a sense of focus for further study of writing centers, their objectives and methodologies, for only through focused research will center directors be able to continue the unified, professional growth they have begun in the last decade.

Gary A. Olson

Introduction

The growth of writing centers is but one part of a search for new vitality in the humanities. This search includes making fundamental changes not only in how writing is taught, but also in how writing is defined. Most teachers can identify good writing, but there is much less consensus on how good writing gets done and how it can be taught. Several new models of the writing process are being proposed, whereas a short time ago classroom teachers had no such models, and few tried seriously to teach writing as a process. Today instructors can inform their teaching from numerous new studies in fields such as rhetoric, cognitive psychology, and sociolinguistics.

The growing pains of writing centers are symptomatic of a general state of flux and tension in the humanities, a condition caused by dropping enrollments and a changing student body. Writing centers are coming of age in the midst of this upheaval because they make room, provide space and time, for students to talk about ideas, to explore meaning, and to freely engage in the trial and error of putting their thoughts into writing.

This congenial environment for learning how to think and to write is based on tutoring, chiefly one-on-one instruction, but also the kind of tutoring that sometimes, though never exclusively, involves small group work. As the number of nontraditional students increased in the 60s and 70s, it became more and more apparent that writing could not be taught to a classroom of twenty, thirty, or more students. Such a pedagogy had always been a marginal method at best. In large classes you can teach grammar, you can teach literature, you can teach rhetorical patterns, but you cannot teach writing. The best way, maybe the only way, to learn how to write is by writing and rewriting. Beyond practicing writing, the writer can also learn a good deal by talking to a sensitive and responsive reader before and during writing and rewriting. The chief pedagogy of writing centers, tutoring, recognizes that writing is at once the most personal and the most social task students engage in. As Kenneth Bruffee explains in this collection, what we know, hence what we write, is a product of social interaction: our talk. Students' writing can improve through close and regular contact with a supportive, yet critical audience. Trained tutors, peer or otherwise, know how to listen and how to engage students in a constructive dialogue that becomes an essential part of the composing process.

As researchers and scholars are redefining what it means to write, so too are writing centers helping to redefine what it means to teach writing. Those who teach in writing centers do not play the role of shaman, guru, or mentor, but instead are the architects and partners of collaborative learning. They redesign the learning environment so that more of the responsibility and the activity of learning is shifted onto the learner. There is a sharing of power, accompanied by the recognition that, since we are all learners, we are all capable of being teachers and that teaching and learning are not separate but complementary activities. In tandem with the new theories of composition that emphasize process, the teaching practices of writing centers are influencing the way writing is taught in the classroom. It is now quite common during classtime to conference and to form small peer groups where students in effect tutor each other. Many teachers no longer mark student papers in private, but instead respond in person during a conference with the author, a practice that is indispensable to writing center pedagogy. Writing centers are one of the chief agents of this movement toward individualization and collaborative learning, but there has been no extensive documentation of their impact.

Most composition researchers and scholars, when looking for areas of inquiry, do not go to writing centers; they go to the classroom. As a result, there is not only an abundance of ignorance about the way writing centers have shaped classroom teaching, but writing center professionals themselves suffer a knowledge gap. As Steve North once noted in a scathing self-indictment, ". . . *we don't know what we are doing.*" A less incriminating observation might be that much more is going on in writing centers than meets the eye. Take for example all of the classroom instructors who have been able to write better essay topics based on feedback from writing center tutors and staff who explain how students react to certain assignments. More real learning is going on than anyone realizes because students are spending more time on what matters and getting more from their contacts with instructors and tutors. There is a flexibiity in the teaching of composition that was not possible ten years ago—teachers and tutors can accommodate a more diverse student body and can talk with students about their writing in a variety òf disciplines, not just English.

Writing centers are doing so much now with collaborative learning that often their practice outstrips their theoretical grasp of principles behind their work. For instance, in the Berkeley writing center peer tutors have been showing selected students videotapes of their tutoring sessions in an effort to stimulate greater involvement, specifically to increase the ratio of student to tutor talk. Tutors have seen significant improvement in both the students' learning behavior and writing, but no one is quite sure how the changes come about. Despite impressive, recent advances in theoretical understanding by specialists, writing centers daily discover new elements in students' writing processes that cry for further investigation. Writing centers now are so close, so intimate with their students' approaches to learning that they often cannot see the forest for the trees. Conjecture and experimentation frequently substitute for more solid understanding. If writing centers are to continue making substantial contributions to classroom practices and curricula, if they are to reach a productive and long-lasting maturity, they must do more than patch together fragments of successful practices.

To begin with, writing centers can ally themselves with faculty who are redefining what it means to teach writing. Writing centers are not alone in meeting the challenge of teaching the new constituency of nontraditional students and the new methodologies of collaborative learning. Faculty from various departments look to the writing center for knowledge and expertise in these areas, but also for a place to share experiences, to compare notes. And more and more faculty from traditional English departments as well are becoming involved with writing center activities. In years to come there will be an increasing demand on writing centers to participate in campuswide efforts to improve the teaching of writing. As traditional faculty look for ways to change their teaching techniques, writing centers will be asked to explain new approaches. Writing centers must draw from their first decade of experience, must gather together their successes (and the shards of their failures), so that they can involve themselves more fully in the new, campuswide interest in teaching composition. There is going to be a greater need than ever before to explain how writing centers do what they do.

The essays in this book suggest many areas for thinking, research, and future study. Certainly more could be written on the group tutorials that Karen Spear feels writing centers underplay, and Patrick Hartwell's conclusions about a tutor's role in helping students translate written-down speech seem a tantalizing invitation to further speculation. But even while writing center staff are concerned with issues that help build their professional profile on the larger, national level, they must remember that a significant source of their strength lies in their responsiveness to the special needs of their local students. Unlike an academic department, writing centers have no claim to a universal discipline. When teachers meet and talk about "English" or "history" or "philosophy," they share an understanding based on a canon of knowledge, but when the talk turns to writing centers, you will find much less agreement about content, purpose, and scope of operations. Rather than a weakness, however, this eclecticism points to an underlying strength: writing centers must be resourceful because they tend to be a school's most concerted response to the individual needs of its students, especially the nontraditional student.

Consequently, writing centers and learning centers are in a very sensitive position (academically speaking) on campus. They must be very responsive to change, and they have a great deal to learn about. They must see their local concerns as their major challenge. When there is a new clientele to serve, whether they be returning women, Asian immigrants, technical writers, or deaf students, writing centers not only face new instructional challenges, but also are in a superb position to make discoveries about language development and composition. Such immediate needs provide writing centers with the opportunity to test existing knowledge and explore new avenues of instruction. What writing centers can learn about teaching writing to their special populations can help all teachers of writing.

By publishing volumes such as this, writing center staff can enlarge their sphere of influence while at the same time take a hand in directing their own growth. No one knows for sure how "big" writing centers will get, how entrenched they might become in the next twenty years on our campuses, but they have made an impression that I think will be strongly felt for a very long time. Writing centers have concentrated on student learning rather than on a "subject" of study. Writing centers stand for an attitude toward students, toward writing, and toward teaching that puts control and responsibility for learning back into the hands of students. Tilly and John Warnock suggest, in their chapter in this book, that this "liberatory" function of writing centers may best be carried out if they remain on the sidelines and avoid being swallowed up by the larger academic units. In other words, whatever the fiscal future of writing centers may be, they will always be important and influential if they remain committed to the kind of tutoring that focuses "on meaning, not form; on process, not product; on authorial intention and audience expectation, not teacher authority or punitive measures; on holistic and human concerns, not errors and isolated skills."

Such an energetic commitment to tutoring presents something of a double-bind to dedicated writing center staff who wish to make a contribution beyond their local realm, to get the word out, to help shape the future by participating in a discourse, but who have a strong obligation to spend their time with students. So, this volume represents a rare gift of time from a few of those many committed professionals, but it is also an invitation to others to get involved. Not only could faculty from various departments (psychology, English, education, sociology, linguistics, rhetoric, come quickly to mind) find fertile ground for study, harried writing center instructors could add new perspective to their work with students if they fought for and got release time to write and publish. The articles in this collection demonstrate that it is well worth the effort.

Thom Hawkins

I Writing Center Theory

1 Peer Tutoring and the "Conversation of Mankind"

Kenneth A. Bruffee
Brooklyn College
City University of New York

The father of "collaborative learning," Bruffee argues that thought and writing are special artifacts grounded in conversation. As such, both are fostered by teaching that emphasizes conversational exchange among peers. Besides providing a theoretical basis for peer tutoring in writing centers, the author answers the most common objections to collaborative learning and suggests how it might be extended to other areas of humanistic study.

The beginnings of peer tutoring lie in practice, not in theory. A decade or so ago, faculty and administrators in a few institutions around the country became aware that, increasingly, students entering college had difficulty doing as well in academic studies as their abilities suggested they should be able to do. Some of these students were in many ways poorly prepared academically. Many more of them, however, had on paper excellent secondary preparation. The common denominator among the poorly prepared and the apparently well prepared seemed to be that, for cultural reasons we may not yet fully understand, all these students had difficulty adapting to the traditional or "normal" conventions of the college classroom.

One symptom of the difficulty was that many of these students refused help when it was offered. Mainly, colleges offered ancillary programs staffed by professionals. Students avoided them in droves. Many solutions to this problem were suggested and tried, from mandated programs to sink-or-swim. One idea that seemed at the time among the most exotic and unlikely (that is, in the jargon of the Sixties, among the most

I am indebted for editorial advice in revising this essay to Marjory Pena, Baruch College, CUNY, and for conversation regarding issues raised in the essay to her and other Fellows of the Brooklyn College Institute for Training Peer Tutors. The Institute was supported by a grant from the Fund for the Improvement of Postsecondary Education.

"radical") turned out to work rather well. Some of us had guessed that students were refusing the help we were providing because it seemed to them merely an extension of the work, the expectations, and above all the social structure of traditional classroom learning. And it was traditional classroom learning that seemed to have left these students unprepared in the first place. What they needed, we had guessed, was help of a sort that was not an extension but an alternative to the traditional classroom.

To provide that alternative, we turned to peer tutoring. Through peer tutoring, we reasoned, teachers could reach students by organizing them to teach each other. Peer tutoring was a type of collaborative learning. It did not seem to change what people learned but, rather, the social context in which they learned it. Peer tutoring made learning a two-way street, since students' work tended to improve when they got help from peer tutors and tutors learned from the students they helped and from the activity of tutoring itself. Peer tutoring harnessed the powerful educative force of peer influence that had been—and largely still is—ignored and hence wasted by traditional forms of education.[1]

These are some of the insights we garnered through the practical experience of organizing peer tutoring to meet student needs. More recently, we have begun to learn that much of this practical experience and the insights it yielded have a conceptual rationale, a theoretical dimension, that had escaped us earlier as we muddled through, trying to solve practical problems in practical ways. The better we understand this conceptual rationale, however, the more it leads us to suspect that peer tutoring (and collaborative learning in general) has the potential to challenge the theory and practice of traditional classroom learning itself.

This essay will sketch what seems to me to be the most persuasive conceptual rationale for peer tutoring and will suggest what appear to be some of the larger implications of that rationale. The essay will begin by discussing the view of thought and knowledge that seems to underlie peer tutoring. Then it will suggest what this view implies about how peer tutoring works. Finally, the essay will suggest what this concept of knowledge may suggest for studying and teaching the humanities.

Conversation and the Origin of Thought

In an important essay on the place of literature in education published some twenty years ago, Michael Oakeshott argues that what distinguishes human beings from other animals is our ability to participate in unending conversation. "As civilized human beings," Oakeshott says,

> we are the inheritors, neither of an inquiry about ourselves and the
> world, nor of an accumulating body of information, but of a con-

> versation, begun in the primeval forests and extended and made more articulate in the course of centuries. It is a conversation which goes on both in public and within each of ourselves. . . . Education, properly speaking, is an initiation into the skill and partnership of this conversation in which we learn to recognize the voices, to distinguish the proper occasions of utterance, and in which we acquire the intellectual and moral habits appropriate to conversation. And it is this conversation which, in the end, gives place and character to every human activity and utterance.[2]

Arguing that the human conversation takes place within us as well as among us and that conversation as it takes place within us is what we call reflective thought, Oakeshott makes the assumption that conversation and reflective thought are related in two ways: organically and formally. That is, as the work of Lev Vygotsky and others has shown,[3] reflective thought is public or social conversation internalized. We first experience and learn "the skill and partnership of this conversation" in the external arena of direct social exchange with other people. Only then do we learn to displace that "skill and partnership" by playing silently, in imagination, the parts of all the participants in the conversation ourselves. As Clifford Geertz has put it, "thinking as an overt, public act, involving the purposeful manipulation of objective materials, is probably fundamental to human beings; and thinking as a covert, private act, and without recourse to such materials, a derived, though not unuseful, capability."[4]

Since what we experience as reflective thought is organically related to social conversation, the two are also related functionally. That is, because thought originates in conversation, thought and conversation tend to work largely in the same way. Of course, in thought some of the limitations of conversation are absent. Logistics, for example, are no problem at all; I don't have to go anywhere or make an appointment to get together with myself for a talk. I don't even need to dial the phone, although I do sometimes need a trip to the coffeemaker. And in thought there are no differences among the participants in preparation, interest, native ability, or spoken vernacular. On the other hand, in thought some of the less fortunate limitations of conversation may hang on. Limitations imposed by my ethnocentrism, inexperience, personal anxiety, economic interests, and paradigmatic inflexibility can constrain my thinking just as they can constrain my conversation. If my talk is narrow, superficial, biased, and confined to clichés, my thinking is likely to be so, too. Still, it remains the case that many of the social forms and conventions of conversation, most of its language conventions and rhetorical structures, its impetus and goals, its excitement and drive, its potentially vast range and flexibility, and the issues it addresses are the sources of the forms and conventions, structures, impetus, range and flexibility, and the issues of reflective thought.

The formal and organic relationship I have been drawing here between conversation and thought illuminates, therefore, the source of the quality, depth, terms, character, and issues of thought. The assumptions underlying this argument differ considerably, however, from the assumptions we ordinarily make about the nature of thought. We ordinarily assume that thought is some sort of "essential attribute" of the human mind. The view that conversation and thought are fundamentally related assumes instead that thought is a social artifact. As Stanley Fish has put it, the thoughts we "can think and the mental operations [we] can perform have their source in some or other interpretive community."[5] Reflective thinking is something we learn to do, and we learn to do it from and with other people. We learn to think reflectively as a result of learning to talk, and the ways we can think reflectively as adults depend on the ways we have learned to talk as we grew up. The range, complexity, and subtlety of our thought, its power, the practical and conceptual uses we can put it to, as well as the very issues we can address result in large measure (native aptitude, the gift of our genes, aside) directly from the degree to which we have been initiated into what Oakeshott calls the potential "skill and partnership" of human conversation in its public and social form.

To the extent that thought is internalized conversation, then, any effort to understand how we think requires us to understand the nature of conversation; and any effort to understand conversation requires us to understand the nature of community life that generates and maintains conversation. Furthermore, any effort to understand and cultivate in ourselves a particular kind of thinking requires us to understand and cultivate the community life that generates and maintains the conversation from which a particular kind of thinking originates. The first steps to learning to think better are to learn to converse better and to learn to create and maintain the sort of social contexts, the sorts of community life, that foster the kinds of conversations we value.

These relationships have broad applicability and implications far beyond those that may be immediately apparent. For example, Thomas Kuhn has argued that to understand scientific thought and knowledge, we must understand the nature of scientific communities.[6] Richard Rorty, carrying Kuhn's view and terminology further, argues that to understand any kind of knowledge, we must understand what Rorty calls the social justification of belief; that is, we must understand how knowledge is generated and maintained by communities of knowledgeable peers.[7] Stanley Fish completes the argument by positing that these "interpretive communities" are the source not only of our thought and the "meanings" we produce through the use and manipulation of symbolic structures, chiefly language; interpretive communities may also be in large measure the source of what we regard as our very selves.[8]

Conversation, Writing, and Peer Tutoring

The line of argument I have been pursuing has important implications for educators, especially those of us who teach composition. If thought is internalized public and social talk, then writing is internalized talk made public and social again. If thought is internalized conversation, then writing is internalized conversation re-externalized.[9]

Like thought, therefore, writing is temporally and functionally related to conversation. Writing is in fact a technologically displaced form of conversation. When we write, having already internalized the "skill and partnership" of conversation, we displace it once more onto the written page. But because thought is already one step away from conversation, the position of writing relative to conversation is more complex than even that of thought. Writing is at once both two steps away from conversation and a return to conversation. By writing, we re-immerse conversation in its social medium. Writing is two steps removed from conversation because, for example, my ability to write this essay depends on my ability to talk through with myself the issues I address here. And my abiity to talk through an issue with myself derives largely from my ability to converse directly with other people in an immediate social situation.

The point is not that every time I write, what I say must necessarily be something I have talked over with other people first, although I may well often do just that. What I say can originate in thought. But since thought is conversation as I have learned to internalize it, the point is that writing always has its roots deep in the acquired ability to carry on the social symbolic exchange we call conversation. The inference writing tutors and teachers should make from this line of reasoning is that our task must involve engaging students in conversation at as many points in the writing process as possible and that we should contrive to ensure that that conversation is similar in as many ways as possible to the way we would like them eventually to write.

Peer Tutoring as Social Context

This practical inference returns us to peer tutoring. If we consider thought as internalized conversation and writing as re-externalized conversation, peer tutoring plays an important role in education for at least two reasons—both resulting from the fact that peer tutoring is a form of collaborative learning. First, peer tutoring provides a social context in which students can experience and practice the kinds of conversation that academics most value. The kind of conversation peer tutors engage in with their tutees can be emotionally involved, intellectually and substantively focused, and personally disinterested. There could be no better source of this than the sort of displaced conversation (i.e., writing) that academics value. Peer tutoring, like collaborative learning in general, makes students—both tutors and tutees—aware that writing is a social artifact, like the thought that produces it. However displaced writing may seem in time and space from the rest of a writer's community of readers and other writers, writing continues to be an act of conversational exchange.

Peer Tutoring as a Context for "Normal Discourse"

The second reason is somewhat more complex. Peer tutoring, again like collaborative learning in general, plays an important role in education because it provides a particular kind of social context for conversation, a particular kind of community: that of status equals, or peers. This means that students learn the "skill and partnership" of re-externalized conversation not only in a community that fosters the kind of conversation academics most value, but also in a community like the one most students must eventually write for in everyday life—in business, government, and the professions.

It is worthwhile digressing a moment to establish this last point. Ordinarily people write to inform and convince other people within the writer's own community, people whose status and assumptions approximate the writer's own.[10] That is, the sort of writing most people do most frequently in their everyday working lives is what Rorty calls "normal discourse." Normal discourse, a term of Rorty's coinage based on Kuhn's term "normal science," applies to conversation within a community of knowledgeable peers. A community of knowledgeable peers is a group of people who accept, and whose work is guided by, the same paradigms and the same code of values and assumptions. In normal discourse, as Rorty puts it, everyone agrees on the "set of conventions about what counts as a relevant contribution, what counts as a question, what counts as having a good argument for that answer or a good criticism of it." The product of normal discourse is "the sort of statement that can be agreed to be true by all participants whom the other participants count as 'rational.' "[11]

The essay I am writing here is an example of normal discourse in this sense. I am writing to members of my own community of knowledgeable peers. My readers and I (I suppose) are guided in our work by the same set of conventions about what counts as a relevant contribution, what counts as a question, what counts as an answer, what counts as a good argument in support of that answer or a good criticism of it. I judge my essay finished when I think it conforms to that set of conventions and values. And it is within that set of conventions and values that my readers will evaluate the essay, both in terms of its quality and in terms of whether or not it makes sense. Normal discourse is pointed, explanatory, and argumentative. Its purpose is to justify belief to the satisfaction of other people within the author's community of knowledgeable peers. Much of what we teach today—or should be teaching—in composition and speech courses is the normal discourse of most academic, professional, and business communities. The "rhetoric" taught in our composition textbooks comprises—or should comprise—the conventions of normal discourse of those communities.[12]

Teaching normal discourse in its written form is thus central to a college curriculum because the one thing college teachers in most fields commonly want students to acquire, and what teachers in most fields consistently reward students for, is the ability to carry on in speech and writing the normal discourse of the field in question. Normal discourse is what William Perry calls the fertile "wedding" of "bull" and "cow," of facts and their relevancies: discourse on the established contexts of knowledge in a field that makes effective reference to facts and ideas as defined within those contexts. In a student who can consummate this wedding, Perry says, "we recognize a colleague."[13] This is so because to be a conversant with the normal discourse in a field of study or endeavor is exactly what we mean by being knowledgeable—that is, knowledge*able*—in that field. Not to have mastered the normal discourse of a discipline, no matter how many "facts" or data one may know, is not to be knowledgeable in that discipline. Mastery of a "knowledge community's" normal discourse is the basic qualification for acceptance into that community.

The kind of writing we hope to teach students in college, therefore, is not only the kind of writing most appropriate to work in fields of business, government, and the professions; it is also writing most appropriate to gaining competence in most academic fields that students study in college. And what both kinds of writing have in common is that they are written within and addressed to a community of status equals: peers. They are both normal discourse.

This point having, I hope, been established, the second reason peer tutoring is important in education becomes clear. As a form of collaborative learning, peer tutoring is important because it provides the kind of social context in which normal discourse occurs: a community of knowledgeable peers. This is the main goal of peer tutoring.

Objections to Peer Tutoring

But to say this only raises another question: How can student peers, not themselves members of the knowledge communities they hope to enter, help other students enter those communities? This question is of course a variation of the question most often raised about all kinds of collaborative learning: Isn't it the blind leading the blind?

One answer to this question is that while neither peer tutors nor their tutees may alone be masters of the normal discourse of a given knowledge community, by working together—pooling their resources—they are very likely to be able to master it if their conversation is structured indirectly by the task or problem that a member of that community (the teacher) provides.[14] The conversation between peer tutor and tutee, in composition or for that matter any other subject, is structured by the demands of the assignment and by the formal conventions of academic discourse and of standard written English. The tutee brings to the conversation knowledge of the subject to be written about and knowledge of the assignment. The tutor brings to the conversation knowledge of the conventions of discourse and knowledge of standard written English. If the tutee does not bring to the conversation knowledge of the subject and the assignment, the peer tutor's most important contribution is to begin at the beginning: help the tutee acquire the relevant knowledge of the subject and the assignment.

What peer tutor and tutee do together is not write or edit, or least of all proofread. What they do together is converse. They converse about the subject and about the assignment. They converse about, in an academic context, their own relationship and the relationships between student and teacher. Most of all they converse about and *pursuant to* writing.

Peer Tutoring and the Humanities

The place of conversation in learning, especially in the humanities, is the largest context in which we must see peer tutoring. To say that conversation has a place in learning should not of course seem peculiar to those of us who count ourselves humanists, a category that includes many if not most writing teachers. Most of us count "class discussion" one of the most effective ways of teaching. The truth, however, is that we tend to honor discussion more in the breach than in the observance. The person who does most of the "discussing" in most discussion classes is usually the teacher.

Our discussion classes have this fateful tendency to turn into monologues because underlying our enthusiasm for discussion is a fundamental distrust of it. The graduate training most of us have enjoyed—or endured—has taught us that collaboration and community activity is inappropriate and foreign to work in humanistic disciplines. Humanistic study, we have been led to believe, is a solitary life, and the vitality of the humanities lies in the talents and endeavors of each of us as individuals.[15] What we call discussion is more often than not an adversarial activity pitting individual against individual in an effort to assert what one literary critic has called "will to power over the text," if not over each other. If we look at what we do instead of what we say, we discover that we think of knowledge as something we acquire and wield relative to each other, not something we generate and maintain in company with and in dependency upon each other.

Two Models of Knowledge

Only recently have humanists of note, such as Stanley Fish in literary criticism and Richard Rorty in philosophy, begun to take effective steps toward exploring the force and implications of knowledge communities in the humanistic disciplines and toward redefining the nature of our knowledge as a social artifact. Much of this recent work follows a trail blazed a decade ago by Thomas Kuhn. The historical irony of this course of events lies in the fact that Kuhn developed his notion about the nature of scientific knowledge after first examining the way knowledge is generated and maintained in the humanities and social sciences. For us as humanists to discover in Kuhn and his followers the conceptual rationale of collaborative learning in general and peer tutoring in particular is to see our own chickens come home to roost.

Kuhn's position that even in the "hard" sciences knowledge is a social artifact emerged from his attempt to deal with the increasing indeterminacy of knowledge of all kinds in the twentieth century.[16] To say that knowledge is indeterminate is to say that there is no fixed and certain point of reference against which we can measure truth. If there is no such referent, then knowledge must be a made thing, an artifact. Kuhn argued that to call knowledge a social artifact is not to say that knowledge is merely relative, that knowledge is what any one of us says it is. Knowledge is generated by communities of knowledgeable peers. Rorty, following Kuhn, argues that communities of knowledgeable peers make knowledge by a process of socially justifying belief. Peer tutoring, as one kind of collaborative learning, models this process.

Here then is a second and more general answer to the objection most frequently raised to collaborative learning of any type: that it is a case of the blind leading the blind. It is of course exactly the blind leading the blind if we insist that knowledge is information impressed upon the individual mind by some outside source. But if we accept the premise that knowledge is an artifact created by a community of knowledgeable peers and that learning is a social process not an individual one, then learning is not assimilating information and improving our mental eyesight. Learning is an activity in which people work collaboratively to create knowledge among themselves by socially justifying belief. We create knowledge or justify belief collaboratively by cancelling each other's biases and presuppositions; by negotiating collectively toward new paradigms of perception, thought, feeling, and expression; and by joining larger, more experienced communities of knowledgeable peers through assenting to those communities' interests, values, language, and paradigms of perception and thought.

The Extension of Peer Tutoring

By accepting this concept of knowledge and learning even tentatively, it is possible to see peer tutoring as one basic model of the way that even the most sophisticated scientific knowledge is created and maintained. Knowledge is the product of human beings in a state of continual negotiation or conversation. Education is not a process of assimilating "the truth" but, as Rorty has put it, a process of learning to "take a hand in what is going on" by joining "the conversation of mankind." Peer tutoring is an arena in which students can enter into that conversation.

Because it gives students access to this "conversation of mankind," peer tutoring and especially the principles of collaborative learning that underlie it have an important role to play in studying and teaching the humanities. Peer tutoring is one way of introducing students to the process by which communities of knowledgeable peers create referential connections between symbolic structures and reality, that is, create knowledge, and by doing so maintain community growth and coherence. To study humanistic texts adequately, whether they be student themes or Shakespeare, is to study entire pedagogical attitudes and classroom practices. Such are the implications of integrating our understanding of social symbolic relationships into our teaching—not just into *what* we teach but also into *how* we teach. So long as we think of knowledge as a reflection and synthesis of information about the objective world, teaching *King Lear* seems to involve providing a correct text and rehearsing students in correct interpretations of it. But if we think of knowledge as socially justified belief, teaching *King Lear* involves creating contexts where students undergo a sort of cultural change in which they loosen ties to the knowledge community they currently belong to and join another. These two communities can be seen as having quite different sets of values, mores, and goals, and above all quite different languages. To speak in one of a person asking another to "undo this button" might be merely to tell a mercantile tale, or a prurient one, while in the other such a request could be both a gesture of profound human dignity and a metaphor of the dissolution of a world.

Similarly, so long as we think of learning as reflecting and synthesizing information about the objective world, teaching expository writing means providing examples, analysis, and exercises in the rhetorical modes—description, narration, comparison-contrast—or in the "basic skills" of writing and rehearsing students in their proper use. But if we think of learning as a social process, the process of socially justifying belief, teaching expository writing is a social symbolic process, not just part of it. Thus, to study and teach the humanities is to study and teach the social origin, nature, reference, and function of symbolic structures.

Humanistic study defined in this way requires, in turn, a reexamination of our premises as humanists and as teachers in light of the view that knowledge is a social artifact. Since to date very little work of this sort has been done, one can only guess what might come of it. But when we bring to mind for a moment a sampling of current theoretical thought in and allied to a single field of the humanities, for example, literary criticism, we are likely to find mostly bipolar forms: text and reader, text and writer, symbol and referent, signifier and signified. On the one hand, a critique of humanistic studies might involve examining how these theories would differ from their currently accepted form if they included the third term missing from most of them. How, for instance, would psychoanalytically oriented study of metaphor differ if it acknowledged that psychotherapy is fundamentally a kind of social relationship based on the mutual creation or recreation of symbolic structures by therapist and patient? How would semiotics differ if it acknowledged that connecting "code" and phenomenon are the complex social symbolic relations among the people who make up a semiotic community? How would rhetorical theory look if we assumed that writer and reader were partners in a common, community-based enterprise, partners rather than adversaries?

And having reexamined humanistic study in this way, we could suppose on the other hand that a critique of humanistic teaching might suggest changes in our demonstrating to students that they know something only when they can explain it in writing to the satisfaction of the community of their knowledgeable peers. To do this, in turn, seems to require us to engage students in collaborative work that does not just reinforce the values and skills they begin with but that promotes a sort of resocialization.[17] Peer tutoring is collaborative work of just this sort.

The Last Frontier of Collaborative Learning

The argument I have been making here assumes, of course, that peer tutors are well trained in a coherent course of study. The effectiveness of peer tutoring requires more than merely selecting "good students" and, giving them little or no guidance, throwing them together with their peers. To do that is to perpetuate, perhaps even aggravate, the many possible negative effects of peer group influence: conformity, anti-intellectualism, intimidation, and the leveling of quality. To avoid these pitfalls and marshal the powerful educational resource of peer group influence requires an effective peer tutor training course based on collaborative learning, one that maintains a demanding academic environment and makes tutoring a genuine part of the tutors' own educational development.

Given this one reservation, it remains to be said only that peer tutoring is not, after all, something new under the sun. However we may explore its conceptual ramifications, the fact is that people have always learned from their peers and doggedly persist in doing so, whether we professional teachers and educators take a hand in it or not. Thomas Wolfe's *Look Homeward, Angel* records how in grammar school Eugene learned to write (in this case, form words on a page) from his "comrade," learning from a peer what "all instruction failed" to teach him. In business and industry, furthermore, and in professions such as medicine, law, engineering, and architecture, where to work is to learn or fail, collaboration is the norm. All that is new in peer tutoring is the systematic application of collaborative principles to that last bastion of hierarchy and individualism, institutionalized education.

Notes

1. The educative value of peer group influence is discussed in Nevitt Sanford, ed., *The American College* (New York: Wiley, 1962), and Theodore M. Newcomb and Everett K. Wilson, eds., *College Peer Groups* (Chicago: Aldine, 1966).

2. Michael Oakeshott, "The Voice of Poetry in the Conversation of Mankind," in *Rationalism in Politics* (New York: Basic Books, 1962), 199.

3. For example, L.S. Vygotsky, *Mind in Society* (Cambridge, Mass.: Harvard University Press, 1978).

4. Clifford Geertz, "The Growth of Culture and the Evolution of Mind," in *The Interpretation of Cultures* (New York: Basic Books, 1973), 76–77. See also in the same volume "The Impact of the Concept of Culture on the Concept of Man" and "Ideology as a Cultural System," Parts IV and V.

5. Stanley Fish, *Is There a Text in This Class? The Authority of Interpretive Communities* (Cambridge, Mass.: Harvard University Press, 1980), 14. Fish develops his argument fully in Part 2, pages 303–71.

6. Thomas Kuhn, *The Structure of Scientific Revolutions,* 2nd ed., International Encyclopedia of Unified Science, vol. 2, no. 2 (Chicago: University of Chicago Press, 1970).

7. Richard Rorty, *Philosophy and the Mirror of Nature* (Princeton, N.J.: Princeton University Press, 1979). Some of the larger educational implications

of Rorty's argument are explored in Kenneth A. Bruffee, "Liberal Education and the Social Justification of Belief," *Liberal Education* (Summer 1982): 8–20.

8. Fish, 14.

9. A case for this position is argued in Kenneth A. Bruffee, "Writing and Reading as Collaborative or Social Acts: The Argument from Kuhn and Vygotsky," in *The Writer's Mind* (Urbana, Ill.: NCTE, 1983).

10. Some writing in business, government, and the professions may of course be like the writing that students do in school for teachers, that is, for the sake of practice and evaluation. Certainly some writing in everyday working life is done purely as performance, for instance, to please superiors in the corporate or department hierarchy. So it may be true that learning to write to someone who is not a member of one's own status and knowledge community, that is, to a teacher, has some practical everyday value; but the value of writing of this type is hardly proportionate to the amount of time students normally spend on it.

11. Rorty, 320.

12. A textbook that acknowledges the normal discourse of academic disciplines and offers ways of learning it in a context of collaborative learning is Elaine Maimon, Gerald L. Belcher, Gail W. Hearn, Barbara F. Nodine, and Finbarr W. O'Connor, *Writing in the Arts and Sciences* (Cambridge, Mass.: Winthrop, 1981; distributed by Little, Brown). Another is Kenneth A. Bruffee, *A Short Course in Writing* (Cambridge, Mass.: Winthrop, 1980; distributed by Little, Brown).

13. William G. Perry, Jr., "Examsmanship and the Liberal Arts," in *Examining in Harvard College: A Collection of Essays by Members of the Harvard Faculty* (Cambridge, Mass.: Harvard University Press, 1963); as reprinted in Bruffee, *Short Course,* 221.

14. For examples and an explanation of this process see Kenneth A. Bruffee, *Short Course,* and "CLTV: Collaborative Learning Television," *Educational Communication and Technology Journal* 30 (Spring 1982): 31ff.

15. The individualistic bias of our current interpretation of the humanistic tradition is discussed further in Kenneth A. Bruffee, "The Structure of Knowledge and the Future of Liberal Education," *Liberal Education* (Fall 1981): 181–85.

16. The history of the growing indeterminacy of knowledge and its relevance to the humanities is traced briefly in Bruffee, "The Structure of Knowledge," 177–81.

17. Some possible curricular implications of the concept of knowledge as socially justified belief are explored in Bruffee, "Liberal Education and the Social Justification of Belief," *Liberal Education* (Summer 1982): 8–20.

2 Liberatory Writing Centers: Restoring Authority to Writers

Tilly Warnock
John Warnock
University of Wyoming

In conceptualizing the modern writing center as a "liberatory lab," the authors assert the center as a means of instruction that frees both the student and the instructor from the bondage of rigid and stifling pedagogies. In such centers, students take responsibility for their own learning and engage in revision—not only revision of writing but also of the world and of themselves.

In many writing centers writing is taught with a focus on meaning, not form; on process, not product; on authorial intention and audience expectation, not teacher authority or punitive measures; on holistic and human concerns, not errors and isolated skills. This kind of teaching, which arises "naturally" out of the writing center situation, proves to have great practical advantages if the center director's goal is truly to teach writing. What is practical about writing centers—cost and time efficient as well as effective— is their "philosophical commitment to individuation through conference teaching," the "one tenet fundamental to all of the most successful writing laboratories." The commitment to individuation rather than to mass production, to growth from within rather than to packaging from without, results in the practical advantage that students learn to conceive ideally, to play with "as if" and the future tenses, to imagine how they might "rewrite" themselves and their worlds. Students learn the practical skills of learning to live in the face of determinate and indeterminate meaning; they learn to revise.

Writing centers and laboratories have continued to flourish despite the disenchantment with the liberal assumptions that spawned them. We wish to argue that though centers may have liberal origins, they continue to grow because they are *liberatory*.[1] The revision from liberal to liberatory seems analogous to broader shifts in our conceptions of writing—from product to process and to performance, from text-centered to reader-centered and context-based. These revisions of terms in composition theory and practice seem in turn analogous to movements being documented in individual and cultural consciousness, shifts Suzanne K. Langer designates as the pervasive "key change" of the modern period, evident in fields as various as physics, art, science, religion, and literature. The change she documents in *Philosophy in a New Key* is to a view that recognizes content as symbolic forms, not as truth in an absolute sense, or, in Kenneth Burke's terms, language as performance, as symbolic action, not language as objective reference. The relationship between symbolic action and liberation is made explicit by Ernst Cassirer: "It is symbolic thought which overcomes the natural inertia of man and endows him with a new ability to constantly reshape his human universe."[2]

As writing teachers, our actions are usually felt to be restricted to the symbolic realm. This is often understood as "merely" the symbolic realm, an assumption reflected in our students' expectation that we ought to respond only to their "style" or "form," not to "what they say." This kind of disenfranchisement is often accepted by teachers, particularly those outside the language arts—if, indeed, it is possible to speak of a teacher actually functioning outside the language arts. But the notion of symbolic action becomes a good deal less restrictive when we give emphasis to symbolic action as an *action*. We do not speak of "mere" action. Action is real, a source of power. For Cassirer and for many others, among them Plato and Kenneth Burke, symbolic action is what is most real. Langer's "key change" is a recognition of this reality, this power.

Teachers, particularly in the liberal arts, sometimes speak of developing students' abilities to reshape their human universes. Teachers in writing centers know, as lecturers and teachers of graduate seminars may not, that these abilities turn out to be not skills in the usual sense, but attitudes that invite revision—revision of the self ("internal revision" as Donald Murray calls it), revision of the language by which the self comes to terms with the universe, revision of the methods which put these terms into action, and finally revision of the world which in turn defines the self. Not all writing centers are liberatory, of course, nor are all actions taken in centers, even by the most liberated of teachers. We want to propose some of the revisions entailed in shifts from the liberal to the liberatory.

The Revision of the Instructor

The first revision concerns the instructor. Writing teachers must first see themselves as writers; they must write so that they can understand writing from the inside out and learn to respect the variety of writing processes, attitudes, readers, and contexts. But this is not all. A liberal understanding, as we are using this term, might take this variety as a sanction for relativism. But a liberatory understanding recognizes also that authority derives from a personal struggle with this variety, a struggle which must be undertaken by each author and which each author is *entitled* to undertake for him- or herself. Thus, the image of the teacher as writer results in a revision of the teacher's relationship with students, for students in liberatory centers also become authors of and authorities on their own texts. Teachers in a writing center usually do not stand,—and if they do, certainly not at the head of their classes—parceling out information at their own discretion, according to their timetable or lesson plan. Writing center teachers often sit comfortably and alertly among their students, listening to papers being read aloud and discussed. Being a writer, having the same relation to "the writing problem" as the students, this sort of teacher does not demand writing formulated according to his or her authority, but instead works with students *in* the process of writing.

Writing center faculty are usually called staff, not faculty, and though the shift in terms may be intended to indicate the less prestigious status of people who work there, certain liberatory tendencies are also implied. A liberatory center staff is composed of part-time, nontenured instructors, graduate students, peer tutors, and tenured faculty. In the center it is impossible to distinguish among the various ranks; in fact, it is often impossible to distinguish between the faculty and the students. Neither age, dress, nor posture will indicate the distinctions; furthermore, the staff are officially students in many cases, and liberatory staff are—significantly—students in their attitudes. The teacher, who listens to students talk about and read papers on issues on which they are authorities, can learn not just new information, not just new symbolic forms, but new relationships to the problems of writing. The teacher is not a traditional teacher-evaluator but a person who assists writers by listening and reading, by helping students imagine an audience, form intentions, and realize them. Writing center teachers honor their own ignorance, and this attitude allows them to act with poise, confident in what they know and others know, and confident that they themselves can revise. Writing center teachers are ready to learn and to listen, empowered with a critical consciousness which comes from understanding language as symbolic action, as having the power to revise the self and the world.

The Revision of the Student

Teachers know that once students develop a critical consciousness toward their own writing, they will very likely have developed such consciousness toward the context for that writing, the world they live in, and thus will be able to *happen to*. However, students may not always, and usually do not at first, come to the center to learn to *happen to* their worlds. They may want at first only to be rescued: "Would somebody proofread this for me?" "How can I pass this course?" But teachers in liberatory centers know that it is cruel to rescue those who will only be thrown back into the same waters again. If students are not taught to swim, or at least float on their own, they cannot "happen" to water. In liberatory centers, then, it is not enough to provide students with what some call "survival skills." The strongest swimmers will not plunge in if they have no place they want to go or think they can get to, and thus they will not survive.

In addition to this attention to motives and purposes, the liberatory teacher realizes that learning to write is also a matter of writing. William Stafford argues for "the value of an unafraid, face-down, flailing, and speedy process in using the language":

> Writers are persons who write; swimmers are (and from teaching a child I know how hard it is to persuade a reasonable person of this)—swimmers are persons who relax in the water, let their hands go down, and reach out with ease and confidence.[3]

Writers can become people who move themselves and the waters that sustain them. The teacher's task becomes redefined further as a new definition of "student" develops in the liberatory center.

The most serious problem most writers have is having no place they want to get to *as writers*. They want, or think they want, any number of things: cars, money, passing grades, correct and complete writing the first time around. But real writing has nothing to do with any of these things, including the last one. In nonliberatory centers, writing is at best a means to an end that is entirely independent of writing: make enough money and you can hire someone to write for you; or write it correctly and completely the first time and then you will not waste any more valuable time than is absolutely necessary on this worthless writing course.

Of course, teachers in liberatory centers do not set out to change the values of students as such nor, of course, do students come to have their values changed. But such teachers do often find that the best and perhaps the only way to change student writing is to help students revise their attitudes towards themselves as writers and towards writing. A crucial part of the change is to restore to students the sense of their own authority and responsibility. In traditional teaching, the students' sense of their own authority in learning is irrelevant, even counterproductive because students must feel themselves void of knowledge in order to accept that which is being given or driven into them. Liberatory learning requires that learners feel confident enough about themselves that they listen to others and evaluate what they learn, transforming some of what they hear into their own purposes, revising their own views in light of the new learning, rejecting what they do not value or believe might have value for them in the future.

More specifically, if the center is to encourage students to assume authorship of their texts and their lives, students must decide whether or not they will attend the center. Classroom teachers may encourage attendance, and adjunct relationships between the center and regular classes may be helpful, but the philosophy of liberatory learning requires that students take responsibility for themselves. Thus, students take an assertive role in deciding what happens to them and to their texts when they come to the center. They determine when they will come, what they will do, whether or not they will return. In short, students evaluate their own learning processes.

Students often need to adjust to this freedom. They bring to the centers the kind of unliberated consciousness that asks only to have their papers proofread, corrected, rewritten by someone other than themselves, to be acceptable to someone other than themselves. This is crucial because writing center staff cannot do that for them—ethical considerations prevent it, if nothing else. So the staff must create a situation that helps to give a sense of options and authority to the writer.

The new role for students in liberatory writing centers allows them to speak what they think, to ask for what they want and need, to give to others, to wait and see. It allows them to draw on their expertise gained gradually in the process of living and interacting with others. Students who say they cannot write will not also say they do not know what they think, and they therefore will be willing to listen to another student's draft and give their opinions. The student can act out familiar life roles that are not permitted in regular classes, where the student is often defined as the one who does not know, who does not even know what is good for him or her. The traditional student role prescribes particular postures, voice tones, politeness rituals, even specific eye contact routines. It entails the attitude of passive receptivity that lacks all wonder and delight. Students are asked to wait in regular classes, but not to wait and learn; they are asked to wait until teachers get to where they want to go, until they "cover" what was planned. Students in regular classes even have to wait until the end of class. In liberatory centers, students wait, listen, and learn, but they also act and determine their own actions, symbolic and otherwise. They read their drafts aloud to others and listen to responses, often conflicting responses, and decide what they will have to do on the basis of the responses. They do not follow criticism obediently, but act on their own critical consciousness.

The Revision of Student-Faculty Relationships

The context of a liberatory center is fundamental to the revisions of "faculty" and "student" and their relationships to each other. In centers, students come and go at will, and they even determine the use of time and materials in the center. In fact, they bring the materials, their own writing, which immediately establishes their authority. Traditional spatial relationships are also revised in liberatory centers. One reason that staff and students cannot be distinguished is that they do not maintain the conventional distance; people move closer, then back, turn away, even stare at each other—as people do in their everyday interactions. Chairs are usually arranged around a table, ideally a round table, and teachers and students alike feel free to sit on desks, to imagine other functions for equipment and space and time than are dictated by the constraints of the traditional setting.

If we were to accept the problematic metaphor of the learning place as marketplace, we could say that the writing center is a buyer's market, with different goods and different rates of exchange than those that characterize the regular class. Although traditional classes do not exist without students, the pretense is that the teacher and the course are permanent while the students are changeable and even expendable.

Power relationships are fluid in liberatory centers, and every effort is exerted to identify victimizing actions. Students and staff are both writers, confronting the same kinds of problems; students and staff are allies. They both develop critical consciousnesses, the capacity to entertain seriously each other's viewpoint, confident that other views can be accepted, rejected, or modified. The understanding of language as symbolic action allows for revision because language is regarded as a performance, not a reference to an absolute truth that cannot be revised because it emanates from a source of incontestable power. Critical consciousness is not power itself (such as is sometimes claimed for knowledge), but it is the necessary condition of power. When language is defined as symbolic action, it becomes a playground for experimenting with ideas, roles, and expectations. It also is an arena for action in which all things are not possible (not all actions are possible all of the time), in which necessities are recognized, and in which revision is defined as an action that changes according to people, purposes, and places, and writing is defined as, among other things, process, product, performance, problem-solving, and thinking. In general, writing is defined as the ability to read a particular situation critically and to decide what kind of symbolic action will work best, given the specific context and motives.

The Writing Center as "Outsider"

Liberatory centers are risk-taking operations, just as liberatory learning is risky business for individuals who allow for revision in themselves. These centers usually exist on the fringes of the academic establishment, often in unused classrooms, old barracks, and basements. Salaries for staff are often low and granted on a year-to-year, even semester-to-semester, basis. The primary materials of the center are the students' own messy texts. The body of knowledge is the students themselves. But despite those obvious signs of "decay," labs flourish and students know where the real action is. Voices are loud, and laughter and tears are frequent. It is these characteristics of the liberatory center scene that nourish liberatory learning because in such contexts faculty and textbooks are not the authorities: students are their own authors.

While we do not suggest that centers must remain in condemned buildings or that staff salaries must remain low, it is probably a mistake for centers to seek integration into the established institution. We are suggesting that the liberatory center remain on the fringes of the academic community, in universities or public schools, in order to maintain critical consciousness. This does not mean a lack of involvement; it means, in fact, active involvement but with a critical distance to assess and evaluate in the light of a theory of liberatory learning. This critical stance is revolutionary and re-visionary, as Cassirer explains in his discussion of a child's first awareness of language as symbolic form:

> With the first understanding of the symbolism of speech a real revolution takes place in the life of the child. From this point on his whole personal and intellectual life assumes an entirely different shape. Roughly speaking, this change may be described by saying that the child passes from a more subjective to a more objective state, from a merely emotional attitude to a theoretical attitude. . . . [T]he child himself has a clear sense of the significance of a new instrument for his mental development. He is not satisfied with being taught in a purely receptive manner but takes an active share in the process of speech which is at the same time a progressive objectification.[4]

This power of revision comes with the understanding of language as symbolic action. This understanding comes to communities and to cultures, as well as to individuals, and the understanding comes, in revised forms, many times. The function of our schools and universities is too often to contradict such consciousness, causing students to deny the revisionary power in and of themselves. Centers are in a unique position to restore that power, that authorial nature, to students and staff.

Notes

1. The notion of "liberatory learning" is today associated most closely with Paolo Friere. See his *Pedagogy of the Oppressed* (New York: Seabury, 1970), and *Pedagogy in Process* (New York: Seabury, 1978). "Critical consciousness" is that consciousness which enables a people to see themselves as agents in their society, not just "knowers" but also "doers." The notion is explained, and practical ways of "teaching" it are proposed, by Ira Short, *Critical Thinking and Everyday Life* (Boston: South End Press, 1980). An analogous notion is "cultural literacy" as this term is developed by C. A. Bowers, *Cultural Literacy for Freedom* (Eugene, Oregon: Elan Publishers, 1974). The argument that conventional composition classes serve the interests of the establishment is made by Richard Ohmann, *English in America* (New York: Oxford University Press, 1976). Recent articles discussing the teaching of writing and language in terms relevant to our discussion of liberatory learning are Kay Fiore and Nan Elsasser, "'Strangers No More': A Liberatory Learning Curriculum," *College English* 44 (February 1982): 115-18; Richard Ohmann, "Reflections on Class and Language," *College English* 44 (January 1982): 1-17; John J. Rouse, "Knowledge, Power, and the Teaching of English," *College English* 40 (January 1979): 473-91; and Gerald Graff, "The Politics of Composition: A Reply to John Rouse," *College English* 41 (April 1980): 851-56.

2. Ernst Cassirer, *An Essay on Man: An Introduction to the Philosophy of Human Culture* (New Haven: Yale University Press, 1944), 62. Kenneth Burke's philosophy of symbolic action may be seen as a rhetorical revision of Cassirer's notion.

3. William Stafford, *Writing the Australian Crawl: Views on the Writer's Vocation* (Ann Arbor: University of Michigan Press, 1978), 22-23.

4. Cassirer, *An Essay on Man,* 131.

3 Writing Center Research: Testing Our Assumptions

Stephen M. North
State University of New York at Albany

North surveys three categories of research that have been done on writing centers and examines their value to the field as a whole. The author then discusses what directions future studies should take. North argues that center directors should begin to test their basic pedagogical assumptions; to illustrate this point he identifies two general assumptions and shows how research projects might be constructed to test them.

I. Current Research

In an essay called "Teachers of Composition and Needed Research in Discourse Theory"—an essay that later won the Richard Braddock Award—Lee Odell argues that teachers of writing have two responsibilities. First, he says, "our primary obligation is to have some influence on the way students compose, to make a difference in students' ability to use written language to give order and meaning to their experience." Moreover, he continues, we "must not only influence our students' writing, but also help refine and shape the discourse theory that will guide our work with students."[1] We must, in other words, not merely accept and operate by our assumptions, but we must test them, challenge them, reshape them. Just plain teaching is not enough.

If what Odell says about teachers of writing in general is true—and I believe it is—then the burden of responsibility on writing center people is perhaps even greater. Not only must we test our assumptions about discourse theory (since we are all, first, teachers of writing); we must also test, to a greater degree than our classroom counterparts, our assumptions about our pedagogy, about *how* we teach writing. For despite the ancient heritage of our primary method of teaching—the tutorial—we are considered by our contemporaries to be at best unconventional and at worst "ad hoc" and essentially futile. Maxine Hairston has this to say about what she calls "writing labs":

24

> Following the pattern that Kuhn describes in his book, our first response to crisis has been to improvise *ad hoc* measures to try to patch the cracks and keep the system running. Among the first responses were the writing labs that sprang up about ten years ago to give first aid to students who seemed unable to function within the traditional paradigm. Those labs are still with us, but they're still giving only first aid and treating symptoms. They have not solved the problem.[2]

We carry, then, more than an average-size burden to be the kind of testers of assumptions Odell describes. Until now, that is not a role we have assumed very well, albeit for good reasons. After all, what might be called the "contemporary" writing center is a relatively recent phenomenon, dating, perhaps, from the 1972 publication of Lou Kelly's book, *From Dialogue to Discourse.*[3] The decade since then has been one of remarkably rapid, in some senses chaotic, growth. Writing centers, writing labs, writing clinics—facilities of all kinds have grown up in reaction to a widespread dissatisfaction with the classroom teaching of writing. The speed of this growth, unfortunately, has enabled writing center staffs to do little more than survive, to do what they can to improve the lot of the writers in their charge, leaving precious little time, money, or energy for research into the hows and whys of their operations. Consequently, writing center research has not, for the most part, been the formal inquiry by which we might test our assumptions. It has tended to fall, instead, into one of three categories.

Reflections on Experience

In this research mode, by far the most common of the decade, a practitioner (or two or more) looks back over something he or she has done (set up a writing center, tried a new recordkeeping system, inaugurated a peer tutoring course), trying to derive, more or less explicitly, guidelines that will help others do the same. Two of the better known and presumably influential examples of such reflective research are Muriel Harris's "Structuring the Supplementary Writing Lab" and Patrick Hartwell's account of establishing a writing lab at the University of Michigan–Flint in 1971, "A Writing Laboratory Model."[4] Both essays offer sound practical advice, a smattering of theory, and uplifting anecdotes; neither is, nor was intended to be, formal or systematic.

Speculation

In this kind of research a teacher or administrator takes a theory or idea (from composition and rhetoric or elsewhere) and uses it either to explain some writing center phenomenon or to make suggestions about what writing centers ought to be. The best known of these are probably

Kenneth Bruffee's articles on peer tutoring as based on theories of collaborative learning.[5] While Bruffee does, of course, call upon experience with his own program in these essays, his main purpose is to bring the implications of collaborative learning theory to bear on the practice of writing centers.

Survey

One might call this third kind of research "counting" or "enumeration." It takes place on at least two levels. On the local level it has been the primary means of writing center evaluation: number of students seen, number of hours tutored, reaction of students to center, reaction of teachers to center, and so on. On the national level it has produced a handful of questionnaire-based studies, the best known of which was "Learning Skills Centers: A CCCC Report," published by NCTE in 1976. Two surveys with a more specific writing center orientation are Mary Lamb's "Evaluation Procedures for Writing Centers" and Maurice Henderson's unpublished dissertation, "A Study of the Writing Laboratory Programs in Two-Year Community Colleges."[6]

Naturally there have been writers who combined two or all three of these kinds of research, especially in longer works. The first was Mark Smith, whose dissertation, "Peer Tutoring in a Writing Workshop," is based on a combination of theory, experience, and evaluation in his writing workshop.[7] My own dissertation, "Writing Centers: A Sourcebook," synthesizes my work as a tutor and assistant director with readings in the research of composition and visits to some thirty-five writing centers throughout the country; and most recently, Mary Croft and Joyce Steward, who between them have at least twenty years of writing center experience, collaborated on *The Writing Laboratory: Organization, Methods, and Management.*[8]

All three kinds of research have been important and fruitful; they are, probably, the hallmarks of a rapidly growing, somewhat unstable field. The reflective research helps to disseminate fundamental information, allowing newcomers to build on the experience of pioneers. The speculative work keeps the field alive, vital, bringing in what might be called new intellectual blood. And the surveys serve two important political purposes: they create a sense of group identity and substance; and they quantify writing centers, making them concrete both for university administrators and writing center directors themselves. The object of such research has been to keep the field growing, moving forward, and it has served this function well.

As writing centers move toward the 1990s, though, they are gaining some measure of professional stability, and we can expect their growth rate to level off. It is no longer necessary for all new writing center directors to compose a reflective essay detailing the experiences of their traumatic first year. There is no need for graduate students to conjure up images of what writing centers are from the bare bones of questionnaires. And while center directors will always have a need for speculative essays—like this one—they will need them in smaller proportion to the total research output. Writing centers are, in short, maturing. As they do so, we must, as Odell argues, turn the focus of our research back onto ourselves. We must ask the hard questions, test the assumptions we have come to take for granted over the first difficult decade of the writing center's existence.

II. Identifying Basic Assumptions

The question naturally arises: What *are* our basic assumptions? Both of the recently published collections of essays on writing centers include an article that deals, in some way, with research. In "Research and the Writing Center" Aviva Freedman moves knowledgeably through the best and most relevant of composition research, concluding with a paragraph about the opportunities for more such research in writing centers.[9] Citing Donald Graves, who "argues for research on the teaching of writing as well as on the process of writing," she points out that "writing centers allow for and practically encourage such research."[10] In "Conducting Research in the Writing Lab" Harvey Kail and Kay Allen take a rather different tack, writing a level-headed, realistic primer (in the best sense of the word) for research neophytes.[11] They offer two bywords, simplicity and integration; point out the relative merits of exploratory and experimental research; give valuable, candid examples from their own efforts; and conclude with a useful annotated bibliography.

What neither article does, however, is single out the issues of greatest import for would-be writing center researchers; neither lays the groundwork for what might be called a research paradigm. That they do not do so is hardly surprising. If there is one thing the ten or so years of often helter-skelter growth of the writing center movement have *not* done, it is to create uniformity. Facilities enlisted under the writing center-writing lab banner now include places as theoretically and functionally diverse as programmed materials-and-tapes labs; peer tutoring drop-in centers; wholesale sentence-combining labs; so-called remedial centers staffed by professional tutors; and so on up to what might be called the full service center, which coordinates the features of a number of models, usually with tutorials as the instructional core. "Writing center" has become more an internal political designation than a pedagogical or theoretical one. Any means of dealing with college writers different from the usual approach of a given institution is likely to be labeled center, clinic, or lab. When it comes time for such places to ally themselves with other facilities of the same label, they can often assume only that they will have in common a nonconventional relationship to their respective curricula. The result is that theory- or pedagogy-based research questions simply cannot meet with universal political approval. Hence, the safest advice for researchers has been to study what is of greatest interest to them in their own facilities.

Such a parochial position seems no longer tenable. Perceptions of writing centers like Hairston's (which is neither the first nor the last such salvo) are in large part a function of the failure of writing center professionals to define clearly what they do, to offer a united theory and pedagogy they have tested themselves. At the risk of creating political dissension, then, I want to assert here that all writing centers—or all places that can be designated writing centers—rest on this single theoretical foundation: that the ideal situation for teaching and learning writing is the tutorial, the one-on-one, face-to-face interaction between a writer and a trained, experienced tutor; and that the object of this interaction is to intervene in and ultimately alter the composing process of the writer.

Surely this is the essence of writing center design. Even in centers where the tutorial is not the primary method of instruction, the *idea* is present; the computer-aided instruction or the slide-tape or programmed materials or the small group work are adopted to duplicate, supplement, or intensify some portion of what the ideal tutorial would address. Peer tutoring, which in its most extreme form (learning-by-tutoring) is concerned almost exclusively with the learning of the tutor, is no exception. There is simply some trading off, the hope being that any loss for the writer will be covered by the gains of the tutor. (As will be noted further on, however, there are questions to be raised about the uses of peer tutors in writing.)

Assuming that even half the 1,500 or so writing centers in America will support this assertion, it is all the more remarkable that in all the writing center literature to date, *there is not a single published study of what happens in writing center tutorials.* There is one fairly well known, unpublished master's thesis, Patricia Beaumont's "A Descriptive Study of the Role of the Tutor in a Conference on Writing."[12] There are, among the reflective researches described above, the inevitable anecdotal accounts of tutorial relationships or the snippets of (often recreated) tutorial dialogue. And there is a parallel and to some extent relevant literature on student-teacher writing conferences, a portion of which is based on what really happens in such conferences.[13] The fact is, however, that our staple instructional method is one we know almost nothing about.

Naturally, there are plenty of adages and sage advice about how such tutorials should be conducted, advice center directors have been forced to concoct and formalize in order to train tutors. But even a quick reading of such advice reveals a variety that scuttles any hopes for a theoretical homogeneity. I will cite just three positions. Some writers treat tutoring in writing as though it were like tutoring in most any other academic area, its aim being the transmission of information (about propriety in written products) and certain "skills" (usually editing).[14] Others treat it as skilled intervention in a complex process, wherein the tutor's object is, in some sense, to help the writer move forward through that process, on the assumption that the only way for the writer to learn to compose is by composing.[15] Still others seem to want tutors to serve as peer editors or peer critics, text experts whose primary task is to pass on their critical insights in tactful, useful ways; in addition, they expect the tutoring to benefit the tutors as much as or more than the tutees.[16] Much more is known, to put it bluntly, about what people *want* to happen in and as a result of tutorials than about what *does* happen.

Clearly, writing center research must begin by addressing this single, rather broad question: What happens in writing tutorials? A few possible sources of information have already been tapped. A number of people have used what seems most obvious: audio- and videotapes of tutoring sessions, although the use of videotapes has been very limited.[17] Thomas Reigstad, in his "Conferencing Practices of Professional Writers: Ten Case Studies," borrows from ethnographic studies to combine audiotaping with an observer-participant who also uses structured interviews to gather information from participants.[18] Thom Hawkins draws upon just a few of the millions of words written in journals by Berkeley tutors over the past ten years.[19] The Bay Area Writing Project also has published a complete version of one such journal.[20] And there is enough precedent in composition research generally[21] and writing centers specifically[22] for case studies of individual writers.

So there has been at least a beginning, an inkling of the kind of work that lies ahead. Possibly the most important work—the work that follows Kail and Allen's bywords, simplicity and integration—are case studies of tutorial relationships that combine, in a form that will have to be arrived at by trial and error, the kinds of data-gathering just listed: tapes, transcripts, interviews, questionnaires, trained observers, self-monitoring, composing aloud, and so on. There are so many questions: How do tutorial relationships begin? How do they change over time? Who decides what happens during tutorials? Are there identifiable "types" of tutorials and tutorial relationships? How do tutors perceive the people they work with? How does this affect the relationship? The list could go on and on.

However, this "grassroots" kind of research, essential as it is, will not be enough. The field cannot drift along at its present limits indefinitely. As prudent as Kail and Allen's bywords are, writing center researchers are going to have to shake them off sometime and engage in work that is neither simple nor integrated—work that is, in fact, complex and disruptive and probably expensive enough to require outside funding. There will be a need, as with the case studies, to create a methodology, one borrowed from disciplines like ethnography, social psychology, and cognitive psychology. These research projects will be the ones that finally test writing center assumptions. The remainder of this essay will be given over to two examples of such assumption-testing studies.

III. Research on the Tutorial Relationship

One of the field's most important assumptions is suggested in the definition of the essence of writing center design, i.e., the notion of a trained, experienced tutor. As noted, there is no widespread agreement on what kinds of training or what sorts of experience are most important. But it seems safe to say that people working in writing centers believe that there are among them individuals who, as a result of training, experience, and perhaps aptitude, are "good" tutors: people who deal with the one-on-one interaction consistently well; who move easily from one student to the next; who seem adept at establishing and maintaining rapport; who seem to make accurate "diagnoses" of students' needs; who adopt strategies that seem well suited to those needs; and who always seem to leave their clients feeling satisfied.

But do such superior tutors exist? Are there people with a gift for tutoring writing, or is our belief in them based on other, mostly irrelevant factors? If such people do exist, is it possible to identify what in fact they do differently—what skill or combination of skills makes their tutorials work better?

A study that might answer these questions would have two parts. First, we would have to identify "good" tutors. Suppose, then, that we selected five well-established writing centers within some reasonable geographic area and asked anyone who had worked in these centers for over a year to list the five best tutors they knew. From these lists (that would include center directors and other staff members), we would select the six tutors whose names appeared most often. These would be the "good" tutors. From the full list of available tutors with over one year's experience, we would select six whose names appeared on *none* of the lists. These would be our "not-so-good" tutors. All twelve tutors would then be invited to participate in the research project, almost certainly for an honorarium or at least for expenses. (All would be told they had been selected by their peers, a minor but necessary deception.)

Next, we would need to devise six of what are called in cognitive psychology *high-fidelity simulation problems*. Basically, we would derive, from real writing center tutorials, six tutoring situations that could be recreated for all twelve participants. The simulations would be conducted in a setting as similar as possible to the participants' usual setting; all the action, however, would be videotaped. The tutees for each situation would be an actor or actress trained to "be" the person from the original, source tutorial; where a piece of writing was involved, we would use the original.

Immediately after working through each simulation, the participants would undergo what is called a *stimulated recall session:* sitting before a replay of the tutorial and able to stop or start the tape, the tutor would be asked by a research assistant to try to remember what he or she was thinking during the tutorial, and his or her recollections would be taped and later transcribed. For each tutor, then, we would have the same six tutorials on videotape and an audiotape or transcript of "stimulated" recollections.

This is a deceptively simplified version of the project, of course. Even as much as is presented here—the polling, the invitations, the logistics of transporting participants, the selection of appropriate simulations, the training of actors, the taping and replaying of seventy-two tutorials, the recording and transcribing of seventy-two stimulated recalls—represents a research project of major, even full-time, proportions and does not even begin to include analysis of the findings. But consider the kinds of analyses that would be possible. We would be able, for example, to determine what kinds of information tutors sought and how they got it. We could find out what sorts of hypothesis-forming tutors did: how early they ventured guesses about what needed to be done, how many such hypotheses they might entertain, how they tested such hypotheses, how they decided—if ever—when a hypothesis became a conclusion, a diagnosis. We could at least begin to discover how much the conduct of a tutorial is a function of the person tutoring and how much a function of the tutoring situation, the problem.

In all this, too, we would hope to discover what differences, if any, exist between the "good" and the "not-so-good" tutors. We might not find any statistically significant differences; on the other hand, the differences might be striking and correctable. We may find that while this study of one-shot tutorials tells us a good deal, we need even more to know what happens in tutorials over time, a problem which will require a methodology more akin to the aforementioned case studies and to Reigstad's borrowings from ethnography.

IV. Research on the Composing Process

A second, and in some writing centers crucial, assumption is that one of the best features of writing center instruction is timing—it is offered to writers when they need it, when they want it. Hence, the drop-in, work-through-one-paper tutorial is not only justified but among a center's strongest offerings. Not all writing centers, of course, offer drop-in services, and a few expressly forbid work on papers not already graded. But as previously noted, no research question can meet with universal approval. And no less eminent a figure than Charles Cooper espouses this service in writing centers: "Through [students'] college years they should also be able to find on a drop-in, no-fee basis expert tutorial help with any writing problem they encounter in a paper."[23]

But do drop-in tutorials work? The case studies should shed some light on the answer, especially as observers are able to compare tutorial content with written products. However, much of the justification for this kind of tutoring stems from claims that it influences the composing process, not merely the composed product; that it changes what writers produce by altering, perhaps permanently, what they *do* when they write.

To test this assumption, we would need to focus rather closely on the composing process of a given writer or set of writers, probably working on one well-defined writing task. Suppose, for example, that we took advantage of the sixty or so students who visit SUNY Albany's center each year for help with the essay portion of their law school applications, selecting (and paying) a small number of them for their participation, half to receive tutoring, half not. Suppose, next, that we introduce these selected prelaw students to composing aloud, giving them a chance to become accustomed to the tape recorder and an observer-prompter and to voicing their thoughts as they compose. We could then collect what would amount to pre- and post-tutorial protocols of them composing the kind of essay asked for in their law school application, as well as observe and tape the tutorial sessions of the half who get tutoring.

People most familiar with protocol analysis in writing (analysis, in this case, of a transcript of the tape that is a record of what the writer thought aloud during writing, plus whatever gets written during the recorded session) warn that it is probably not an accurate diagnostic tool. It is, to begin with, an intrusive method, one that very likely distorts composing; moreover, it cannot claim to capture, in one or two sessions, the "normative" composing habits of a single writer. Nevertheless, it would seem a safe enough method here to probe for the kinds of changes we could expect to find among the tutored group: a more careful, conscious analysis of audience, a heightened, more probing search for appropriate voice, a greater tendency to move from generalizations to specifics, and so on. If these kinds of changes turn out to be observable in the composing processes of the tutored group and not in the untutored group, could we find in the records of the tutorial sessions reasons why this should be so?

If so, what tutor behaviors seemed to generate them? If not, are there other changes not merely attributable to the inherent instability of the research method? What are these? In either case, do the apparent changes in composing behavior turn up in the written products? In what ways? And, whatever the impact of the tutoring, do follow-up composing-aloud sessions, say four weeks later, still reflect that impact, or is the effect short-term?

V. Further Assumptions and the Aims of Research

There are plenty of other assumptions that need testing. Consider, for instance, some of our notions about peer tutoring: that the best peer tutors are likely to be those successful in writing (and, often, grammar); that peer tutoring benefits the tutor as much as the tutee; that, in fact, there even *is* such a thing as peer tutor. The term, after all, is taken from a literature that seldom ventures beyond the high school level and almost never into writing. What does it mean in a college setting? What do people have to have in common to be peers in a writing tutorial, and how is the relationship different from other tutorial relationships?

Or consider our relationship with instructional materials of all kinds. We assume that there are "parts" of writing that are best or most efficiently learned without a tutor's direct assistance: editing, usually, but also revision or invention. Is this true? What *do* people learn during the time we send them to work on a programmed text, a computer terminal, or a slide-tape presentation?

These are the kinds of questions we need to answer, the assumptions we need to test. Our primary purpose, naturally, is to make writing centers work better for the writers they serve. We have, however, a second aim: to *challenge* another set of assumptions, those of our colleagues who, like Maxine Hairston, do not believe that writing centers work. The next ten years should tell the tale. By 1995 we will either have some answers—or we won't be around to need them.

Notes

1. Lee Odell, "Teachers of Composition and Needed Research in Discourse Theory," *College Composition and Communication* 30 (February 1979): 39.

2. Maxine Hairston, "The Winds of Change: Thomas Kuhn and the Revolution in the Teaching of Writing," *College Composition and Communication* 33 (February 1982): 82.

3. Lou Kelly, *From Dialogue to Discourse* (Glenview, Ill.: Scott, Foresman, 1972).

4. Muriel Harris, "Structuring the Supplementary Writing Lab," (ERIC ED 124 966, 1976); Patrick Hartwell, "A Writing Laboratory Model," in *Basic Writing: Essays for Teachers, Researchers, and Administrators,* ed. Lawrence Kasden and Daniel Hoeber (Urbana, Ill.: National Council of Teachers of English, 1980), 63–73.

5. See, for example, Kenneth A. Bruffee, "Collaborative Learning: Some Practical Models," *College English* 34 (February 1974): 46–57; "The Brooklyn Plan: Attaining Intellectual Growth through Peer-Group Tutoring," *Liberal Education* 64 (December 1978): 447–68; or "Two Related Issues in Peer Tutoring: Program Structure and Tutor Training," *College Composition and Communication* 31 (February 1980): 76–80.

6. Mary Lamb, "Evaluation Procedures for Writing Centers: Defining Ourselves through Accountability," in *New Directions for College Learning Assistance: Improving Writing Abilities,* ed. Thom Hawkins and Phyllis Brooks (San Francisco: Jossey-Bass, 1981), 69–83; Maurice Henderson, "A Study of the Writing Laboratory Programs in Two-Year Community Colleges" (Dissertation, Indiana University of Pennsylvania, 1980).

7. Mark Smith, "Peer Tutoring in a Writing Workshop" (Dissertation, University of Michigan, 1975).

8. Stephen M. North, "Writing Centers: A Sourcebook" (Dissertation, State University of New York at Albany, 1979); Mary Croft and Joyce Steward, *The Writing Laboratory: Organization, Methods, and Management* (Glenview, Ill.: Scott, Foresman, 1982).

9. Aviva Freedman, "Research and the Writing Center," in *New Directions,* ed. Hawkins and Brooks, 83–93.

10. Freedman, 91.

11. Harvey Kail and Kay Allen, "Conducting Research in the Writing Lab," in *Tutoring Writing,* ed. Muriel Harris (Glenview, Ill.: Scott, Foresman, 1982), 233–45.

12. Patricia Beaumont, "A Descriptive Study of the Role of the Tutor in a Conference on Writing" (Master's thesis, University of San Diego, 1978).

13. See, for example, Adela Karliner and Suzanne Jacobs, "Helping Writers to Think: The Effect of Speech Roles in Individualized Conferences on the Quality of Thought in Student Writing," *College English* 38 (January 1977): 489–505; Thomas Reigstad, "Conferencing Practices of Professional Writers: Ten Case Studies" (Dissertation, State University of New York at Buffalo, 1980); or Richard Beach, "Development of a Category System for the Analysis of Teacher-Student Conferences" (Paper presented at the Annual Meeting of the Conference on College Composition and Communication, Washington D.C., 1980).

14. Deborah Arfken, "A Peer Tutor Staff: Four Crucial Aspects," in *Tutoring Writing,* ed. Harris, 111–22; and, in the same book, Phyllis Sherwood, "What Should Tutors Know?" 101–104.

15. Aviva Freedman, "A Theoretic Context for the Writing Lab," in *Tutoring Writing,* ed. Harris, 2–12; and, in the same book, Anita Brostoff, "The Writing Conference: Foundations," 21–26.

16. Kenneth A. Bruffee, "Staffing and Operating Peer-Tutoring Writing Centers," in *Basic Writing,* ed. Kasden and Hoeber, 141–149; Marvin P. Garrett, "Toward a Delicate Balance: The Importance of Role Playing and Peer Criticism in Peer-Tutor Training," in *Tutoring Writing,* ed. Harris, 94–100.

17. Beaumont, "A Descriptive Study"; Karliner and Jacobs, "Helping Writers to Think"; Freedman, "Research and the Writing Center."

18. Reigstad, "Conferencing Practices."

19. Thom Hawkins, "Intimacy and Audience: The Relationship between Revision and the Social Dimension of Peer Tutoring," *College English* 42 (Sept. 1980), 64–69.

20. Jackie Goldsby, *Peer Tutoring in Basic Writing: A Tutor's Journal,* Classroom Research Study No. 4, (Berkeley, Ca.: University of California, Berkeley Bay Area Writing Project, 1981).

21. Charles K. Stallard, "An Analysis of the Writing Behavior of Good Student Writers," *Research in the Teaching of English* 8 (Fall 1974): 206–18; Sharon H. Pianko, "The Composing Acts of College Writers: A Description" (Dissertation, Rutgers University, 1977); Sondra Perl, "Five Writers Writing: Case Studies of the Composing Processes of Unskilled Writers" (Dissertation, New York University, 1978).

22. Harvey Kail and Kay Allen, "Conducting Research," in *Tutoring Writing,* ed. Harris, 233–45.

23. Charles Cooper, "What College Writers Need to Know" (Third College Composition Program, University of California at San Diego, 1979), 16.

4 A Philosophical Perspective on Writing Centers and the Teaching of Writing

Lil Brannon
New York University

C. H. Knoblauch
State University of New York at Albany

The authors argue that in order for writing centers to be effective, center personnel, as well as their colleagues in the classroom, must ground their pedagogy in "sound conceptual premises." They critique methods of instruction based on traditional, analytical views of discourse and suggest principles of a research-based approach. To illustrate the differences in pedagogical effectiveness between the approaches, the authors thoroughly examine a sample of student writing and a corresponding writing protocol. In addition, they discuss the complementary functions of the writing center and composition classroom.

In her book *The Making of Meaning* Ann Berthoff suggests that writing teachers who seek to be effective must become philosophers and researchers in their field. She means that instruction cannot be purposeful and directed unless it proceeds from sound conceptual premises that teachers understand, remain conscious of, and continually modify in light of their own experiences with students.[1] It is probably safe to say, though, that most teachers and tutors are not typically philosophers and that they do not see their interactions with students as a basis for research. Instead, they teach unself-consciously from recollections of how they were taught and from hearsay about what "everybody does," supported by the outmoded assumptions, false analytical distinctions, regimented methods, and prescriptivist emphases enshrined in textbooks.[2]

Several decades of research in rhetoric and composition, linguistics, psychology, and instructional theory have begun to yield both plausible and preferable substitutes for traditional ideas and methods. But as Maxine Hairston has recently noted,[3] despite a growing sophistication among researchers and theorists, the majority of teachers and tutors continue to do what they have always done, seldom reading the available literature, seldom seeking (or receiving) a rigorous conceptual preparation for their work, and seldom pausing, amidst the demands of the classroom, to reflect on what they do, why they do it, and what they are really trying to accomplish.

The Analytical View of Discourse

The first step toward improved understanding must be dissatisfaction with ideas and practices currently sustained only through custom and philosophical laxity rather than deliberate intellectual commitment. For instance, given the directions of recent composition theory and the accumulating weight of corroborative research, it is simply startling that so many teachers and tutors still work from building-block and stage models of composing, still regard writing as an exercise in manipulating artificial formal constraints, still teach by enumerating the constraints, step by step, in lecture-discussion, and, finally, drill students in obedience to each. In this traditional setting, writing-as-product is analyzed into components—words, sentences, paragraphs, essay frames, modes of discourse, and the like. Writing-as-process is similarly analyzed to yield stages of activity, thereby, in effect, making it no longer a process: find a subject and a thesis, make an outline, write the lead sentence of an attractive introductory paragraph, draw a conclusion, edit the text, and so on. Each of these process and product components then becomes the basis for isolating a "skill": spelling, diction, and punctuation; writing correct sentences; writing general-to-specific paragraphs; argumentative writing and, separately, persuasive writing; comparison-contrast—all are skills. Potentially, hundreds of such skills could be distinguished, depending only on how thorough an analysis one wished to make. For example, one could isolate subskills of sentence construction—subject/verb agreement or forming adverbial clauses—or one could distinguish five, ten, or thirty different paragraph structures, implying a different skill for each. There is no end to analytical inquiry—just as a pie can be divided into pieces of different size or shape and into different numbers of pieces, limited only by the intent of the cutter and the sharpness of the blade. And while such cutting is possible, does it tell us anything useful about how to make a pie?

In any case, from such inquiry "units of instruction" are born, representing an idiosyncratic sampling of all the available "skills" and "subskills" fitted to the constraint of available class hours. Large, interesting units get included in writing courses—"the deductive argument," "the extended definition," "the research paper"; small, less interesting units— "the comma" and "the topic sentence"—belong to the writing center, where they are often labeled in terms of deficiencies associated with them, for instance, "the comma splice". Tape modules, computer cassettes, and workbook drills stand ready in the writing center for activities whose tedium could otherwise represent a threat to the mental health of live teachers (though no one worries, seemingly, about the threat to live students).

There are several philosophical problems worth thinking about in connection with the alliance between an analytical view of discourse and the teaching of writing. One problem is that not every historical analysis of discourse is true and useful even for research, let alone pedagogical ends. The old folk wisdom that paragraphs begin with topic sentences followed by predictable sequences of tapered subordinations is demonstrably false[4] and therefore unworthy to be taught. The ancient analysis of orations into five or six parts, from exordium to peroration, certainly described what classical rhetoricians wanted ceremonial composition to look like, but it did not distinguish the features of all coherent writing. Modern subdivisions of essays into introduction, background, body, and conclusion are similarly unnecessary to meaningfulness. Teaching them as though they were is philosophically unacceptable.

A second, larger problem deserves even more thought: the mere possibility of distinguishing parts in some whole does not mean that the parts really enjoy independent status or that they should be taught as discrete entities and in some preferred sequence. Writing can easily enough be broken into words, sentences, and strings of sentences; into planning, stating, and revising; into thesis, argument, and conclusion; or into a considerable variety of other "parts" according to one's point of view. But doing so implies nothing at all about the value of teaching, say, word choice separate from or earlier than the making of independent clauses or about the usefulness of introducing either outside the context of composing as an integrated process. Analysis can afford a nomenclature for describing and talking about an otherwise undifferentiated, continuous reality. But the resulting models should not be mistaken for the richer phenomena they schematically represent; the memorizing of some model of composing and the mechanical practicing of "skills" that it appears to describe as discrete activities should not be taken as equivalent to learning how to write.

This fact introduces a third, closely related problem: not all analytical schemes have equal value in the classroom merely because they enjoy equivalent measures of descriptive validity or research merit. James Britton's distinction of expressive, transactional, and poetic modes[5] has research plausibility and evident value for distinguishing the complicated relationships among writers, subjects, and readers. But the teacher who asks students to practice "expressive writing" as though it were a genre, structure, or strategy of discourse that a writer consciously manipulates as such is perverting Britton's model by applying it to performance rather than to the study of completed texts for which it was designed. Similarly, all classifications of "forms" of discourse, whether sentence patterns, paragraph structures, essay models, or other analytical abstractions, have questionable utility in the classroom or the writing center, partly because of what they imply about writing and partly because of the emphasis they create in instruction. They imply the existence of prefabricated structures which writers simply select and "fill up" with content—like pie crusts. Worse, they exaggerate the importance of formal propriety while undervaluing the writer's personal (and personalized) search for meaning. Hence, whatever the merit of formalist criticism for describing discourse, a preoccupation with formal absolutes in writing centers or courses is inappropriate because writers do not *perform* with an explicit sense of those absolutes. Form is a gradually achieved consequence of the search for meaning, not a preconception.

The Pedagogy of Form and the Pedagogy of Meaning

Writing teachers and tutors need to become more philosophically deliberate about these issues before they can hope to refine their classroom and writing center methods. They also need to give less credence to unexamined tradition and more to an empirical regard for what writers do and how they learn to do it. Tutors have two excellent laboratory subjects near at hand: themselves and their students, their own composing processes and those of the writers they tutor. Nothing informs so quickly about composing as watching people do it while remaining open-minded and reflective about what one sees. To illustrate, consider the following paragraph and the change of view about it that can come from knowing how the writer constructed it. The paragraph was written by a first-year college student who was also asked to compose aloud into a tape recorder so that the teacher could gain insight into the choice-making process as it occurred.[6] First, the paragraph:

> Jane, I imagine, is a wonderful friend. Being her brother, I don't qualify as a friend. We have a superficial friendship only to keep our parents' sanity. (To give an example, sitting at the dinner table, she will complain about the juicy thick steak that she is not eating. I will offer to take it off her hands for her. But rather than give it to her brother, she will march into the kitchen and throw it out.) This doesn't last long though. As soon as the folks are asleep, she starts in. Monday night football will have a tied score. There is five

minutes left and the Steelers are on the ten yard line and all of a
sudden, I am confronted with I Love Lucy. It is really too bad that
she is so bright and talented and uses that as a weapon.

A traditionalist might view this paragraph in purely formal terms,
regarding it not as one moment in a writer's continuing struggle to conceive and convey something of personal significance but as a violation of
ironclad principles of paragraph structure. It lacks unity, coherence, and
emphasis; it lacks a topic sentence and any clear pattern of subordinations;
its examples are not closely tied to the general statements they are
supposed to modify. *Friendship,* the traditionalist might say, should have
been defined right at the start since that is the broadest idea in the
paragraph. Then the writer should have explained why he and his sister
could not be friends, offering an example or two—but more pertinent
examples than those now included in the paragraph. Finally, since the
concluding sentence introduces new information unconnected to the issue
of friendship and the writer's relationship to his sister, it should be
discarded in favor of a summary of the paragraph's "main points." In
short, structural prescriptions might well dominate over an effort to find
out what actually mattered to the writer, what the writer intended to say
by means of the choices he made. Teachers commonly allow their models
of the Ideal Text, their private notions of formal propriety, to deprive
writers of control over their own purposes, interpreting any deviation
from the Ideal Text as a skill deficiency.[7] These teachers might say that
the writer of the statement above lacks ability to organize paragraphs
correctly, with topic sentences, supporting examples, and appropriate
conclusions. The writer should work at paragraph development drills.

But let us now eavesdrop on the writer's own process of discovering
meanings by looking at his writing together with the transcript of his oral
composing. Brackets indicate when the writer is talking and when he is
writing portions of the paragraph.

> [Talking] Now, alright, let's see. [Writing] Sister dearest, starring
> Jane. [Talking] You understand, the names have been changed, to
> protect—so she doesn't know—all right. [Writing] Jane is, I [Talk-
> ing] imagine—i-m-a—you're going to have to correct the spelling,
> anyway. [Writing] imagine, is a wonderful friend [Talking] friend,
> n-d, that's right. [Writing] But unfortunately [Talking] no—I have
> an inescapable, marvellous invention [Writing] I, being her brother,
> am not her friend [Talking] Let's see. Oh, okay—out loud [Puts in a
> period] [Writing] Not that we don't try to be friends [Talking] f-r-i-
> e-n-d-s. No, that's silly. [Reading] Not that we don't try to be friends
> [Laughter and talking] It's just that over the years we've learned
> how to be enemies. Hmm. When she came back from school—she is
> taking a semester off from school—I figured, you know, we're both
> mature people, we can be friends—but, nooo. Oh, I'm not writing

anymore. Gotta write, not talk. I can talk and write? Okay. But this doesn't make any sense. [Reading] Jane is, I imagine, a wonderful friend. But being her brother, being her brother [Talking] You know, that doesn't make any more sense either. Wait a minute—could I just change that around? Let's see: being her brother, I am not her friend. [Reading] Being her brother [Writing] though [Reading] I am not her friend. [Talking] Let's see. I'll start all over again. Jesus, I've got to learn to spell. [Writing] is a wonderful friend. [Talking] n-d. [Writing] Being her brother, I don't qualify as a friend. [Talking] Period. [Writing] We have a superficial [Talking] i-c-i-a-l [Writing] friendship [Reading] a superficial friendship [Writing] Only [Reading] Only [Writing] to keep my our parents' sanity. [Talking] I hope she never sees this! 'Cause even though she's smaller than me she packs a punch. Let's see. This has to be short, so I can't go into past history or anything—Oh, I can start with past history? [Writing] To give an example, sitting at the dinner table, she will complain about the juicy thick steak [Talking] e-a-k? [Writing] that she is not eating. I will offer to take it off her hands for her. But [Talking] Uh, oh, you aren't supposed to start—oh, I don't know, okay. [Writing] rather than give it to her [Talking] Wonderfully sweet—blow your own horn, David! [Reading] to her [Writing] brother, she will march [Talking] c-h [Writing] into the kitchen and throw it out. [Talking] Sweet girl. Hmm. Do you want me to just write what I am thinking? Or is, do I have to write—like an essay—I should talk what I am thinking? Okay, cause that's not what I've been doing. All righty, then, I will put a line through "sweet girl." I need a cigarette. Let's see, so . . . . [Reading] Jane, I imagine, is a wonderful friend. Being her brother, I don't qualify as a friend. We have a superficial friendship only to keep our parents' sanity. To give an example, sitting at the dinner table, she will complain about the juicy thick steak [Talking] Well, that's not an example of keeping our parents' sanity. That's an example of her insanity. So, that doesn't make any sense—um, I guess I have to, uh, give an example of what I said before that. All right. [Reading] I don't qualify as a friend. We have a superficial friendship only to keep our parents' sanity. [Talking] So, I'll put that in parentheses 'cause that should not follow what I just said. [Reading] I don't qualify . . . . We have a superficial friendship only to keep our parents' sanity. [Writing] This doesn't last long. As soon as the folks are asleep, she starts in. [Talking] Let's see. An example of how she starts in. Let's see. [Reading] This doesn't last long. As soon as the folks are asleep, she starts in. [Talking] Mostly minor stuff—just enough to pick at you. [Writing] Monday night [Talking] g-h-t [Writing] football will have a tied score. There is five minutes and the Steelers [Talking] S-t-e-e-l-e-r-s [Writing] are on the ten yard line and all of a sudden [Talking] d-d-e-n [Writing] I am confronted with I Love Lucy. [Talking] Granted, my caring about football is as ridiculous as her caring about "I Love Lucy," but certain things are important—But you see, writing takes an awful lot longer than the time we've been given—like most of this—if I just had longer—this would all be trashed, right off, and I would start probably in a very different way

and never mention "I Love Lucy." Well, I would, I don't know—"I
Love Lucy" is kind of interesting—I have yet to get up to the present
time—she threw the steak out when she was much younger—now
she is on to bigger and better things—well, she is very good at getting
her way about things—when it comes to, like, getting money out of
our parents, she's really wonderful at that—I get tipped with the
terrible guilts if I feel that I want something from them—I just, if it
doesn't work the first time, I give up—but she will go at it and go at
it until she gets what she wants. So why don't you write that instead
of Monday night football? But the folks are asleep . . . . Hmmm.
Let's see. I'd have to work that one out later. This all has yet to be
rearranged. This is only supposed to be one paragraph. If I could
write a paper, I could push all of this around in different places, and
by the end of the paper—or probably scratched out. Hmm. [Writing]
Actually, I love [Talking] Her dearly. Scratch that one out, too.
Let's see. . . . Taping myself makes me silly. It upsets her a lot that
I'm older than her, and my parents always treated us a little
differently—you know, I expected to be semi-responsible, and to be
able to take care of things, while they really don't expect anything
like that from her, you know. [Writing] It is really too bad that she
is so bright and talented but does [Talking] e-s [Writing] not [Talk-
ing] Hmm. No, that's wrong. [Reading] that she's so bright and
talented [Writing] and uses that as a weapon.[8]

What can be learned from this narrative? Though the writer feels
awkward at having to write and talk at the same time, we nonetheless
glimpse something of the true nature of composing—its messiness, the
starts, stops, and restarts, the groping and tentativeness, the labored
articulating of meanings and the struggle to tie them together as a
coherent statement. This writer is in pursuit of a significance that matters
but that also persistently eludes him. Each assertion is a distinct effort to
close on what the writer wishes to say about his relationship to his sister,
but each causes dissatisfaction as well because of its inadequate or
incomplete rendering of his experience. In short, the writer behaves and
feels like the rest of us, like all writers regardless of their expertise, testing
and reformulating ideas, following false trails, looking backward and
forward in order to decide what to say next, wondering how to make
connections, toying with language, getting distracted and stalling, associating freely, nitpicking over technical details, rambling, revising, and
forever registering discontent with the results of his labor. Underlying all
of these activities, meanwhile, and giving them a sense of direction and
momentum, is the writer's own growing awareness of intent: his desire,
not merely to complete an assignment, realize some formal absolute, or
imitate a teacher's notion of verbal decorum, but to make valuable
statements about the meaning of his own experience.

The most telling point of disjunction between this writer's narrative of
his composing and the hypothetical traditionalist critique of his paragraph

offered earlier is the fact that "the meaning of friendship" is not really what the writer wishes to discuss, though "friendship" is indeed the first and most general concept he introduces. His concern, instead, is to learn about his relationship with his sister, to make sense of his feelings toward her and perhaps to ponder as well their different relationships with their parents. The teacher who allows a preoccupation with the "correct" forms of paragraphs to dictate how writers will be required to function would surely, in this instance, sacrifice the writer's purpose in favor of a personal agenda. The student writer, recognizing a possible confrontation of goals, would quickly enough capitulate to the teacher's wishes and compose the teacher's paragraph about friendship—but at what cost to motivation, to his sense of the value of composing and his own accomplishment as a writer?

It is worth noting the harm already done to him by teachers who have so exaggerated formal and technical constraints that his awareness of them actually impedes his effort to pursue the meanings he values. Time and again he worries about whether he has said things the "right way": he has to "correct the spelling" ("I've got to learn how to spell"); his statement must be "short" ("This is only supposed to be one paragraph") so he cannot "go into past history or anything"; he should not begin a sentence with *but;* he is nervous about whether or not he is allowed to "just write what I am thinking." These issues repeatedly interrupt his train of thought, betraying the tension between his desire to make meaning and an imposed requirement to follow orders of some sort. In view of his genuine inexperience at making connections explicit for a reader, the concern of his past teachers for inculcating mechanical rules seems rather inappropriate.

There are intriguing clues in the narrative to suggest that this student writer is becoming more aware, as he writes, of what he means and how he can convey it. And, interestingly, he is already aware that he has not yet achieved the result he is after. Far from supposing that his paragraph represents completed writing, he is quite sensitive to the evolving shape of a discourse, perhaps more so than the traditionalist instructor who views the paragraph as a "product" to be evaluated for evidence of skill deficiencies: "Writing takes an awful lot longer than the time we've been given—like most of this—if I just had longer—this would all be trashed . . . and I would start probably in a very different way and never even mention 'I Love Lucy'"; "This all has yet to be arranged"; "If I could write a paper, I could push all of this around in different places." More important, the writer really is making progress toward the coherence he seeks, although the completed paragraph does not yet reflect it. He recognizes a problem with the example of his sister's throwing out the steak: it does not effectively modify what precedes it. A teacher's criticism of its lack of relevance would have minimal value for the writer, therefore, since he already understands the difficulty. He knows too that the reference to Monday night football and "I Love Lucy" should be "trashed" in favor of less superficial instances of the strain in his relationship with his sister. The example of her skill at manipulating their parents and his resentment of her seeming freedom to be less responsible than he are more suited to his purpose; presumably, he would exploit them if he had more space and time. The mysterious last sentence in the paragraph, which some teachers might be inclined to call irrelevant, is a reference to this unexpressed example: his sister uses her intelligence, inappropriately he believes, to get money from their parents. The writer's narrative, then, is rich in potential for more writing and so, too, is his paragraph if a tutor can see it in the right light.

The tutor (or teacher) who has achieved a philosophical perspective on composing and an awareness of how writers actually work would be less likely to approach this student's writing in a formalistic way. The tutor's responses to the paragraph would be aimed at assisting the writer's ongoing pursuit of his own intentions, the making and conveying of meanings that he values. The tutor might recognize, for instance, that the writer has not yet reached the point where he can say exactly why he and his sister are not friends, but that the key to their strained relationship seems to lie in her rather selfish behavior as suggested in the writer's examples, both those expressed in the paragraph and those in the composing-aloud narrative. The tutor might ask questions about the writer's reactions to his sister's behavior: why it bothers him so much, whether her age justifies it or not, whether he believes that there is yet some hope for the friendship he seems to wish for at least implicitly in the paragraph. Questions such as these mean that the writer needs to do more writing, perhaps a longer statement in which he can make the connections among statements and examples more explicit for the reader. The tutor should not assume that he or she knows what the writer wants to say, nor should the tutor have a plan to help him say it "the right way." The tutor simply should serve as a sounding board, offering the writer some strategic questions whose answers, which it is the writer's business to supply, may well enhance the coherence of his writing.

The Complementary Functions of Center and Classroom

Of course, everything that has been said here about gaining philosophical perspective and observing writers at work applies equally to classroom teachers and writing center tutors. Indeed, our most important point is that tutors, far from performing an adjunct or support service, do essentially the same work as their classroom counterparts—and do it under conditions that can be particularly beneficial to writers. The tutor, like the classroom writing teacher, is preeminently a reader whose informed, facilitative responses to writers not only provide them with the feedback needed to make more effective choices, but also dramatize for them the nature of writing as a process of making and communicating meaning. The tutor is not, therefore, a mechanic specializing in superficial maintenance, any more than the classroom teacher is a dispenser of prefabricated, all-purpose formal shells into which writers pour their "content." Ideally, teachers and tutors are interchangeable because their tasks are equivalent: creating incentive to write by taking writers' meanings seriously and guiding writers by responding to their discourses in ways that enable them to perceive the uncertainties their choices have created in readers. What changes between the classroom and the writing center is not the skill of the teacher or the focus of the work, but only the context of reader response. That difference is significant and worth discussion, but it is not finally as important as the similarities of attitude, outlook, and method that relate classroom teachers and writing center tutors.

The advantage of the classroom is the presence of many different readers, other students as well as the teacher. A writer can receive multiple responses to his or her own work and can learn from responding to the work of others. The disadvantage, however, is that the teacher reader's attention is diffused among many writers so that no one of them can receive the close, immediate support that is most desirable. Furthermore, most of a classroom teacher's responses are written rather than oral and are returned days after students' initial composing has occurred; because time is limited the responses are abbreviated as well as delayed and distant.

The center, by contrast, offers immediate, close, and extensive support to individual writers in a setting where writers and readers can converse directly about the motives for authorial choices and the potential reactions of an audience, where more writing can take place on the spot in answer to questions that enable the writer to reconceive ideas or reevaluate strategies. A tutor is freer to look over a writer's shoulder, to inquire about purposes and choices even as the writer is coming to discover them, to represent the reader's perspective at the moment of composing, thereby concretizing the needs and expectations of audiences for writers who may not fully have considered them.

The writer of the paragraph cited earlier surely could have profited from this kind and quality of attention. A tutor could readily have elicited in conversation much of the information contained in the enlightening, but also rather awkward and sometimes ambiguous, orally composed narrative. Knowing the unarticulated line of thought of which the paragraph is an inadequate visible sign, the tutor could have supported the writer in discovering a fuller expression of his meaning. The writing center, then, can be, in certain ways, more flexible than the classroom to anticipate the special requirements of individuals; it is not a substitute for the writing course, but neither is it subordinate to, the classroom. It is an alternative resource, with its distinctive advantages, available whenever writers, at any level of competence, desire the focused attention of a discerning reader.

A Philosophical Pedagogy

But this view of the writing center's function, and of methods pertinent to tutorial work, assumes the larger philosophical perspective on the nature of composing and the teaching of writing which we have been discussing. A tutor who has no concern for a writer's meanings is not more effective than the classroom teacher merely because of the tutorial environment. Indeed, students are commonly more reluctant to visit writing centers than to suffer through coursework when tutoring emphasizes the same drill-on-skill pedagogy: spending an hour (often of one's free time, no less!) on the subordinate clause unit of a workbook is even less agreeable to normal human beings than practicing comparison-contrast in the classroom.

Purposeful instruction derives from philosophical awareness; an understanding of relationships between the concepts pertinent to a subject, the objectives of one's teaching, the means available to achieve those objectives and a sense of how people learn and how the learning can be encouraged. If the teaching of writing has been impoverished in the past, the reason is not the fact that writing centers have failed to supplant classrooms. The reason is that teachers in both places have failed to master their disciplines. Let us all, as conscientious writing teachers, take pains to insure that we have finished our own homework before we insist too strenuously that students knuckle down to theirs.

Notes

1. Ann E. Berthoff, *The Making of Meaning* (Montclair, N.J.: Boynton/ Cook, 1981).

2. In Chapter 1 of *The Composing Processes of Twelfth Graders,* NCTE Research Report, no. 13 (Urbana, Ill.: National Council of Teachers of English, 1971), Janet Emig demonstrates this point. The writers she interviewed seldom used outlines or any other "textbook formulas" when they composed.

3. Maxine Hairston,"The Winds of Change: Thomas Kuhn and the Revolution in the Teaching of Writing," *College Composition and Communication* 33 (February 1982): 76–88.

4. Richard Braddock, "The Frequency and Placement of Topic Sentences in Expository Prose," *Research in the Teaching of English* 8 (Winter 1974): 287–302.

5. James Britton et al., *The Development of Writing Abilities (11–18)* (London: Macmillan Education, 1975; distributed in the United States by the National Council of Teachers of English).

6. This technique, called protocol analysis, has been used by many researchers, particularly Emig (cited above) and Linda Flower, "Writer-Based Prose: A Cognitive Basis for Problems in Writing," *College English* 41 (September 1979): 19–37.

7. For an extensive explanation of this concept, see Lil Brannon and C. H. Knoblauch, "Students' Rights to Their Own Texts: A Model of Teacher Response," *College Composition and Communication* 33 (May 1982): 157–166.

8. For further discussion of this protocol, see C. H. Knoblauch and Lil Brannon, *Rhetorical Tradition and the Teaching of Writing* (Montclair, N.J.: Boynton/Cook, 1983).

5 The Writing Center and the Paradoxes of Written-Down Speech

Patrick Hartwell
Indiana University of Pennsylvania

Hartwell explores the paradoxes of "written-down speech"—writing that simply transcribes spoken language—in order to develop a pedagogy suitable for writing centers. In this context he makes a strong case for the self-destructive effects of writing instruction based on rules of grammar.

I want to explore some of the paradoxes faced by college students writing at the level I think of as "written-down speech"—that is, students who can only transcribe their spoken language onto paper, without recourse to the cohesive devices, structural links, and organizational frameworks of written discursive prose. Doing so will enable me to suggest why writing centers—and particularly writing center tutors—are so effective in improving the writing of such students.

The Paradox of "Writing Errors"

James L. Collins and Michael M. Williamson provide a formal analysis of "written-down speech," which they call "semantic abbreviation in writing," because the full cues to meaning needed in writing are abbreviated, as they would be in ordinary speech, where the shared context of a speaking situation would provide those cues.[1] Collins and Williamson identify three features of writing at this stage. The first is *formulaic expression,* the transfer to the page of stock verbal expression which would require more specification in writing, as the expression "very interesting" in the following passage:

> He showed a very interesting movie on how to fight a fire with a fire extinguisher. The first part of the movie, they showed people that had no experience at all on how to fight a fire. . . .

The writer makes the claim, "very interesting," but does not move to develop it.

48

The second feature is *personal exophora,* the use of personal pronoun without a clear reference. (*Anaphora,* Greek "to carry again," is a normal pronoun reference; *exophora,* Greek "to carry without," is an unconnected reference.) An example of personal exophora is the use of *they* in the second sentence of the passage above—a perfectly natural statement in ordinary speech, but lacking a clear reference in writing (thus it might be revised to something on the order of "the directors showed people").

The third feature is *demonstrative exophora,* the use of an article or pronoun without a clear reference, as in the sentence below.

You should always aim at the base of *the* fire.

Here the second definite article presumes a fire shared by reader and writer. The writer intends a more general statement, "the base of a fire." Indeed, unless the pronoun *you* has a precise reference in the context, the writer intends a still more general claim:

One should always aim at the base of a fire.

Despite the precision of formal classification, I think writing center staff members can learn to identify written-down speech intuitively and with adequate precision. They might ask of a piece of writing, Is the writer trapped by the connections between writing and speaking (written-down speech), or is the writer able to make more productive use of those connections?

Here is a sample of written-down speech, a report written by an adult student enrolled in a CETA-sponsored employment training program:

Something Burning

[1] It was raining very hard on July 8, 1980, and Ron Grierson from the Flint, Fire Equipment Co. give a demostration on how to use a fire extinguisher. [2] He told us about Class A, fire which is the one that contain paper and garbage, and the only one that can be put out with water. [3] Then class B, fire, which is a liquid fire like greese lighter fluid, oil, gasoline, or any thing that boils.

[4] Next he told us about Class C, which is an electric fire. [5] He said for this the first thing you should do is pull off the main switch of the house, then use the extinguisher on the fire, and if the fire is too big call the fire department and get out of the house.

[6] He showed us a very interesting movie on how to fight a fire with a fire extinguisher. [7] The first part of the movie, they showed people that had no experience at all on how to fight a fire; they did not know the proper way to use the fire extinguisher.

[8] Then they were tought the right way to use a fire extinguisher, and when they went to use it they knew how to pull the pin from it and the proper way to aim at a fire; they were tought to aim at the base of the fire, instead of aiming at the middle of it and spreading it

[9] Then in the afternoon we went out side and everyone took there turn at using the fire extinguisher. [10] We were toled to go up

on the fire, with the wined to our back, and to never turn our back
on the fire, but back away when the fire is out. [11] You should
always aim at the base of the fire.[2]

This writer has a maturity, a level of understanding, that she cannot
adequately transfer onto paper. Certainly there is a fine irony in the
opening sentence, whether or not the writer was fully conscious of that
irony. The central lesson—"you should always aim at the base of the
fire"—is clearly mastered, though perhaps by memorizing it. (A demonstrator, before an actual audience, would indeed say, "You should always
aim at the base of the fire," and the writer transfers that speech directly to
the page.) But the shape of the paper—five paragraphs, each about the
same length—seems to be controlled by assumptions about English papers
(every paper has five paragraphs) rather than controlled by the logic of
the writer's subject-matter, which has three divisions: the lecture, the film,
and—apparently after the rain stops—the demonstration outside.

Many writing center staff members, particularly as they begin their
work in a center, tend to see such a writing sample, and the student
behind it, with a model provided by their own experience in writing
classes. They see themselves as "little English teachers," and their sense is
that "little English teachers" do what big English teachers do: identify
errors in writing and provide rules of grammar to correct them. But such
a model will not be much help in working with students at the level of
written-down speech.

For one thing, the notion "error in writing" turns out to be a surpris-
ingly fuzzy one. I have used this sample in workshops and seminars with
English teachers, and I occasionally ask the teachers to mark every error
in the sample, using the correction symbols they normally use. As might
be expected, the result is a dizzying profusion of symbols and labels, even
when readers agree on errors, as with the problems of tense and agreement
in sentences 1 and 2. But more than that, teachers differ in their perception
of error. Do we ask the writer to capitalize the first letter in "class B fire"
(sentence 3) to match "Class A fire" (sentence 2) and "Class C" (sentence
4), or do we prefer the lower case version or initial capitals all across
("Class B Fire")—or do we notice the issue at all? Do we correct "liquid
fire like greese lighter fluid" (sentence 3) to "liquid fire like greasy lighter
fluid" or to "liquid fire like grease, lighter fluid" or even to "liquid fire,
like grease, lighter fluid"? Do we change the occurrences of *back* in
sentence 10 to *backs,* reading it as "with the wind to our [individual]
backs, and to never turn our [individual] backs on the fire"? Or do we
leave it unmarked, implying a different, but equally correct reading: "with
the wind to our [collective] back, and to never turn our [collective] back

to the fire"? And usage questions, such as "everyone took [their] turn" (sentence 9) and "to never turn our back" (sentence 10), are still more complex in the responses they evoke.[3]

In fact, it may be that giving this student "rules of grammar" to correct "errors in writing" may work against her ability to improve her writing. The problems in the use of the comma in sentences 1, 2, and 3 probably appear because the writer has overgeneralized a rule of grammar, "Always separate the name of a city from the name of a state with a comma": Flint, Michigan. We might even speculate that the misspelling "toled" for *told* in sentence 10 grows out of the writer's concern with past tense markers (the same word is correctly spelled in sentences 2 and 4) and that the same misspelling may explain "wined" for *wind* in sentence 10.

Indeed, when we look beyond narrowly defined errors in writing, we can see that this writer has larger problems in expressing herself to a reader. She is uncertain about tone—the flat understatement of the body of the paper does not match the urgency of the final sentence. She is equally uncertain about her reader (note, for example, the shift from *we* to *you* in sentences 5 and 11). Like most basic writing students, she is tied to a narrative order, unable to recast her experiences in a discursive mode, and she has more trouble—both in structure and in correctness—with the classification of fires in the first two paragraphs than with the experiences that follow, which more readily lend themselves to narration. She uses semicolons correctly (in sentences 7 and 8)—the use of the semicolon had recently been discussed in her class. But beyond that, she seems limited to written-down speech, so that along with "errors in writing" come what are finally more serious needs.

A Diagnostic Method

Perhaps the best way to isolate the special needs of writers at the level of written-down speech is to ask them to read their writing aloud so the gap between what is written and what is meant can be heard as well as seen. The following sample is a partial transcription of this writer reading her essay into a tape recorder. I provide phonetic transcriptions of her pronunciation in brackets and identify most of the instances in which what she reads departs from what she wrote. I might note, to begin with, that she consistently reads the words *a, the,* and *about* with their formal stressed pronunciations, as "aye," "thee," and "ayebout," rather than with their informal pronunciations, suggesting that she has a rather artificial view of "reading aloud" and perhaps of reading and writing more generally.

Something Burning

[1] It was raining very hard on July 8, 1980, and Ron Grierson

    [ðiy] *no pause*   [geyv ey] [deməstreyʃən]
from the Flint, Fire Equipment Co. give a   demostration on how

    [ey]   [eybawt] *no pause pause*
to use a fire extinguisher. [2] He told us about Class A, fire which

  [ðiy]   [conteynz]
is the one that contain paper and garbage, and the only one that

               no sentence
               intonation   *no pause*   [ey]
can be put out with water. [3] Then class B, fire, which is a liquid

    [griys // layter fluwId //]   *no pause*
fire like greese lighter fluid, oil, gasoline, or any thing that boils.

                         [ɔn]   [fayrz]
[4] Next he told us about Class C, which is an electric fire.

          [ðiy]   [wiy]   [pʏl ðiy . . .]
[5] He said for this the first thing you should do is pull off the

                    [ðiy]   [ðiy]
main switch of the house, then use the extinguisher on the fire,

    [ðiy]   [ðiy]
and if the fire is too big call the fire department and get out of

[ðiy]
the house.

           [impɔrtnt]
[6] He showed us a very interesting movie on how to fight a fire

with a fire extinguisher. [7] The first part of the movie, they

showed people that had no experience at all on how to fight a fire;

they did not know the proper way to use the fire extinguisher.

          [tɔt]
[8] Then they were tought the right way to use a fire

[ðɛn]—*followed by great difficulty*

extinguisher, and when they went to use it they knew how to pull

[ɪt]

the pin from it and the proper way to aim at a fire; they were

[tɔt]

tought to aim at the base of the fire, instead of aiming at the

sentence
intonation

middle of it and spreading it

no pause

[9] Then in the afternoon we went outside and everyone took

[tɔld]

there turn at using the fire extinguisher. [10] We were toled to go

[wɪnd]

up on the fire, with the wined to our back, and to never turn our

[bæks]

back on the fire, but back away when the fire is out. [11] You

should always aim at the base of the fire.

This reading has to give a jolt to the little English teacher in all of us. Without any instruction, the writer, reading her work aloud, corrects essentially all errors of grammar, spelling, and, by intonation, punctuation. The written forms, "Flint, Fire Equipment Co.," "Class A, fire," and "Class B, fire," are read without the pauses suggested by the commas; tense, agreement, and plural forms are corrected ("he *gave* a demonstration"; "the one that *contains* paper and garbage"; "never turn our *backs* on the fire"); the series construction of "grease, lighter fluid, oil, gasoline, or anything that burns" is read appropriately; the fragment of "sentence" 3 is read as part of the previous sentence; the shifting references to *we* and *you* are in part regularized (in sentence 5 she reads *you* as "we"); and the misspellings *toled* and *wined* are read correctly as "told" and "wind." The writer for the most part adjusts to her misreadings: when she reads *an* in "an electric fire" (sentence 4) as "on," she adjusts her syntax to make sense, "on electric fires." There are some gaps, of course: the pronunciation "demostration" matches its mispelling (aside from *interesting* and *extinguisher*—certainly learned spellings—it is the only Latinate word in the passage); the writer does not notice the usage problems in sentences 9 and 10; and, more importantly, most of the discourse problems of written-down speech remain.

Nevertheless, asking the student to read her work aloud has provided us with an essential first step in diagnosis. It has given us an insight into what the writer thinks "reading aloud" means. It has allowed us to see, at point after point, what the writer intended to communicate. It has allowed us to see that the errors in writing, which loomed so large in our first reading, are not really that important: the writer has the tacit language skills to correct almost all of them.

But there's a further paradox here. When this writer read her work aloud, for all practical purposes she corrected all her errors. Yet she did not notice that what she read departed from what she had written. Indeed, in the larger experiment from which this sample was taken, seventeen of

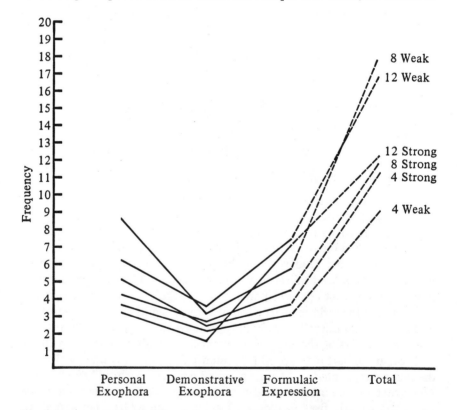

Fig. 1. Patterns of semantic abbreviation for groups of strong and weak writers in grades four, eight, and twelve. (Reprinted from James L. Collins and Michael M. Williamson, "Spoken Language and Semantic Abbreviation in Writing," *Research in the Teaching of English* 15 [1981]: 32. Copyright © 1981 National Council of Teachers of English. Reprinted by permission.)

the eighteen CETA adult students corrected essentially all of their errors of grammar, spelling, and, by intonation, punctuation—but none of their errors in usage—when they read their work aloud. Yet none noticed that what they read departed from what they had written. The problem of the writer at the level of written-down speech is not the problem of "correcting errors"; clearly these errors are naturally corrected in oral reading. Rather, the problem is more abstract: writers at the level of written-down speech need to develop a sense of "text as text" that will allow them access to their natural language abilities.

Collins and Williamson, whose analysis of "semantic abbreviation in writing" was cited at the beginning of this essay, performed an experiment that sharpens this sense of paradox. They gathered writing samples from fourth-, eighth-, and twelfth-grade students judged to be "strong" or "weak" in writing ability, and they analyzed those samples for the features of semantic abbreviation discussed earlier. Their results are summarized in Figure 1; the reader can get the quickest sense of those results by skimming down the righthand column.

The strong writers, though tightly grouped, show a slight increase in semantic abbreviation—an increase suggesting that stronger writers learn to exploit the productive links between speaking and writing. The weaker writers show an entirely different pattern of development. As they move through school, they rely more and more on semantic abbreviation, on written-down speech. The results of the Collins and Williamson experiment allow me to draw a first negative conclusion: as weak writers move through school, they behave in increasingly counterproductive ways as writers *in spite of* instruction.

The Paradox of Writing Instruction

Let me now carry the paradox one step further, to develop some evidence that supports an even stronger claim: that weak writers behave in counterproductive ways *because of* instruction.[4] William D. Page and Gay Su Pinnell, in a recent book on reading comprehension, discuss an informal experiment in which fourth-grade students were asked to write brief answers to three questions, Why do people read? What do people do when they read? and How do people learn to read?[5] The experiment isolated the students' models of reading rather effectively, and, as we might expect, better readers had a better sense of what reading was all about. Accordingly, I have begun to ask students to respond, in a sentence or two, to three parallel questions: Why do people write? What do people do when they write? and How do people learn to write?

I have preliminary data from several third-, fourth-, and fifth-grade classes, from eighth- and ninth-grade classes, and from several college freshman classes. In each case, instructors were asked to single out students they considered "strong" writers and "weak" writers. Here are representative answers to one question, "What do people do when they write?" First, answers by elementary students deemed "strong" writers:

> When they begin they think of stuff to write.
> They think of what they are going to write. They ask a person if it sounds good.
> They really open their minds and futures.
> They share their thoughts with someone.
> Some people write storys and poems so you wont be bord.
> They relax.
> Think and learn.
> Write letters to thery frendes. Write letters to you'r Grandmother.

Compare these to the answers of elementary students labeled by their teachers as "weak" writers:

> They hold the pendil tightly.
> They sit up straight.
> They write people name.
> Make letters.
> They waste ink or lead.
> Move there fingers. And write neat.
> They moiv there hand and they moive the pencicle.
> Hold the crat. [crayon?]
> They have a piece of paper and a pencil.
> People our suposed to sit down when they write so they dont mess up there paper.
> After they write it they make sure it's neat. They copy it down.
> They write letters and numbers.

Here are representative answers from eighth- and ninth-graders. First the "strong" writers:

> They tell about things like a story about someone or even theirself.
> They get stuff across to other people.
> Actually, their making symbols and shapes to stand for words.
> They use their mind to guide their hand to express their thoughts.
> They get stuff across to people or they entertain people.

Now the "weak" writers:

> Just write stuff down on a piece of paper.
> The hold a pencil and move their hands.

> They put the point of the pencil to the paper and start making words and letters.
>
> Think about what there going to say.
>
> They use up extra energy.

The same pattern appears with college students. Here are responses to What do people do when they write? by college freshmen labeled "strong" writers:

> They are conveying thoughts and ideas.
>
> People explain their ideas, theories, stories and imagination with each other when they write.
>
> People try to translate their feelings or beliefs on paper.
>
> When people write they often do so to express their opinion or ideas. When you write you don't have a time limit and you can take your time and express yourself in the best possible way.
>
> I think when people write they sometimes reveal thoughts and feelings which would otherwise be locked inside them.
>
> When people write they are expressing themselves in a way unlike no other.
>
> What I think people do when they write is to go to another world, another dimension. Writing lets you experience all sorts of things, and it is all at your fingertips.

Here are responses by college freshmen considered weaker writers:

> They gather information, organize it, and then supposedly make sense out of it.
>
> They express their view.
>
> People write through English grammar, punctuation, etc.
>
> When people write they combine any previous knowledge on the subject with research information.
>
> Carefully arrange sub units under a main topic in a logical, easy to read manner.
>
> First you pick your topic, then you make sure that you have enough information. Then you rewrite and check the spelling and copy it down.
>
> Using correct usuage and grammer.
>
> When people write they verbally express themselves through ideals, comments and personal experiences. They express their overall views on the given topic and later draw conclusions in a patterned coherent fashion.
>
> They make contact between the head of a pencil or pen to paper or other serfaces. They make letters that form words that other people can read and understand.

These results have to give a further jolt to the little English teacher in all of us—and one would hope, a fatal jolt. Who learns what English teachers tell them? Weak writers. They learn a mechanical view of writing, dominated by a rigid sense of form and a strong, even dominant, concern with grammatical correctness. In a parallel study, Mike Rose analyzed the writing processes of fluent and weaker college writers, and he found that the weaker writers had the most rigid models of the writing process, models he characterized as made up of "rigid rules, inflexible plans, and the stifling of language."[6] Better writers go beyond what teachers and textbooks tell them; they somehow grasp a more productive model of writing.[7]

In fact, we can explore this paradox even further. Let's suppose that weaker writers want to improve their writing—given their model of writing, what do they do? Answer, using the responses of the elementary students: they sit up straighter, they form their letters more neatly, and they hold the pencil more tightly. Answer, using the responses of weaker college writers: "they verbally express themselves"; they "supposedly make sense out of it"; they try harder to use "correct usuage and grammer." In other words, the more weaker writers try, the less they improve, because their model of writing enforces behavior that is counterproductive to the mastery of adult literacy.

The Value of "Tutor Talk"

These paradoxes begin to explain why writing center tutorials can be so useful for students at the level of written-down speech. Textbooks aren't going to be much help for such students ("rules of grammar" only get the writer of "Something Burning" into trouble), and "teacher talk" has clearly been counterproductive (note that the comments of our weaker writers imitate "teacher talk"). But what might be characterized as "tutor talk" can be immensely productive; it can provide an accessible way for writers at the level of written-down speech to move toward the special code of literate behavior. There is, of course, a developing body of information about the value of peer tutoring; I would like to supplement that information by examining a converging range of speculation about the transmission of literacy, speculations by sociolinguists, cognitive psychologists, and learning theorists, that should lead us back to a powerful justification of "tutor talk."

Sociolinguist Roger Shuy criticizes conventional models of literacy—models like that of the little English teacher—and substitutes an "iceberg model" to explain classroom or writing center interaction.[8] At the top of the iceberg, the small portion we can be consciously aware of, is the learning that we can see, that we can know about in a formal way. Much more crucial, from his perspective, is the learning below the surface of the teacher's or tutor's conscious awareness, for example, the tacit force of the models we glimpse when we ask people, What do people do when they write? Good advice, from this perspective, is "Learn to trust your instincts, not your rules."

Cognitive psychologist Frank Smith, in a recent book on writing, refines this perspective.[9] He argues that it would be impossible to learn to write if we viewed learning to write simply as the discrete mastery of individual skills, noting that the average college graduate can spell, use, and understand between 150,000 and 200,000 words, in itself an impossible learning task. (We would come to a similar conclusion if we tried to list, as discrete learning tasks, everything that the writer of "Something Burning" would have to master to become a stronger writer.) What must happen in the mastery of literacy, Smith argues, is some more subtle transfer of more complex information, very much like the child's natural acquisition of spoken language. He characterizes this transfer with the words "demonstrations, engagement, and sensitivity."

The teacher-tutor is in fact constantly demonstrating adult literate behavior, although most of that demonstration is below the conscious awareness of the demonstrator. The learner, in turn, must have a certain engagement with that demonstration, a willingness to learn. And the demonstrator needs to be sensitive to the needs of the learner, to translate the learning task to the capabilities of the learner. For students at the level of written-down speech, this translation takes place through dialogue, through tutor talk, not through rules of grammar. "Trust people," Smith concludes, "not programs."

Reading theorists, as noted, have found that better readers have a better grasp of the purposes and goals of reading. Thus, they speak of "metacognitive awareness," our ability to monitor our own learning, and of "metalinguistic awareness," our ability to monitor our own language use.[10] The writer of "Something Burning," who writes "one that contain paper and garbage" but reads "one that contains paper and garbage," does not need little English teachers and "rules of grammar"; she needs a supportive environment that will help foster an awareness—a metalinguistic awareness—of the special needs of the many codes of written discourse. The writing center can provide such an environment.

Employing the Paradoxes

There are no simple answers to the paradoxes of written-down speech, and there is no single right way to deal in a writing center with the writer of "Something Burning." Reading aloud helps, obviously enough, and in a center forced to emphasize grammatical detail on a drop-in basis, it might be enough to isolate for the writer the places where she departs in reading from what she wrote, stressing that she already has the tacit language skills to make the necessary corrections. In a different writing center, with more time available, it might be useful to ask the writer to try some exercises designed to foster metalinguistic awareness.[11] In yet another context the tutor might rely on the tacit force of tutor talk and simply ask the writer to talk through her experiences and her reaction to them. A sensitive tutor, for example, might isolate the formative change offered by the writer's misreading of "an interesting movie" as "an important movie," focusing on that shift as a way to orient the writer to the needs of a reader. That would not be "useful work" from a little English teacher's point of view; in fact, it would be using a "mistake" in a positive way. But it might be productive work, given the paradoxes of written-down speech.

Thus my conclusion is a positive one, in spite of these paradoxes. A writing center provides an environment rich in a humane commitment to human communication. If tutors will learn to trust their instincts, writers will learn to trust theirs.

Notes

1. James L. Collins and Michael M. Williamson, "Spoken Language and Semantic Abbreviation in Writing," *Research in the Teaching of English* 15 (February 1981): 23–36.

2. This sample was submitted as part of a graduate research project by Frankie Miller, Delaware Technical and Community College, and Bruce Stanley, Reading Area (Pennsylvania) Community College. The name of the individual in sentence 1 has been changed, and the location in sentence 1 has been changed from the unexpected "Indiana, Pennsylvania," to the more expected "Flint, Michigan."

3. For responses to usage, see Joseph M. Williams, "The Phenomenology of Error," *College Composition and Communication* 32 (May 1981): 152–68, and for perceptions of error, see Sidney Greenbaum and John Taylor, "The Recognition of Usage Errors by Instructors of Freshman Composition," *College Composition and Communication* 32 (May 1981): 169–74.

4. This claim is strongly developed, along somewhat different lines, in a paper by Mike Rose, "Remedial Writing Courses: Do They Limit More Than Foster Growth in Writing? A Critique and a Proposal" (University of California, Los Angeles, 1982).

5. William D. Page and Gay Su Pinnell, *Teaching Reading Comprehension* (Urbana, Ill.: ERIC/RCS and National Council of Teachers of English, 1979).

6. Mike Rose, "Rigid Rules, Inflexible Plans, and the Stifling of Language," *College Composition and Communication* 31 (December 1980): 389–401.

7. These more productive models are discussed in Patrick Hartwell, "Writers as Readers" (Paper presented at the Annual Meeting of the Conference on College Composition, Dallas, March 1981; available from ERIC as ED 199 211).

8. Roger Shuy, "A Holistic View of Language," *Research in the Teaching of English* 15 (May 1981): 101–12.

9. Frank Smith, *Writing and the Writer* (New York: Holt, Rinehart and Winston, 1981). Three chapters are available as articles in *Language Arts:* "Demonstrations, Engagement, and Sensitivity: A Revised Approach to Language Learning," 58 (September 1981): 103–12; "Demonstrations, Engagement, and Sensitivity: The Choice between People and Programs," 58 (September 1981): 634–42; and "Myths of Writing," 58 (October 1981): 792–98.

10. Carol Chomsky presents a lucid discussion of this point of view in "Developing Facility with Language Structure," in *Discovering Language with Children,* ed. Gay Su Pinnell (Urbana, Ill.: National Council of Teachers of English, 1980), 56–59; more technical are Ann L. Brown, "Knowing When, Where, and How to Remember: A Problem of Metacognition," in *Advances in Instructional Psychology,* vol. 1, ed. Robert Glaser (Hillsdale, N.J.: Lawrence Erlbaum, 1978), and Ellen Bouchard Ryan, "Metalinguistic Development and Reading," in *Language Awareness and Reading,* ed. Lynn H. Waterhouse et al. (Newark, Del.: International Reading Association, 1980). I wish to thank a colleague at Indiana University of Pennsylvania, Dan Tannacito, for pointing out to me the relevance of this line of inquiry.

11. For a general discussion of metalinguistic awareness, see James L. Collins, "Speaking, Writing, and Teaching for Meaning," and Barry M. Kroll, "Developmental Relationships between Speaking and Writing," both in *Exploring Speaking-Writing Relationships,* ed. Barry M. Kroll and Roberta J. Vann (Urbana, Ill.: National Council of Teachers of English, 1981); for practical examples, see Patrick Hartwell and Robert H. Bentley, *Open to Language: A New College Rhetoric* (New York: Oxford University Press, 1982).

6 Promoting Cognitive Development in the Writing Center

Karen I. Spear
University of Utah

Spear presents a cognitive model for developmental writing in general and tutorials in particular. Her essay includes speculation about why writing centers should exist and a challenge to the most fundamental of writing center practices: the one-on-one tutorial.

Lawrence Kohlberg and Rochelle Mayer, in a 1972 *Harvard Educational Review* article, argue that intellectual and moral development are the only defensible aims of education. This "progressive" philosophy, they believe, invalidates the two other principal educational philosophies: the romantic self-actualization model and the mechanistic social welfare model, both of which seek to manipulate and control students' thoughts and behavior. "A notion of education for development and education for principles," the authors conclude, "is liberal, democratic, and nonindoctrinative. It relies on open methods of stimulation through a sequence of stages, in a direction of movement which is universal for all children. In this sense, it is natural."[1]

The cornerstone of Kohlberg's argument is the concept of developmental *stages,* a universally invariant, hierarchical progression of thought processes. Each successive stage reflects a different thought structure, increasingly differentiated and integrated as compared with the preceding structure. "Stage theory" approaches yield what Kohlberg terms "a functional epistemology of mind," a description of the cognitive and moral behavior evident at each stage and an understanding of the conditions necessary for progression from one stage to the next. The role of education, then, is to provide opportunities for learners to traverse completely their cognitive map, perhaps to accelerate the stages but certainly to facilitate movement to the highest possible levels of thinking and ethical judgment. Kohlberg's position is similar to those of a number of stage theorists, beginning with the extraordinarily influential work of Jean

Piaget. Though particular theories differ in some of their details, they mutually affirm the overall concept of stages, supporting Kohlberg's claim that development is the appropriate aim of education.

The developmental underpinnings of the various stage theories are particularly relevant to the role of the writing center. The existence of the writing center is testimony to educators' conviction that writing is fundamental to higher education. Yet, if the explicit mission of the writing center is to help students, especially basic writers, succeed in college by improving their writing, the implicit mission is to nurture the cognitive abilities that make good writing possible. Andrea Lunsford's thesis that basic writers "have not attained that level of cognitive development which would allow them to form abstractions or conceptions" affirms the need for a developmental approach in the writing center.[2] Carl Bereiter, in "Development in Writing," seems to concur, emphasizing that growth in writing stems from other, more basic forms of development—cognitive, social, moral, and probably linguistic.[3] My aim is to present an overview of three principal stage theories as they pertain to basic writers' cognitive development, to explore their implications for instruction, and to suggest a rationale for the existence of writing centers that goes beyond their usual role of promoting mastery learning and providing support for the larger writing program.

Basic Writers and Formal Operations: Developmental Goals

Piaget's description of thinking at the "formal operations" level sets forth an ideal standard of adult thinking. Formal operations, which begin sometime during adolescence, include a number of thought processes that are not present in earlier stages of thinking. Piaget calls these preceding stages sensori-motor, preoperational, and concrete operations. (See Figure 1.) Few if any basic writers have fully achieved formal operational thinking. Thus, the characteristics of formal operations not only clarify the cognitive goals of basic writing instruction, they also suggest the kinds of activities basic writers ought to engage in to stimulate and reinforce this level of thinking.

There are five primary characteristics of mature, formal operational thought. First, students become capable of abstract thinking. They can hold large bodies of information in their minds and manipulate ideas without needing concrete referents. Consequently, they come to reflect on and evaluate ideas, assuming a metaperspective that involves awareness not just of thought contents but of thought processes. In writing, this perspective is closely related to an awareness of structure that leads to coherence. Second, students are capable of what Piaget terms "hypothetico-deductive" thinking: the ability to formulate hypotheses and make deductions from them. Third, students engage in propositional thinking, devising assumptions for the sake of argument without requiring that the assumptions be valid. Students are able to arrive at a variety of possible propositions and devise criteria by which to accept or reject them. Propositional thinking leads to a fourth characteristic of formal operations, combinatorial logic. Students become aware of the potential relationships among variables in a field and are able to consider the possible effects of manipulating one or more variables while holding the others constant. For example, a student would recognize the multiple and related causes of a complicated problem like inflation and consider the effects of manipulating interest rates, credit, the money supply, unemployment, job programs, and so on. The ability to consider possible combinations leads to more deliberate, controlled problem solving, not the random, trial and error approaches that predominate at earlier stages. Fifth, students reach proficiency in setting up hierarchical classifications, perceiving subordinate nd superordinate relations and establishing criteria for membership in the various classes.[4]

Each of these general characteristics is fundamental in writing; they are analogues for skills that researchers have identified throughout the composing process, from exploring a topic to organizing and revising an essay. And with each of these operations, basic writers in the writing center have difficulty. John Butler, in his essay "Remedial Writers: The Teacher's Job as Corrector of Papers," highlights these students' inability

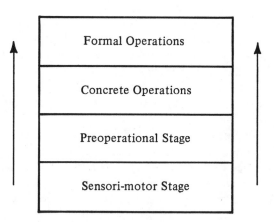

Fig. 1. Jean Piaget's stages of cognitive development.

to deal particularly well with the concrete much less the abstract or, in Piagetian terms, the formal.[5] Butler demonstrates basic writers' tendency to correct grammatical and syntactic faults in their writing as they read their papers aloud, projecting onto the page the sounds they hear in their minds. Lunsford's eye-opening study, "The Content of Basic Writers' Essays," extends this image of the basic writer, who is still at the stage of concrete operations.[6] Among her observations, Lunsford includes writers' tendencies to focus on personal experience rather than general principles (even when the focus is inappropriate to the topic), to view oneself as a victim of the powerful but anonymous "They," to take a conservative position on political and social issues, and, though not mentioned explicitly by Lunsford, to prefer, ironically, "safe" intellectual topics rather than those that call for personal experience and self-exploration. From the standpoint of developmental theory, these writers simply have not reached the cognitive level that most of them are capable of. Their deficiencies result less from lack of knowledge than from, as Martin Sleeper points out, "the need to reorganize" knowledge into more complex structures.[7]

Evidence from research in the development of historical thinking implies that basic writers' failure to reach the formal operational level is not uncommon. R. N. Hallam, a British historian, found from empirical investigations that in qualitative subject areas such as history, "children were reasoning at a lower level than had been expected, reaching, for the most part, the formal operational level at a chronological age of 16:2 to 16:6 years."[8] Further, substituting mental for chronological age, Hallam found that formal operations do not occur until 16:5 to 18:2 years, by contrast to formal operations in quantitative areas, which begin four to six years earlier.[9] What this illustrates is a phenomenon Piaget called "horizontal décalage," the gradual broadening of intellectual capabilities across content areas. Hallam's research, along with Kohlberg's, suggests that linguistic and judgmental reasoning are the last to reach formal operations, perhaps because of the complicated issues of values and independent decision making involved here. Piaget himself conceded that faced with new and bewildering tasks (such as writing for basic writers), people regress to earlier levels of thinking.[10]

This point of view requires that we look at basic writers' problems with language in a different way. Rather than replacing poor language structures with better ones, instructors are faced with introducing new cognitive operations. Writing center personnel therefore need to consider writing assignments that not only exercise the features of formal operations but that also elicit students' awareness of these new approaches to the problems and issues they are writing about. To do this effectively, instructors need a clear understanding of the thinking processes that basic writers tend initially to employ.

Basic Writers and Dualistic Thinking

William Perry's theory of intellectual development helps clarify some of the constraints on basic writers' thinking by exploring the complicated interplay of intellect and identity. Based on an elaborate study of Harvard undergraduates, Perry proposes a nine-stage model of intellectual and moral development, from "dualistic," right-wrong thinking to principled, committed thinking or, as Perry describes it, "a progression from thinking to metathinking, from man as knower to man as critic of his own thought."[11] Figure 2 presents a simplified version of Perry's model. The study, successfully replicated with other student populations, focuses on students' assumptions about the nature of truth, authority, and individual autonomy to illustrate how these assumptions restrict learning, especially during the early stages of cognitive development.

Perry's study is important for understanding basic writers because it takes us beyond what we can infer about their cognitive behavior from their writing to a more direct apprehension of the writers themselves. Another approach to understanding the cognitive development of writers, due largely to the influence of Piaget's theory of decentering and Lev Vygotsky's observations of children's "inner speech," has been to focus on problems resulting from *egocentricity*.[12] On the basis of Perry's study, however, egocentricity is a deceptively simple description of a complicated array of preconceptions embedded in a specific cognitive style. The first two positions in Perry's model, the dualistic positions, reveal the dynamics of this style.

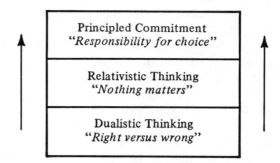

Fig. 2. A simplified version of William Perry's model of intellectual development.

For Perry, students' intellectual development during the college years is largely a process of overcoming the predominate assumption that Truth is synonymous with Authority, a position Perry calls "basic dualism." Although most students in his study had begun to move beyond the extremes of this initial position, it dominates the thinking of the immature and is particularly descriptive of the basic writer. At this stage, students structure their experience by dividing it into two camps:

> This division is between the familiar world of Authority-right-we, as against the alien world of illegitimate-wrong-others. In the familiar world, morality and personal responsibility consist of simple obedience. . . . In the educational aspect of this world, morality consists of committing to memory, through hard work, an array of discrete items—correct responses, answers, and procedures, as assigned by Authority. In this structure's most primitive form, Authority's omniscience is so taken-for-granted that no distinction is made between Authority and the Absolute. "Truth" and "what they say" function as tautological alternatives of expression, as do "right" and "what They want."[13]

These attitudes produce four significant departures from widely accepted assumptions about good writing. First, a person functioning dualistically insists on rules, formulas, and explicit instructions, convinced that success will result from strict obedience and conformity to expectations. For some basic writers these rules are conquerable through hard work; for others they are so overwhelming that they keep students from returning to the writing center. As a result, many basic writers seem to expend their energies fruitlessly, trying to divine the rules of the game, either the center's or those of the referring instructor. They cannot accept the fact that there is no clear, one-to-one correspondence between a teacher's expectations and a student's achievement. Consequently, writing center staffs need to recognize that these students' strategies derive from the values associated with dualistic thinking and to instill in basic writers the confidence necessary to identify and pursue their *own* goals. In so doing, they can bring students closer to a more mature view of writing— that good writing results from allowing oneself to discover and explore one's own ideas and from finding personal methods for making and expressing these discoveries.

Second, dualistic thinking is decidedly arhetorical. If Authority is indeed omniscient, a writer need not be excessively concerned with clarity. Authority will always "know what I mean" because "I am writing to tell Them what They want and what They already know." Such writing is not so much self-expressive as it is confirmatory, the written equivalent of the spoken "you know. . . ." Moreover, Authority is the only conceivable audience for one's writing—because Authority is giving the ultimate reward, the grades. Grades, in turn, primarily reflect procedural and quantitative performance (how long the paper is, how much time the student spent, how closely the paper conforms to the assignment), since recognizing the relative merit of a theme is outside the province of dualistic thinkers.

Third, interpretative tasks are virtually impossible because one writes to convey absolute truths. "A salient characteristic of this structure, and the source of its innocence," says Perry, "is its lack of any alternative or vantage point from which a person may observe it. Detachment is impossible, especially regarding one's own thought."[14] From this naiveté derives the quality of assured conviction that much basic writing conveys, the complacent innocence that justifies the most outrageous clichés and stereotypes. This characteristic runs counter to our understanding that prewriting is essentially an exploration of alternatives and that the process of writing is one of gaining increased perspective not just on the message but on the "transaction" between writer and audience.

Finally, because of their crippling dependence on Authority as source of truth, dualistic thinkers fail as makers of meaning. In other words, with their thinking restricted to discrete particles of information, these students are unable to perceive implicit connections among ideas or to supply those connections from their own musings on a topic. This failing seems to occur partly because of the conviction that the reader (the Authority) already knows how the parts fit together and partly because establishing meaningful connections among ideas involves considerable ability to interpret information and hypothesize about it—activities that are outside the cognitive reach of the dualistic thinker. In basic writers this tendency results in what Mina Shaughnessey calls "sentences of thought" rather than "passages of thought" since "the mind is not allowed to play upon the topic, to follow out the implications that lie within statements."[15] In short, the features of dualistic thinking are completely at odds with the necessities of formal operations that basic writers need to achieve to overcome their difficulties with writing.

A study of students' journals in an experimental course at the University of Minnesota helps to confirm these traits as characteristic of dualistic thinkers' writing.[16] Students in the course, all of them freshmen or sophomores, were described as either dualistic or relativist. In Perry's model relativistic thinking replaces dualistic as students begin to recognize multiple points of view and understand their contextual relevance. Perry equates the transition from dualism to relativism with the Fall, "man's taking upon himself, at the serpent's suggestion, the knowledge of values and therefore the potential of judgment."[17]

The journals that the two groups produced differed significantly. The relativists wrote extensively, using the journal for self-reflection and clarification of ideas. The dualists had trouble writing at all, largely because they perceived the journal as an assignment, externally imposed, rather than internally initiated and self-rewarding. Both groups found the journal difficult, but their difficulties varied greatly. The relativists worried about issues such as coherence and complexity of ideas, on both logical and rhetorical grounds. The dualists worried about grades. The relativists were frustrated at not being articulate enough to express all their ideas; the dualists were just frustrated—overwhelmed by the open-endedness of the journal assignment.

I do not wish to imply that all dualistic thinkers are basic writers or that dualistic thinking is the only trait that describes a basic writer. Secondary school background, writing experience, and the language environment at home and among peers all must have a bearing on the basic writer. But since most basic writers seem to be dualistic thinkers, the characteristics of dualistic thinking profoundly influence their writing. Reliable measures have been devised to place students at the various positions on Perry's scale, and they should be used in a sound research design. Meanwhile, if inferences based on the model are correct, researchers can follow up on the pedagogical implications of existing studies to consider directly the developmental needs of basic writers.

For instance, the assessment of students' journals at Minnesota was part of a larger study to determine the effects of various instructional techniques on students at different stages of development. The vehicle for the study, a literature and psychology course called "Themes in Human Identity," dealt with conflicts and paradoxes in the assigned readings in an attempt to influence students' cognitive development. Instructors were concerned with moving dualistic thinkers toward an awareness of multiple points of view and relative perspectives and relativistic thinkers toward commitments based on individually realized principles. The underlying assumption of the course was the notion that improving "students' abilities to analyze and synthesize seems to require helping them to alter their assumptions about the nature of knowledge and values."[18] This assumption reinforces James Moffett's assertion[19] that what inexperienced writers lack is not knowledge but awareness—in the case of basic writers, both audience awareness and self-awareness.

The pedagogical findings for dualistic thinkers emphasize the need for carefully sequenced assignments in the writing center. "For dualistic thinkers, it seems to be important for subject matter to be selected, sequenced, and presented to explicitly guide the student through relativistic operations. Such guides allow the students to practice relativistic skills and, also, to stretch their subjective paradigm for perceiving the world."[20] Specifically, the teaching of dualistic thinkers in the Minnesota course relied heavily on experiential learning, in class and out, as well as collaborative learning, both placing heavy emphasis on recognizing alternative points of view. Experiential teaching consisted essentially of varied role playing activities. Students assumed the roles of characters in novels, authors, psychological theorists, and so on to learn to project themselves into unfamiliar situations, empathize with another point of view, and comprehend the "field" of foreign situations, not just the discrete particles. Collaborative learning similarly emphasized alternative points of view, but it also helped to break the fusion of Authority and Truth. Equally important, small group experience seemed to satisfy the need of dualistic thinkers for security while they were being asked to confront ideas in new ways. Likewise, instructors attempted to provide the kind of structure these students need by giving explicit procedural directions for assignments, whether written or experiential. Interestingly, the students in this group made the greatest developmental gains.

Implications for Writing Center Practices

These findings confirm some writing center methods and suggest that we reconsider others. Writing centers seem especially committed to and successful in creating a secure, friendly, learning environment. Both groups of students in the Minnesota study found trusting relationships with teachers and discussion leaders essential—the relativistic students because they needed "space" for experimentation without risk of failure, the dualistic students because they needed personal encouragement as they began to redefine the nature of Authority. Writing centers that teach writing as a process also seem to be serving their students' developmental needs. This approach satisfies the dualist's need for direction, but it also diverts attention from particle to field as students are asked to consider larger "chunks" of writing in an organized way. Sentence combining, a familiar technique in the writing center, probably helps students move beyond dualistic thinking as well. Its emphasis on alternative combinations, especially in paragraph- and essay-length exercises, introduces students to relativism and field dependence. One peril, however, in the early stages of relativistic thinking is the recognition of alternatives without the ability to make qualitative discriminations. Students recognize options but fail to try them all, convinced that one choice is as good as another. An essential countermeasure is, as the Minnesota researchers found, group learning situations in which students can be asked to provide reasons for their choices.

The Tutorial Reconsidered

The importance of group learning in the Minnesota study calls into question one of the most fundamental of writing center practices: the one-on-one tutorial. If, as Perry suggests, the fusion of Truth and Authority is the crucial issue for dualistic thinkers, the one-on-one relationship may actually reinforce the fusion. Implicit in the relationship is the tutor who knows and the tutee who does not. One reason why peer tutoring may succeed over faculty tutoring is that peers are not automatically endowed with the same degree of omniscience as a faculty or a staff member. However, trainers need to ensure that their peer tutors do not tacitly fulfill basic writers' authority needs by becoming the authorities that the writers want them to be. Training models that emphasize nondirective communication skills seem most appropriate because of their emphasis on clarification, judgment, and decision making rather than didactic instruction.

Nevertheless, the one-on-one relationship may not foster long range developmental goals. No matter how nondirective a tutor may be, the tutee cannot experience multiple points of view and thus cannot easily make the transition into relativistic thought. Even when those in authority attempt to provide alternatives, the dualistic thinker, according to Perry's findings, simply questions their credentials as authorities or rejects the subject matter itself. Said one freshman in response to a general education course in science:

> That seems to be the excuse that natural science people give for these courses, they're supposed to teach you to arrive at more logical conclusions and look at things in a more scientific manner. Actually what you get out of that course is you, you get an idea that science is a terrifically confused thing in which nobody knows what's coming off anyway.[21]

Among basic writers, this response translates as annoyance with instructors for being too vague and lack of respect for writing.

On the other hand, dualistic thinkers seem more tolerant of diversity when it comes from their peers. Among them, dualistic thinkers are more willing to receive and offer alternatives. Group learning, therefore, helps to disengage Truth from Authority, eventually redistributing both to the group members. As a result, students assume greater responsibility for their ideas as well as increased skill in evaluating them. Because all these attitudes are crucial to writing development, writing centers might better serve their students by substituting small group sessions for one-on-one tutorials.

Mastery Tests and the Teaching of Form

The Minnesota study also calls into question the role of mastery tests in the writing center. A seventy-five year tradition of research has conclusively demonstrated the irrelevance of usage testing to writing competence (research that has nevertheless failed to affect many educators); the developmental approach provides another challenge to such tests.[22] Mastery tests keep basic writers' attention focused on particles, reinforcing their restrictive cognitive style. Moreover, this approach offers yet another variation on the Authority theme. Getting the right answers is enough; understanding concepts and principles is unnecessary; quantity replaces quality. In short, mastery tests steal time and energy from basic writers' real writing problem: communicating something effectively to someone else.

At the level of the whole composition, the same limitations apply. Writing from imitative models, such as model description paragraphs or comparison-contrast essays, or writing to meet specific criteria, such as word lengths and specified numbers of pronouns or transition words, prevents students from concentrating on the communicative "field" of writing in favor of mastering discrete particles as prescribed by Authority. In contrast, James Moffett's *Active Voice* demonstrates that instructors can meet basic writers' needs for structure by supplying guidance on the composing process rather than on the composition—guidance that has a far more long-lasting impact on subsequent independent work.[23] All the implications of the Minnesota study suggest that when students in the writing center focus their energies on whole pieces of discourse in settings that invite genuine communication, their developmental needs, specifically in writing and more generally in thinking, are being served.

Basic Writers and Ethical Development

For Perry, the higher reaches of cognitive development involve ethical concerns—how one responds to complex problems, how one understands relativity, how one makes responsible decisions, how one evaluates actions and ideas. In other words, high level thinking manifests itself in issues involving values and judgments. Underlying Perry's work and the research associated with it is the conviction that cognitive development and its extension into ethical development can be enhanced through an understanding of the characteristics and limitations of each stage. Once these stages are understood, instructors are better able to devise appropriately sequenced instructional techniques and to evaluate existing methods. Lawrence Kohlberg's model of moral development elaborates on the connections between cognitive growth and ethical behavior. These connections bear heavily on the academic purpose of the writing center, but they also suggest that the writing center serves a much larger social purpose.

Like Perry's theory, Kohlberg's has been extended beyond its initial research population of Harvard undergraduates and has consistently received confirmation of both its hierarchical and universal properties.[24] Figure 3 shows Kohlberg's three-stage model. Essentially, Kohlberg identifies a *preconventional* stage in which morality is governed primarily by external consequences of reward and punishment, a *conventional* stage in which one not only conforms to personal and social expectations but actively identifies with and supports the social order, and a *postconventional* or principled stage in which one consciously seeks to identify and validate one's own moral standards regardless of those held by the social group.

Though these stages seem fairly obvious, the conditions for progression from one to the next are less so. Alexander Smith summarizes the conditions this way:

> Higher stages of moral development demand the ability to see perspectives other than one's own. Thus the development of role taking ability is a necessary process if the full development of moral reasoning is to occur. . . . Moral reasoning [also] has a strong cognitive core. Understanding and using higher forms of moral reasoning require the ability, in Piagetian terms, to be at a formal operation stage. The level of moral reasoning will not surpass the general level of cognitive reasoning. On the other hand, moral reasoning does not necessarily reach its optimum level and may lag behind cognitive development.[25]

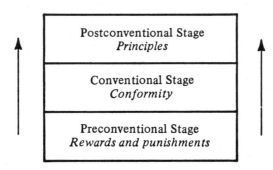

Fig. 3. Lawrence Kohlberg's three-stage model of moral development.

Add to this three other points. First, Hallam's study and others show that many college students are not yet thinking fully at the level of formal operations.[26] Their qualitative and judgmental abilities seem to lag behind their quantitative-skills. Such is the case with basic writers in the writing center. Second, according to a nationwide longitudinal study of several thousand high school, college, and graduate students, individuals continue their moral development as long as they are in school; when they leave school, however, their judgments tend to stabilize.[27] Third, Kohlberg finds that principled, postconventional moral development is essentially an adult, not an adolescent, phenomenon.[28] Nor is age alone responsible for the shift to higher levels of development. Says Kohlberg, "Personal experiences of choice involving questioning and commitment, in some sort of integration with stimulation to cognitive-moral reflection, seem required for movement from conventional thought."[29]

Writing involves precisely these activities—choice, questioning, commitment, and reflection. If writing instruction is carried out according to a legitimately sequenced model, writing can spur on students' cognitive development, moving them toward more fluent and disciplined engagement in these processes. To the extent that mature writing stems from the ability to anticipate other points of view and to reflect with detachment upon the value of one's ideas, it lays the cognitive foundation for continued moral development. Consequently, the writing center is more than a humane safety net to give struggling students one last chance to succeed in college. It can have both long and short term effects on students' lives. By consciously nuturing their cognitive development *and* by helping them continue in higher education, the writing center can benefit the larger society, ensuring that it will be composed of morally principled, responsible members.

Although students in the writing center will not reach postconventional moral development, they can move from dualistic to relativistic thinking and thus begin to work more comfortably at the level of formal operations. These achievements are the necessary forerunners of cognitive and ethical maturity. If writing center personnel view their role as a developmental one, their services are more likely to result in the coherent perspective and detached, independent thought that basic writers—and prospective citizens—need.

Notes

1. Lawrence Kohlberg and Rochelle Mayer, "Development as the Aim of Education," *Harvard Educational Review* 42 (November 1972): 494.

2. Andrea Lunsford, "Cognitive Development and the Basic Writer," *College English* 41 (September 1979): 39.

3. Carl Bereiter, "Development in Writing," in *Cognitive Processes in Writing,* ed. Lee W. Gregg and Erwin R. Steinberg (Hillsdale, N.J.: Lawrence Erlbaum, 1980), 74.

4. For a useful guide to Piaget's theories and their applications, see Roger W. Bybee and Robert Sund, *Piaget for Educators,* 2nd. ed. (Columbus, Ohio: Merrill, 1982).

5. John Butler, "Remedial Writers: The Teacher's Job as Corrector of Papers," *College Composition and Communication* 31 (October 1980): 270–77.

6. Andrea Lunsford, "The Content of Basic Writers' Essays," *College Composition and Communication* 31 (October 1980): 279–83.

7. Martin Sleeper, "A Developmental Framework for History Education in Adolescence," *School Review* 84 (November 1975): 95.

8. R. N. Hallam, "Piaget and Thinking in History," in *New Movements in the Study and Teaching of History,* ed. Martin Ballard (Bloomington: Indiana University Press, 1970), 164.

9. R. N. Hallam, "Logical Thinking in History," *Educational Review* 19 (June 1967): 191.

10. Bärbel Inhelder and Jean Piaget, *The Growth of Logical Thinking from Childhood to Adolescence,* trans. Anne Parsons and Stanley Milgram (New York: Basic Books, 1958), 248–51.

11. William G. Perry, *Forms of Intellectual and Ethical Development in the College Years: A Scheme* (New York: Holt, Rinehart and Winston, 1970), 71.

12. Jean Piaget, *The Language and Thought of the Child,* trans. Marjorie Gabain (New York: Meridan, 1955), and L. S. Vygotsky, *Thought and Language,* ed. and trans. Eugenia Hanfmann and Gertrude Vakar (Cambridge, Mass.: MIT Press, 1962).

13. Perry, 59.

14. Perry, 62.

15. Mina Shaughnessey, *Errors and Expectations: A Guide for the Teacher of Basic Writing* (New York: Oxford University Press, 1977), 227–28.

16. Carole Widick and Deborah Simpson, "Developmental Concepts in College Instruction," in *Encouraging Development in College Students,* ed. Clyde Parker (Minneapolis: University of Minnesota Press, 1978), 27–59.

17. Perry, 60.

18. Widick and Simpson, 47.

19. James Moffett, *Teaching the Universe of Discourse* (Boston: Houghton Mifflin, 1968), 195.

20. Widick and Simpson, 33.

21. Perry, 74.

22. In *The English Teacher's Handbook* (Cambridge, Mass.: Winthrop, 1980), 274, Stephen and Susan Judy offer a bibliographic review of research on the relation between usage study and writing ability, dating back to 1906.

23. James Moffett, *Active Voice: A Writing Program across the Curriculum* (Montclair, N.J.: Boynton/Cook, 1981).

24. Lawrence Kohlberg and his associates have conducted research in Taiwan, Mexico, and Turkey to obtain cross cultural verification of the theory. See Kohlberg and Gilligan, "The Adolescent as Philosopher: The Discovery of the Self in a Postconventional World," *Daedalus,* 100 (1971): 1051–86, and Kohlberg and Kramer, "Continuities and Discontinuities in Childhood and Adult Moral Development," *Human Development* 12 (1969): 93–120.

25. Alexander Smith, "Lawrence Kohlberg's Cognitive Stage Theory of the Development of Moral Judgment," in *Applying New Developmental Findings,* ed. Lee Knefelkamp, Carole Widick, and Clyde Parker (San Francisco: Jossey-Bass, 1978), 57.

26. In addition to Hallam's research, cited earlier, see Michael A. Zaccaria, "The Development of Historical Thinking: Implications for the Teaching of History," *The History Teacher* 11 (May 1978): 323–40, and Randall Freisinger, "Cross Disciplinary Writing Workshops: Theory and Practice," *College English* 42 (October 1980): 154–66.

27. James R. Rest et al., "Age Trends in Judging Moral Issues: A Review of Cross Sectional, Longitudinal, and Sequential Studies of the Defining Issues Test," *Child Development* 49 (1978): 263–79.

28. Lawrence Kohlberg, "Continuities in Childhood and Adult Moral Development Revisited," in *Collected Papers on Moral Development and Moral Education,* ed. Lawrence Kohlberg (Cambridge, Mass.: Moral Education and Research Foundation, Harvard University Graduate School of Education, 1973), Chapter 4.

29. *Ibid.,* 41.

7 Priorities and Guidelines for the Development of Writing Centers: A Delphi Study

Bené Scanlon Cox
Middle Tennessee State University

The author applies the Delphi technique to writing center administration in order to determine the priorities of writing center directors. Her study yields a list of ranked priorities that is organized into a set of guidelines for the future development of writing centers. Scanlon's essay is a timely effort to provide direction for the field of writing center administration.

As new writing centers continue to emerge and as established centers develop in the 1980s, they face problems of directing services, successfully integrating themselves into curricula, modifying their pedagogy, and adjusting their priorities to serve the changing needs of students, faculty, administrators, and others. Writing centers continually adapt to new roles as, for instance, training grounds for composition teachers, research laboratories for writing specialists, adjuncts for remedial services, and resource centers for composition. However, the absence of clear priorities and guidelines for future development is a major problem because the staff of each center must rely largely on its own experience and knowledge to provide the rationale to direct services and even to justify survival. Progress towards solving these problems lies in approaching systematically and collectively the priorities for future functions of writing centers. In order to determine priorities essential for successful writing center operation, I conducted a research project aimed at soliciting and collating experts' opinions.

Survey Design

The purpose of the study was to achieve expert consensus on ranked priorities for future planning of writing centers and to construct guidelines for establishing new writing centers and developing existing ones. I first examined the range of writing center functions in view of experts' analysis

77

of their future importance and relevance. Then, using the Delphi fore-casting technique, I surveyed a sample of writing center directors to determine a consensus of rank-ordered priorities necessary for planning the future of writing centers; from their consensus I generated guidelines for the development of writing centers.

The study employed a form of the Delphi technique: a rapid-succession survey meant to gather expert speculation about future events. This survey method assumes that groups of experts provide reliable conjectures about the future and that experts in the field "will make conjectures based upon rational judgment and shared information rather than merely guess-ing and will separate hope from likelihood in the process."[1] Commenting on criteria for selecting predictive experts, Olaf Helmer and Nicholas Rescher state:

> The first and most obvious criterion of expertise is of course knowl-edge. . . . We expect his [the expert's] information and the body of experience at his disposal to constitute an assurance that he will be able to select the needed items of background information, determine the character and extent of their relevance, and apply their insights to the formulation of the required personal probability judgments.[2]

Moreover, Helmer and Rescher state that the expert must prove capable of employing her or his knowledge and experience "to bear effectively on the predictive problem in hand."[3] Selection of experts in a Delphi study does not approximate a random sample because expertise serves as the criterion. Thus my sample is not representative of writing center directors throughout the United States. I selected mainly directors who have worked several years in writing center development and who represent various types of postsecondary institutions, including two-year, four-year, public, private, state, and regional colleges and universities. I considered primarily the publication and research record of center directors but I also included experts who have developed and expanded centers and have received recognition primarily for these activities.

The Delphi technique has been used to survey panels of experts ranging in number from seven to 400[4]; however, Frederick Cyphert and Walter Gant report the modal frequency as approximately fifty respondents.[5] The Delphi community for this study consisted of thirty-six experts, yielding a respectable number of participants and limiting the possible Questionnaire 1 responses to a manageable number.

In Round I, I requested that respondents submit at least three, but no more than five, priorities which should be included in planning the functions of college or university writing centers over the next five years. I asked respondents to phrase priorities as complete statements and allowed them to clarify each by adding a sentence or two. Twenty-six respondents agreed to participate and returned Questionnaire 1. The responses resulted in 115 statements concerning future priorities for writing centers. I reduced these to thirty-seven statements, taking into consideration shades of meaning and clarifications where necessary.

In Round II, I mailed respondents Questionnaire 2, which consisted of the thirty-seven priorities expressed as generic statements with instructions for participants to rate the importance of each. I attained results from this round by attaching a numerical value to each response from most to least important. With the return of twenty-two usable responses to Questionnaire 2, I tabulated responses to determine consensus for each item. Then in Round III, I forwarded Questionnaire 3 to each respondent. On this questionnaire I compiled three columns of revised information for each item and included a fourth column for the participant to enter a new rating. I asked participants to reconsider their original rankings and attempt to reach a group consensus on each item. The responses to Round III formed a hierarchical list of twenty priorities for future functions of college and university writing centers. I divided those responses into primary, secondary, and tertiary priorities.

Primary Priorities

The four highest-ranked items concern the writing center's responsibility to meet students' needs: (1) address the immediate needs of students through trained instructors who diagnose writing problems and provide instruction and practice for writing improvement; (2) help students become self-directed, independent writers; (3) build students' confidence by improving their abilities to use language acceptably; and (4) help students who have problems with more advanced writing tasks. Priorities in this category emphasize not only the student-centered role of the writing center, but also its function as helper and tutor.

Secondary Priorities

Generally, the second group of rankings concerns practical aspects of center administration: (1) secure administrative and faculty support; (2) integrate the writing center within an established academic department; (3) integrate writing skills instruction into the total university curriculum; (4) employ only instructors and directors who desire the positions; (5) regularly evaluate the total writing center program, with emphasis on teaching and learning processes, and revise it as necessary; (6) encourage the administration's support of remedial programs by characterizing the writing center as a means of retraining students and maintaining the academic standards of the college or university; and

(7) discourage the image of the writing center as a "dumping ground" for academic failures.

Many comments from respondents indicated that these mid-range priorities are nevertheless indispensable to effective center functioning— the necessity of some having been learned by trial and error—and that ineffective functioning resulted from the director's poor planning or disinterest. The director's responsibilities include careful guidance of the writing center and, equally important, the encouragement of support from administrators and other faculty members within the institution.

Tertiary Priorities

The third group of rankings slightly overlaps the second. It centers on philosophical approaches to methodology and writing center auxiliary services, that is, those beyond the remedial and developmental functions: (1) assume responsibility for teaching all skills of grammar transcription, e.g., spelling and punctuation; (2) open the services of the writing center to all students, faculty, staff, and administrators; (3) develop resources to offer full support for all writing faculty and to become an information clearinghouse with such material as current journal articles, an idea file, and teaching technique information; (4) augment the training of graduate students in English by serving as an information source and by offering opportunities for practical experience; (5) teach conventions of the written language as conventions; (6) teach critical thinking; (7) develop a basic skills file; (8) augment teacher education by serving as an information source and by offering opportunities for practical experience; and (9) expand the variety of center teaching materials, including equipment such as tape recorders, files, filmstrips, films, and programmed materials. These priorities fall from middle to lower range in importance and involve the expansion of functions of well-established writing centers. Furthermore, they reflect priorities that suit the needs of institutions according to their local purposes and goals.

Guidelines for Center Development

This ranked list reflects a consensus of experts' views of priorities for college and university writing centers. Guidelines established from these ranked priorities should aid administrative personnel in planning, establishing, and developing writing centers. These guidelines deserve special consideration because they (1) derive from the Delphi study incorporating a panel of experts from a cross section of colleges and universities, (2) represent the consensus of experts rather than the extremes, and

(3) offer a planning tool to be assessed along with individual institutional characteristics such as size, goals, scope, student profile, and so forth.

In the following guidelines I have included seventeen unranked priorities with the twenty ranked ones. I grouped priorities into four areas, dividing concerns into categories and subordinating them according to experts' recommendations for priority consideration. The four principal areas are (1) establishing the writing center's philosophy of service to students, (2) creating administrative policy, (3) expanding services, and (4) providing teaching and research models. The subgroups are priorities requiring immediate attention—those ranked in the top twenty—and those deserving secondary consideration—the seventeen unranked statements of the Delphi group. This arrangement allows a director or planning committee reviewing writing center development to focus on one particular area or to consider a comprehensive set of recommendations.

Guidelines

I. Establishing the writing center's philosophy of service to students
   A. Primary considerations
      1. The writing center should address the immediate needs of students through trained instructors who diagnose writing problems and provide instruction and practice for writing improvement.
      2. The center must help students become self-directed, independent writers.
      3. The center should build students' confidence by improving their abilities to use language acceptably.
      4. The center staff must discourage the image of the writing center as a "dumping ground" for academic failures.
      5. Justification of writing center existence should be in terms other than "student success rate," especially as expressed in student retention statistics.
      6. The writing center should assume responsibility for teaching all grammar skills.
      7. Staff of the center should teach conventions of the written language as conventions.
      8. The center should teach critical thinking (inferences, assumptions, arguments).
      9. The staff should establish a basic skills file.
   B. Secondary considerations
      1. Tutors should teach writing as a tool for concentrated, extended analysis.
      2. Tutors should teach form as the concrete representation of the

page and style as appropriate to the type of writing under study, e.g., literary, business, and so forth.

3. The center should teach critical reading.
4. The center should strive to cultivate in students respect, appreciation, and affection for language, particularly the English language, and for dialectal diversity.

II. Creating administrative policy
   A. Primary considerations
      1. The writing center must secure administrative and faculty support for success in budgeting, reinforcing goals, and developing programs.
      2. The center should be integrated into an academic department, preferably English (since on most campuses it is responsible for the composition program), to assure continuity and academic interest in the program.
      3. The center should employ only instructors and directors who desire the positions.
      4. The director should evaluate the total writing center program regularly, with emphasis on teaching and learning processes, and effect necessary program revision.
      5. The director should encourage administrative support of remedial programs by characterizing the writing center as a means of retaining students and maintaining the academic standards of the institution.
   B. Secondary considerations
      1. The director should minimize administrative procedures and staff.
      2. The director and staff should create an appropriate physical environment to encourage all students to use the facility as a writing room and as a place to discuss ideas and to test assumptions.
      3. The director should control the number of students in the center for effective, individualized instruction.
      4. The center should reduce its dependence on federal funding and other "soft" money.

III. Expanding services for students, faculty, and others
   A. Primary considerations
      1. The center should help students who have problems with more advanced writing tasks, such as abstracts, reports, and term papers.
      2. Eventually the writing center should open services to all students, faculty, staff, and administrators.

3. The center should augment the teacher education program by serving as an information source and by offering opportunities for practical experiences.
4. The center should serve as a faculty resource center, offering full support to all writing faculty, and as an information clearinghouse with current articles, an idea file, teaching technique information, and so on.
5. The center should obtain a wide variety of equipment such as tape recorders, files, filmstrips, films, and programmed materials.
6. The director should train and educate tutors by collaborative learning methods.
7. The center may provide public school teachers with training and experience in teaching writing, establishing writing centers, and defining "basic skills."

B. Secondary considerations
1. The center should help students prepare for standardized tests such as the LSAT and GRE.
2. The center should serve as the resource and procedure center for all out-of-class testing of writing skills.

IV. Providing teaching and research models
A. Primary consideration: Writing skills instruction should be integrated into the college or university curriculum through collaboration of the director and permanent center staff with other faculty and curriculum planning committees.
B. Secondary considerations
1. The center should offer a model of writing instruction to guide and direct other faculty members.
2. The center should provide a place to conduct research on the composing process.
3. The center should serve as a place to conduct research in fields related to the composing process, such as linguistics, language development, rhetorical theory, and measurement of writing ability.
4. The center should cooperate with researchers by offering a cumulative data base and experimental situations for research in teaching writing.

The writing center promotes the art and practice of heuristics because its tutorial methods and individual or small-group instruction create immediate situations in which questions about teaching and learning receive prompt attention, consideration, and, in some cases, solution. The center can prove to be an experimental base for finding methods to teach writing for various learning styles or patterns. When skills instruction becomes integrated into the college or university curriculum, then we can learn more about how to teach writing and about how students learn to write.

Notes

1. W. Timothy Weaver, "The Delphi Forecasting Method," *Phi Delta Kappan* 52 (1971): 268.

2. Olaf Helmer and Nicholas Rescher, "On the Epistemology of the Inexact Sciences," *Management Science* 6 (1959): 43.

3. *Ibid.*

4. Norman Dalkey and Olaf Helmer, "An Experimental Application of the Delphi Method to the Use of Experts," *Management Science* 9 (1963): 458.

5. Frederick R. Cyphert and Walter L. Gant, "The Delphi Technique: A Case Study," *Phi Delta Kappan* 52 (1971): 273.

II Writing Center Administration

8 Establishing and Maintaining a Writing Center in a Two-year College

Gary A. Olson
University of North Carolina, Wilmington

This essay is intended as a primer for those who wish to establish a writing center. The essay begins with an outline of methods for convincing administrators that a writing center can be a feasible and valuable operation and includes discussions of salient topics such as center funding, location, staff, tutor training, and administration. Sample writing center forms, which directors can adapt for their own use, are also provided.

The writing lab is no longer a university phenomenon. Junior and community colleges are establishing centers and report a high degree of success. Although there are many obstacles to establishing a center in the two-year college, a determined and creative faculty member can overcome them. The following are several interrelated areas pertinent to establishing a center.

Selling the Idea

Obtaining departmental and administrative support involves selling the idea of a writing center. Initial opposition to establishing a writing center, even from one's own department, can be surprising. Opposition may arise from the fact that centers commonly are associated with remediation and a resulting fear on the part of some instructors that if a center is established, they must be failing at their jobs. If such sentiment exists, the prospective writing center director might point out that a center actually makes instructors' jobs easier by assuring that students are writing at higher levels of proficiency than they would otherwise.

It is essential to convince those who are skeptical about a writing center's utility that the center is effective in countering the so-called "literacy crisis." In fact, it is easy to argue that the community college *needs* a center more than a four-year college does because the two-year college sometimes attracts students with low competency levels. Because two-year colleges often have open enrollment, the potential for attracting such students is great. The prospective director might therefore argue that it is the *duty* of the community college to offer this service in order to be fully responsive to the needs of all students. Since the two-year college is specifically service oriented, one can easily argue that a center is a necessary part of the essential service it offers the public. In fact, the director might point out to administrators that establishing a center is a concrete step and shows legislators and taxpayers that the school *is* doing something about literacy. Also convincing to administrators are statistics from other colleges indicating the rate of student use of centers each semester. Some administrators are not even aware that such centers exist, and this statistical information can be persuasive.

If intense resistance is likely, the prospective director might first prepare a feasibility report: a formal persuasive paper arguing for the project's implementation. The feasibility report should be based on as much factual information as possible—projected cost, funding sources, physical location—and should include alternatives when possible, for instance, several sources for funding. In other words, the director constructs the projected center on paper and then submits it to the chairperson and dean, saying, "See, it *can* work."

Funding

There are two funding sources: external and internal. Locating funds outside of the college is not impossible. Usually, external funding takes the form of a one-time grant. It is important not to rely on external sources for continued funding, but grants can provide the initial investment necessary to establish the center. External funding can come from several sources.

First, corporations and large businesses occasionally award grants to educational projects showing a clear need. A corporation bases its decision on a grant proposal. If the applicant's school operates a grants office, its personnel will assist in devising proposals. Telephone calls can help target companies likely to accept a grant proposal for writing centers. Second, state organizations and agencies, both public and private, sometimes award grants. One such organization is a state committee for the humanities or similar organization. Most organizations require specific proposals, budgets, and justification. Third, federal agencies sometimes award funds for writing centers. According to Peggy Jolly of the University of Alabama at Birmingham, several schools in Alabama are receiving funds for their centers from the Support for Developing Institutions Project (SDIP) of Title III in the Department of Education.

The most reliable sources of funding are internal, however. Again, the best procedure is to devise a feasibility report *before* approaching the administration; this is akin to the grant proposal in external funding. There are two likely internal sources: the supporting department or departments and the college administration. Departmental funding is perhaps the most secure because once the center is established, the department is likely to continue to support it—although bureaucrats and legislators who are searching for "nonessential programs" are more likely to question the center's existence if it is they who fund it. Once the center has been created by some initial investment, the center will not be much of a drain on departmental funds; the initial investment, then, is the most important. Perhaps the most desirable situation is to secure an initial investment externally or from the general administrative fund and to receive annual funding from the sponsoring department, with occasional grants of "soft money" from the administration. (For a more detailed discussion of this subject, see Chapter 9 in this collection.)

Materials

Stocking the center with adequate materials is dependent upon the level of funding. Several tables—round ones, if possible—are necessary. Many directors agree that round tables are superior to square or rectangular ones because they allow the tutor to sit next to rather than opposite the student, thus breaking down the traditional teacher-student relationship and contributing to a relaxed atmosphere. Tables can often be obtained from within the college, perhaps by convincing the head librarian or cafeteria director to donate some of theirs. In choosing chairs, it is probably best to avoid the wooden straightback type and to opt instead for the molded-plastic type or, ideally, a cushioned chair. These particular types of chairs and tables are recommended because it is important that students be as physically comfortable as possible, especially since many will feel uncomfortable or resentful about attending the center in the first place. Finally, the center should have adequate lighting.

These three items—tables, chairs, and lighting—are the essentials as far as materials are concerned. Given great financial pressure, it is possible to survive, though barely, with the essentials only, but there are other materials the director should try to obtain: a chalkboard or two; one or more bookshelves to store resources; a receptionist desk where students can make appointments and sign in; and a filing cabinet for storing student records and copies of examinations. Also, a wall clock and telephone are useful. The clock is important when the center has an appointment system and many students; the telephone enables students to call and make or cancel appointments.

Perhaps the most directly useful materials are diagnostic and competence exams and a collection of composition and English texts. The director can accumulate a modest library of center resources by collecting complimentary copies of recent texts from publishers and by soliciting from colleagues unused and unwanted texts. These books contain chapters and exercises that can supplement individualized instruction, and tutors can use them as reference material. Diagnostic and mastery exams can be used for diagnosing problem areas when the student first comes to the center and for determining whether the student has mastered those areas after instruction. ("Before" and "after" test scores can be used not only to determine student progress, but also to show administrators that the center itself is effective. The director can do this by recording before and after scores of all tests and calculating rough mean scores at the end of the semester, e.g., "Students exhibiting problems in subject/verb agreement averaged 60 percent on diagnostic exams and 95 percent on exit mastery exams this semester.") The same kinds of tests can serve as practice exams. Diagnostic, practice, and mastery exams can be constructed from composition workbooks in the center's resource collection.

Locating a Physical Center

The ideal center would be a new or renovated building, centrally located. Some schools use trailers or small frame houses owned by the college; however, it is more realistic to attempt to requisition a room or suite of rooms. A center can survive with one room, but a suite is more appropriate—one or two rooms for tutoring and another for a receptionist and a waiting area. It is essential that the tutoring room be neither cramped nor windowless. Too often centers are relegated to dingy, windowless, basement closets adjacent to the boiler room, hardly a propitious environment for learning. Even a classroom transformed into a center is better than a room which has the potential of stifling learning; in fact, the most likely target is a large classroom or two adjoining classrooms, which the director must convince the appropriate administrator are not too much to invest in a quality writing center. Wherever the center is situated, it should have an atmosphere that is friendly and favorable to learning. Posters on the walls, for example, encourage the feeling that the center is a place for help, not a "clinic" for "doctoring."

Staffing

Staffing the center is perhaps the most difficult problem two-year colleges encounter because they have neither graduate students nor juniors and seniors. But this obstacle *can* be overcome. First, the center can use faculty tutors, a procedure that may or may not be a problem, depending upon colleague support. Some schools arrange to have all English professors spend one or more hours per week in the center. Others provide release time: nine hours per week in the center, for example, might be considered equal to teaching one course. There are many possible compensatory arrangements.

Second, the center can employ peer tutors. As compensation, tutors can receive work-study payment or credit hours for tutoring. Tutoring can also be made part of an internship, perhaps in English education. It may even be possible to convince some students to work as volunteers. Peer tutors are economical, usually relate well to other students, and afford the director maximum control of the staff.

Third, the center can solicit volunteer English teachers from local high schools. This is not as difficult as it may seem. Experience in individualized instruction is a marketable skill; some teachers are happy to gain this experience. Many are interested in the personal enrichment to be gained from working in college programs and may work simply for the opportunity of acquiring ideas and methodology for their own classrooms. Our best tutor one year was a volunteer from a local secondary school.

Fourth, if the college is situated near a university or four-year college, it may be possible to arrange to have English majors or graduate students from that institution work in the center on internships. Since more and more colleges and universities are requiring on-the-job internships, it may be easy to arrange a program with a nearby school.

Ancillary Staffing

By answering the phone and making and canceling appointments, a receptionist helps the center operate at maximum efficiency because tutors are then free to spend their time tutoring. If the dean has allocated the center a budget, the director can hire part-time help at minimum wage. Alternatively, the director can hire a receptionist through work-study, assuming funds are available; in fact, if the center uses work-study peer tutors, the receptionist job is a good way to break in new tutors. Again, the center can also use volunteers as receptionists. Often it is possible to find students who will donate some time, especially with the promise of being allowed to tutor in the future.

Center Director

Ideally a full-time director is responsible for all administrative tasks—devising schedules, training tutors, and so on—and spends some time tutoring as well. However, it is more likely that the director will work only part-time in the center. In return for the position, a faculty member should receive two or at least one release time per semester. A third possibility is a codirectorship with split release time.

Tutor Training

Tutor training is perhaps the director's most important task and the primary means of influencing the type of center the school will have, from a traditional grammar lab to a modern center emphasizing the "writing process." Even with faculty tutors, it is probably best to conduct a weekly meeting to discuss problems. With peer tutors the best method is to select prospective tutors in the first term of their freshman year and to ask them to attend a credit course on composition and tutoring methods, ideally taught by the center director. The initial instruction can be supplemented by weekly staff meetings designed to guide tutors while they are working in the center. It is important to note that English majors are not necessarily the best tutors; a student with patience, a receptive attitude, and a facility in explaining complex ideas often will prove to be a better tutor than someone who simply displays a good knowledge of the material.

If it is impossible to offer an initial course to prospective tutors, they might be required to attend an intensive one- or two-day training workshop before the semester begins and to have passed the freshman English requirement with a certain grade. It might be a good idea to enlist the help of colleagues in this workshop. Requesting assistance is not only a good method of using their expertise to help the cause but is also a way to help acquire their support for the center.

The center director must determine the content of training sessions, but there are a few important steps the director should take: warn tutors against publicly disagreeing with a grade a student has received on a paper; caution them against proofreading papers; ask them to avoid the temptation of making corrections and telling students what's what instead of leading the student to the answer; and encourage tutors to work only on one or two major problems at a time rather than overloading the student with too much criticism.

Operational System

Most centers use a dual system: referral and walk-in. The walk-in system is one in which the center remains open during certain hours of the week for students who voluntarily seek help. The walk-in program can operate with an appointment or "open door" system. Since the appointment system helps avoid "grid lock" during rush hours, it is efficient. Regardless of the system, though, it is important to allocate some time for students who seek help on their own. Operating without walk-in hours fosters the perception that the center exists solely for remediation.

Under the referral system a teacher sends a student to the center for assistance on a mandatory basis. The student must attend the center each week for a specified time period, usually one-half hour. Either the referring teacher or the tutors determine the duration of the student's attendance during the semester. A referral system can be collegewide (any instructor from any department can refer a student) or limited to a department (only English professors can refer students). The policy usually depends upon how many tutors and how much support the center has.

A third system of writing center operation is a credit course offered through the center. Some schools offer one-, two-, or three-credit courses as a supplement to the standard English requirement. Usually, the center course substitutes for a nonexistent remedial English course. An entry placement test determines whether an incoming student needs the supplementary course. Although these credit course arrangements are common and seem to please administrators because they believe they are getting their money's worth from the center, many directors believe this arrangement attempts to make the center something it is not. They argue, quite persuasively, that the center is meant to be a place where students can obtain intensive individualized instruction and that a college should offer a remedial course in conjunction with the center, not through it.

Hours of Operation

The director must determine what hours the center will remain open. Center hours are contingent partly upon the hours tutors have available. The center will be most effective if it offers maximum access to students. In other words, it should remain open for some time each day, ideally during school office hours and for a few hours one or two nights a week. (Some centers even open on Saturdays.)

Centers should have double tutor coverage throughout the day, though this may be impossible due to limits on tutors and funds. Having two tutors working during all open hours allows one tutor to be free at all times for students who drop in without appointments. In this arrangement, the tutors trade off unscheduled time so that one tutor does not spend the entire day tutoring while the other is idle.

Most directors determine their semester operating hours after they devise the tutors' semester schedules. While some directors believe that scheduling the same tutor for more than two hours at a time decreases his or her effectiveness because of fatigue, others believe it is best to schedule tutors in large blocks, say, five hours on Monday and five on Tuesday. Perhaps this choice can be left to the tutors themselves since each will feel differently about the matter.

Forms

Writing center directors are now turning to business administration to discover ways to eliminate unnecessary forms and to make others more succinct. While adequate records are important, the paper flow should be restricted. Records help justify the center's existence, and reducing their number saves money and time. An efficient center needs between two and six mimeographed forms.

An information form—on which students can record their name, address, telephone number, and English class in which they are enrolled— along with a worksheet—on which tutors can record a brief summary of each student conference and the time the student spends in each meeting— constitute the core of the student's file. (See Sample Forms 1 and 2.)

A center operating on a referral system obviously needs a referral form. This form should have lines for the instructor's signature, the student's name, the class the student is having trouble with, the date, a brief description of the problems the student is experiencing, and perhaps a question asking the instructor how long he or she wishes the student to work in the center. (See Sample Form 3.) This form binds the student to regular attendance and lets center personnel know that they should send an absence notice to the student's instructor should that student miss an appointment.

The absence notice (Sample Forms 4 and 5), usually on a half sheet of paper, informs the instructor that a referral student has missed an appointment. The weekly or monthly report (Sample Form 6) provides a summary of areas the student has worked on and indicates how many times the student has visited the center. (See Chapter 10 for a detailed discussion of writing center forms.)

Data Collection

Data collection is the principal means of justifying a center's existence to administrators. A report at the end of each term specifying exactly how many students attended, the total number of operating hours, and so on provides the concrete information administrators need to judge the center's success. They also can use it in requesting money from *their* superiors. Moreover, the center director can use this information to justify expansion.

Sample Form 1
Student File Questionnaire

1. Name: _____ Date: _____

2. College address: _____ Phone: _____

3. Major: _____ Student #: _____

4. Home address: _____

5. Classroom instructor: _____ Course: _____

6. How would you rate your English preparation?

    Excellent _____ Good _____ Fair _____ Inadequate _____

7. Mark (1) in the areas in which you feel most adequately prepared. Mark (2) in the areas in which you feel that you have average preparation. Mark (3) in the areas in which you feel inadequately prepared.

    Expository writing _____ Critical writing _____

    Mechanics:

        Grammar _____ Vocabulary _____ Spelling _____

        Punctuation _____ Speech _____

8. How would you rate your own study skills and habits?

    Good _____ Average _____ Inadequate _____

    ****

9. Objectives in the Writing Center: (to be completed by tutor)

    _____ Spelling _____ Verb tenses _____ Sentence variety

    _____ Punctuation _____ Subject-verb agreement _____ Fragments & run-ons

    _____ Apostrophes _____ Pronouns _____ Paragraph development

    _____ Vocabulary _____ Essay structure _____ Other _____

Sample Form 2
Writing Center Report

Name of student: _____ Phone: _____

Walk-in or referral? _____

Instructor: _____

Name of tutor: _____ Appointment time: _____

To the tutor: Write a brief report on each tutorial session with each student. Include such things as topic of discussion, specific problems, progress made (if any), and student's attitude. If the student does not appear, please so indicate.

_____

Date: _____ Time: _____

_____

Date: _____ Time: _____

_____

Date: _____ Time: _____

_____

Sample Form 3

The Writing Center is located _____

The telephone number is _____

Writing Center Referral Sheet

(Please send this form via campus mail to: Director, Writing Center. Have your student come in for an appointment.)

I wish to refer the following student to the Writing Center for tutorial assistance. I wish the student to attend the Writing Center for 30 minutes per week for _____ weeks (please specify).

Name: _____

Class: _____ Date: _____

In the space below indicate particular weaknesses that you have observed in the student's written work. If you wish him/her to have tutoring on specific assignments, it would help if you would supply us with copies of those assignments. (Use the back of this form if you need more space.)

_____
(Please sign on line and circle appropriate title.)

Advisor

English Instructor

Other _____

Sample Form 4

Absence Notice

To: _____ Dept.: _____

From: The Writing Center

Date: _____

According to our records, _____ has missed

his/her appointment for the week of _____. Please ask

this student to come to the Center as soon as possible.

Thank you.

Sample Form 5

To: _____

From: The Writing Center

_____ has not come to the Writing

Center to make an initial appointment. Please ask this student to

come to the Center as soon as possible.

Thank you.

Sample Form 6

Monthly Attendance Report

To: _____ Dept.: _____

From: The Writing Center

Date: _____

According to our records, _____ has

attended the Writing Center _____ times for a total of _____

hours this semester. The student has worked on the following areas:

_____

_____

_____

_____

_____

_____

_____

_____

_____

_____

_____

_____

_____

_____

_____

_____

_____

_____

Typically, there are five types of data the director should collect: (1) the number of students attending during the term (the more students, the more successful the center appears on paper); (2) the number of student conferences; (3) the total time spent in conferences during the term; (4) the average time per conference; and (5) the number of hours tutors have spent in the center.

Scheduling

An appointment system is probably the most efficient way to handle conferences because it imposes discipline on center scheduling; without an appointment system, students are liable to crowd into the center during certain times, leaving other times in which no one shows up. It is possible to use fifteen-minute appointments if the center is cramped, but many directors believe that students should receive at least thirty minutes of individual instruction. If tutors are unable to see students for this long because of a lack of tutors or an influx of students, it is best to supplement individualized work with center resources such as exercises from textbooks. It is probably best to have students work with the same tutor each visit; this adds a sense of continuity to the instruction students receive.

Advertising

Advertisement allows the director to inform the student population of center services and is helpful because it keeps the center visible to faculty and administration. The basic medium of advertisement is the poster. A flashy ad, on colored paper, with some kind of illustration printed on it will catch students' attention. Also, small brochures can be quite effective. Another medium is the faculty memo informing instructors about the referral system and asking them to announce the walk-in hours in their classes. In addition, tutors can visit classes to make personal announcements. If a school has no student newspaper or radio station, the local media usually will run free public service announcements. Regardless of the medium, the ad should include a standard disclaimer: "The writing center will not proofread your papers or help you write them, but it will help you learn editing and proofreading techniques."

9 The Bottom Line: Financial Responsibility

Peggy Jolly
University of Alabama, Birmingham

The problems of financing developmental programs in general and writing centers in particular have plagued educators and administrators for years. This essay is a comprehensive discussion of financing a writing center. The information in this essay will be valuable to directors of prospective writing centers, but it also will be helpful to directors who wish to expand existing centers.

Historical Perspective

Remedial, compensatory, developmental: the terminology changes as the attitudes about preparatory instruction evolve. Whatever name the program goes by, the idea of tutorial instruction is not new. According to Frederick Rudolph, "In 1870 there were only five states in the country where none of the colleges was doing preparatory work: all five were in the Northeast, four of them in New England where the academy movement was strong; and all five were states where the idea of private higher education was so strong that the land-grant foundations of 1862 were added to existing private institutions."[1] Today, even New England is not exempt from the need for preparatory courses in college. One researcher estimates that "nationally 60 percent of all persons who enter community college needs some developmental work, and that percentage is rising."[2] This pattern also exists in four-year colleges and universities, both public and private.

While the notion of providing tutors for postsecondary education is not new, the method of providing the service is. Traditionally, the upper income social class routinely hired tutors for their children; indeed, private tutoring often was seen as the main avenue to learning.[3] The tutors themselves were relatively poor, or at least not members of the wealthy class, and sold their services to make money to pay their own tuition fees. Honor societies and social organizations on occasion offered a pool of tutors whose services were made available to those less fortunate academically, but not socially, than the tutors themselves. Tutor-tutee relationships, though, generally served to establish the image of the "poor" tutor who rendered a service to those able to pay for time and knowledge and to reinforce the distance between the haves and the have-nots.

"Free tutoring" was first made available to athletes and World War II veterans during the 1950s through university athletic funds and the G.I. Bill. Veterans alone contributed vast numbers of students to the postsecondary educational system. An estimated one-third of the 11 million World War II veterans took advantage of the educational assistance program.[4] Many of these students were admitted into college without regard for their academic preparation. This resulted in the need for individualized tutoring on a scale much larger than had existed before. Of course, the tutoring was not free; someone had to pay for it, but, in a break with tradition, the someone in this case was not the student receiving the service.

During the 1960s, another invasion hit the postsecondary system: the influx of large numbers of low income, educationally disadvantaged students for whom tutorial services were a necessity if the open admissions colleges were to prove more than merely a revolving door. These students often were unable to afford the cost of private tutoring which they so desperately needed. Once more tutoring was "free," but again free only to certain students. The cost of these services was the responsibility of the individual institution or the government agency providing financial aid to students.

By the late 1960s, tutoring was available for three distinct groups: athletes and veterans, financially disadvantaged students, and the wealthy. The cost of services for the first two groups was assumed either by the college or by the federal government; the cost for the third group was assumed by the individual receiving the service. This system, admittedly inequitable, ignored a fourth, large population: the middle-class, academically deficient students who were paying for their own educations. Their access to tutoring was limited, first because they were not poor enough to be subsidized by government funds, second because they had no special service status to offer to the college, and third because they were not wealthy enough to hire private tutors. Support for "equal access" soon corrected this oversight.

Current Trends

Today "the general philosophy that pervades preparatory programs is that tutoring should be free, voluntary, and available to any student, not restricted to economically disadvantaged or wealthy students," or to those whom the college endows with special status.[5] The physical arrangement of the tutorial service has also changed. Rather than offering individualized one-on-one study sessions off campus and not on school time, modern tutorial facilities are housed on campus and are open during the school day. While the one-on-one relationship still predominates, the tutorial facility is likely to have a number of concurrent sessions at any given hour of its operation. Computers, self-paced instructional materials, and audiovisual aids are available to supplement the books and professional knowledge that used to be the standard "equipment" in a tutorial session. Staffing of these facilities has increased to include a director, clerical personnel, and several tutors who not only instruct students, but also set up programs of instruction, develop curriculum, and record data relevant to the students and facility.

Funding the Modern Center

Providing funds to support the modern tutorial service has proved burdensome, indeed impossible, for some institutions. The cost of a modest tutorial program serving only 300 students each year was estimated in 1980 to be over $100,000.[6] This base cost, which will necessarily increase over time and, ironically, with an effective program, is already prohibitive for schools facing decreased funding and reduced student populations. This situation poses a dilemma for postsecondary administrators. While few deny the need for tutorial services, they nevertheless must determine the place of the program in the mission of the institution and its cost in relation to other services before they underwrite the expense.

The source and amount of funding apportioned for tutorial support often depend more on the priority of the program than on its cost. Stephen Walsh, president of Saint Edwards University in Austin, Texas, notes that most tutorial programs begin as high profile, special projects designed to meet the needs of a particular group of students. As an administrator, Walsh's continued support of such a program depends on two factors: justification of cost and potential integration of the service into the mainstream of the activities deemed consistent with the mission of the university.[7] Donald Rippey[8] and Andrea Lunsford[9] echo these same sentiments, which they have found coincide with their experiences as directors of tutorial programs.

Origins of a Center

A tutorial services program available to all students usually begins on a modest basis, perhaps as a pilot project. The data collected from the program then can be used to justify the need for continued service. The pilot program often is funded by "soft money," external grants appropriated for a specified length of time or from discretionary administrative funds. For new programs, "hard money," budgetary funding for a specified ongoing cost, is generally token, perhaps in the form of release time for one or more faculty members to staff the service.[10] Continuation of the soft money may be difficult at best, impossible at worst, and may actually be detrimental to establishment of a sound program because of administrative restrictions and time demands that are imposed. As Nancy Vandett has found, "Shuffling of papers, collecting meaningless data to justify the grant, elimination of certain students, or restriction of course offerings may all go with grant funding."[11]

Administrators are influenced positively by what they perceive to be advantageous to them. Supplying evidence that the tutorial program benefits the institutional image and coffers as well as students is thus necessary for the program's survival. "One of the most powerful arguments that can be made for developmental programs," says Rippey, "is that they reduce attrition and increase the holding power of the college."[12] This holding power can be translated into dollar figures by determining the annual minimum income each student brings to the university, either directly through tuition or indirectly through appropriation from the state legislature or other funding bodies. At his school Rippey estimates that each student produces in some form or another $1,000 each year. Thus, high risk students who might normally be expected to leave the institution after a semester or two would actually net several thousand dollars each in revenue for the school if time spent in a tutorial program allows them to achieve basic skills that permit at least temporary success in college.[13] This is the type of justification that convinces an administrator to continue financial support of a program.

The amount and source of funding available to a tutorial service depend on the type and location of the facility as well as on the anticipated number of students it will serve. Tutorial services have evolved into two primary types since their inception some twenty years ago: academic services and student services.

The Academic Tutorial Center

The academic tutorial center is closely associated with the discipline it serves: English, math, reading, and natural sciences—in that order—being most prevalent. These laboratories, or centers as they now are commonly called, cater to specific needs identified by the faculty of the particular disciplines. The English faculty, for example, may have noticed that growing numbers of students display marked ignorance of basic skills such as grammar and mechanics and may have requested tutorial assistance to remedy this problem. Thus, the need for a writing center is identified and plans for such a facility can begin.

Funding

Funding for this unit will initially be the responsibility of the department. Since a realistic budget cannot be determined accurately before the demand for such services has been established, a small pilot project is the most sensible approach. Staffing, equipment expenditure, and operating costs will necessarily be limited until some reasonable expectation of expenditure is determined. Staffing for the pilot project will include a director and perhaps as few as one or two tutors, most often people who are already on staff and whose salaries have been budgeted through the department. Thus, salary funding for the center staff is included in the line item budget, covered through release time.

Even though the writing center staff serves both the academically disadvantaged student and eases the work of the full-time teaching faculty, the work itself is usually perceived to be low-status, unrewarding, and unremunerative. Indeed, full-time faculty members who direct or tutor in these centers generally are released from only part of their full-time teaching duties. In this instance the traditional image of the "poor tutor" whose services are undervalued is perpetuated. Tutorial work is seen as part-time or peripheral to the "real" teaching that goes on in the department. Nevertheless, in the center located within an academic unit, equipment expenditures and funding of salaries are secure, if limited, as long as the service can justify its worth to the satisfaction of the administrator in charge of departmental budgets. Growth of the academic center will necessarily be limited; it cannot reasonably expect more than a small proportion of the departmental budget, but the core operation may be more secure than the elaborate student service tutorials.

The Student Service Tutorial

Student service tutorials, as the name implies, are designed to meet a variety of student problems. In addition to the basic academic tutoring available in the smaller, self-contained units, these centers may include testing, advising, and skill development programs. More expansive centers reach outside the university to include student recruiting, job placement, and community service programs.

A large, comprehensive program is necessarily more expensive than an academic skills unit. Its staffing pattern generally resembles that of the university itself, with a director of each specific area, a cadre of tutors, and support personnel, including clerical staff. Because the student service tutorial is not uniquely identified with any one academic unit, it is housed most often in a common area such as a student center or administrative building. It becomes a unit of the university separate from any single department.

Funding

Despite the considerable expense of a service operation, its high visibility and diversity allow it to recover costs that might be difficult for a smaller academic unit that is neither so visible nor so diverse. Such a service has access to more avenues of revenue, both internal and external. The student service tutorial is the responsibility of the vice president for student services in large universities and deans in smaller ones; it thus has access not only to line item funds in the budget but also to discretionary funds. Additionally, because the service tutorial offers academic programs usually not available in individual disciplines, it can reasonably request departmental funds to help support the operation. Staff, too, can be recruited from academic units through release time rather than by hiring additional personnel from outside the university. Student workers, either peer tutors or clerks, can be secured from graduate assistantship programs and honor organizations or can be hired through work-study programs.

Day-to-day operating expenses can be prorated over the academic units being served as well as through the student service area. Furthermore, soft money is more readily available to the student service tutorial than to the academic unit. The sheer diversity of services offered allows opportunity for a wider variety of grants. If the service includes community programs, it can solicit contributions from business leaders or charities to support its efforts.

Basically, the difference in funding opportunity and the effectiveness in procuring money for the student service tutorial as opposed to the academic unit is simply that the visibility of the former catches the attention of high-level administrators. The economic stability of the service tutorial often depends on the support of the university's chief officers. Yet, at the bottom line, the security of the tutorial unit is directly proportional to the clout of the supporting administrator.

Alternative Funding Sources for Centers

There are, however, some steps an individual director can take to ensure financial stability. These steps are relevant to either academic or student services, although some may be more appropriate to one than to the other. Since several of the sources I will discuss provide soft money only, I must stress that the core of the program—director's salary, tutors' salaries, housing—should be funded from somebody's line budget. Having that core supported by hard money means that the program will continue. Expansions and refinements made possible by soft money may be so well accepted that they eventually will be included in the line budget, but a director should never commit to soft money the essential parts of the service.

In addition to the sources already mentioned—academic budgets, discretionary funds, student support areas—Martha Maxwell has listed some fifteen other funding sources.[14] While this list is by no means comprehensive, it does give a director a starting place to seek funds. Individual programs often have access to monies unique to their university's structure or to their community. These sources can be valuable not only for providing economic support, but also for indicating leads to other sources.

Maxwell's funding sources can be divided into three general categories: internal, local external, and national external. While some of the sources overlap, most are distinct enough to identify as belonging to one group or another. The most important characteristic of each, certainly, is that it has an established pattern of providing funds to worthwhile causes. The director's job is to convince the funding agency that the center is worthy of its generosity.

Before seeking financial support, a director must outline clearly the areas to be funded and the projected amount of funding. A writing center budget contains four major areas: salaries, physical facility, equipment, and operating expenses. Since support of all these areas is not appropriate for any one funding source, it is first necessary to consider seriously which one is most likely to be supported by a particular source. Second, the director must reasonably estimate the amount of money needed. Costs should reflect past performance, although most funding sources will not argue with anticipated increases based on inflation and growth. Third, the director must always remember that in bargaining for funds, an agreement is being made: while the funding source may appear generous and disinterested in the proposed use of its money, do not be misled. Any source is exchanging money for something. Decide what "something" it wants in return—good public relations, a solution to a specific problem, or measurable growth of student progress—and attempt to supply it. Not only does this approach increase the chance of receiving the funding, but it also enhances the relationship between the director and potential funding agency.

Local Funding Sources

Local funding sources are in-house university agencies which may include but are not necessarily limited to the academic unit sponsoring the center.

It is reasonable to expect departmental funding for three of the basic costs of the operation—salaries, physical facilities, and operating expenses. For example, at the University of Alabama in Birmingham, the English Lab director is a faculty member. Tutors include graduate assistants who spend a portion of their assistantship hours in the lab and part-time English faculty who, for working ten hours a week in the lab, are paid the equivalent stipend of teaching one class. In other departments, tutors may be students who are hired through a work-study program and are paid minimum wages for working twenty hours a week, or tutors may be paraprofessionals hired from the community. A tutoring arrangement that involves no expenditure has students work a given number of hours in the center as a course requirement. This is particularly appropriate in courses such as Advanced Composition or Educational Methods.

Funding of physical facilities might seem a departmental responsibility, but in reality it is an institutional expense. While the space occupied by the tutorial unit is normally assigned to an academic department, the cost is prorated throughout the school. The average cost for a new tutoring facility—not just taking over existing rooms— is 6 percent of the cost of the entire building.[15] This cost, of course, can be prohibitive for a department. In existing buildings the costs of furnishings, heating, lighting, cooling, and maintenance are included in the indirect costs of the school. Other expenses such as telephone lines and computer time are usually billed to the sponsoring department.

Operating expenses may be another area that is outside a departmental budget. While the bills for paper, pencils, and photocopying may be absorbed by the departmental budget, the copier and its inherent expenses are usually charged to a central account such as the school's operating expenses.

Outside Departments

A center, especially an English center, may request financial aid from outside departments. An English center that can improve its own students' writing skills certainly can help the communication skills of students in business, sociology, nursing, and education. In return for the offer to work with students from other departments, the center director can ask for financial assistance, tutors from that discipline, paper, texts, or duplicating privileges. An outside department may be happy to help an existing facility that produces better skilled students with minimum outside involvement.

Occasionally, center directors should visit faculty meetings in outside departments to determine what types of support services the faculty want. Open houses for outside faculty members are vital links in communication with departmental clients. Developing curricula and study aids tailored to specific academic units, screening students for reading and writing problems, and improving general writing, reading, and study skills all enhance the reputation of the center and often result in financial support from a variety of disciplines.

Discretionary Funds

Another way of securing local funds is to appeal to the administration for discretionary monies. This appeal is especially effective if directors can show they have interdepartmental support since an administrator can better justify an expenditure that helps the entire school, not just one part of it. When soliciting administrative funds, start with the chief officer. The more powerful an administrator, the more clout she or he will have with those who control budgets at lower levels. It is difficult for a department chair to deny funds to a center that has the financial as well as the verbal support of the chancellor or president.

Charging Students

If a center needs further funding at the local level, the director might consider a direct charge to the students. This method of funding, though, should be used with caution and only as a last resort since it undermines the philosophy of equal access to all students. There are three types of student charges: student activity fee, registration fee, and direct charge to the student. All three methods will require administrative approval.

The student activity fee is common to most schools. Traditionally this fee is used to support student organizations, activities, and publications. The problem with adding a charge to support a developmental center is twofold: first, it increases the student's costs at a time when tuition is rising so quickly that some students can no longer afford the cost of education; second, by requiring students who neither need nor desire the service to pay for it, the charge imposes on the nonuser the obligation of subsidizing those who will use the center.

A second method of directly charging students is to include a registration or lab fee in the tuition of students enrolling in freshman English. In addition to having the same limitation as the student activity fee, this method creates another problem: deciding what to do about students who want or need tutoring but who are not enrolled in freshman English.

A third method is to impose a direct charge on students who come to the center for tutoring. While this method would eliminate the subsidy and nonenrollment problems, it could nevertheless restrict the access of some students who need the service but who are unable to pay for it. In most developmental centers it seems that a disproportionate number of ill-prepared students are from economically disadvantaged groups. This payment-on-demand program not only would discriminate against these students, but also would return the tutoring service to its traditional role: catering to the wealthy.

Local External Sources

The second funding category available to developmental center directors is local external sources. These sources are as diverse as profits from vending machines to endowments from trust funds. An enterprising director can secure monies by remembering the barter principle: something is being exchanged for something else.

Entrepreneurial Sources

Commercial ventures such as vending machines—dispensing soft drinks, coffee, snacks—can be launched on a profit percentage agreement with the sponsoring company. Installation of these machines will require approval from the administration, but a strategically located vending machine will produce a tidy sum with little involvement from the center staff.

Another money-making project for a writing center is production of educational materials that may be distributed locally or nationally. For example, other center staffs may be able to use curriculum materials that have proved effective in improving students' basic skills. A national market might be interested in developmental and administrative strategies that have a record of success at the local level. Development of the materials will necessarily demand time and energy from the center staff, but a successful publication will have a dual effect: not only are royalties generated, but the center also becomes more visible, thus increasing its perceived worth and, perhaps, the number of potential sources of income.

A variation is securing royalty rights from an established author. Perhaps in return for publicity, a local author can be encouraged to endow a staff position in the center. Convincing the author to part with a portion of his or her royalty income will depend on the director's ability to persuade the potential donor that support of the center is a worthwhile venture.

Grants

The most substantial sources in this category, though, are the many grants available to a center director. Agencies often fund academic projects, support salaries for services, or purchase equipment that can be used in a specified way. While directors tend to think of national agencies only, many local ones do exist. Almost every university has a grants officer or department that can provide a comprehensive listing of potential funding sources. Because some grants are restricted to use with particular groups of students, the guidelines and limitations available from the university's grants office will prove invaluable.

Besides the more obvious organizations such as chambers of commerce, rotary clubs, and humanities groups, a number of less publicized opportunities exist. Large banks, particularly those with trust departments, often administer trust funds that endow grants; these monies may or may not be restricted as to use. Athletic organizations, both teams and sponsors, occasionally provide financial support for aspiring athletes. In the South, state organizations such as the Alabama Committee for the Humanities and Public Policy offer grants to support academic services such as tutorial centers. Regional groups, too, like the Arts Endowment for the Gulf States, have grant monies available. Similar organizations are located throughout the country.

A word of caution: these sources generally offer soft money in relatively small amounts that is never guaranteed to be appropriated more than once. Also, the process of applying for a grant, receiving approval, and being funded can be time consuming; it is not uncommon for funds to be received a year after the initial proposal. Finally, these grants are rarely given without some stipulation—for instance, that the monies be used for particular groups of students, for specified methodologies, or for purchase of certain types of equipment. To ensure compliance with the agreement, the center director will be asked to submit in writing periodic reports on the project and expenditures. These stipulations can be both frustrating and time consuming.

The most important consideration, though, is to realize that while these monies are important, they are no substitute for the budget that funds the core of the program. To depend too heavily on these soft monies is to invite disaster for the continuation of the tutoring facility. Enjoy these monies and use them for special projects, but never commit the essential elements of the center to external funds.

Federal Sources

A final source available to the center director is perhaps the most profitable: federal grants. These grants can be applied for either by an individual or by a group. Sources of federal grants are listed in national registers available in the school's grant office or from public libraries and the government printing office. These registers include valuable data such as guidelines for applicants, proposal formats, deadlines, evaluation methods, amount of funding available, numbers and types of proposals previously funded. From this information, the director can learn how to tailor the proposal to fit the expectations of the funding source and thus enhance the chance of acceptance.

The Department of Education is a large agency the center director should consider first for possible funding. This agency is responsible for dissemination of huge amounts of money both to individuals and groups. Some grants can be renewed for several years. For example, the Support to Developing Institutions Program under Title III of the Department of Education has for the past decade provided large grants to developmental programs. "Developing institution" does not necessarily refer to recently founded schools. It also includes particular school programs that are new and innovative. Tutoring facilities qualify for funding under this broad interpretation. The University of Alabama in Birmingham is one of the schools that has benefited from such a grant. The Title III monies appropriated to UAB over a three-year period have amounted to almost $1 million; of this amount, over $100,000 has gone directly to the support of the English Lab. Similar sums have been used for the Math Lab and for student services in a number of areas.

While this type and level of funding can be a boon, there are some drawbacks. First of all, the monies are provided for a specific length of time (three years), to bolster particular pedagogies and purchase equipment with the understanding that the school administration gradually will assume financial responsibility of these programs. Second, the Title III grants require periodic evaluation and review of the programs, including outside consultants who partially determine the effectiveness of the facility. Thus, uses of the grant monies are strictly specified. Any proposed expenditure that does not appear on the original budget must be requested in writing and approved in Washington before it can be executed. Finally, the extensive paperwork required by the Title III agency has necessitated creation of a local bureaucracy just to oversee administration of the grant. But if director and school can work within these limitations—both administrative and temporal—these federal funds certainly can provide substantial financial support for local programs.

Other agencies that provide grants for individual programs include the American Council of Learned Societies, Department of Agriculture, National Institute of Health, National Institute of Justice, National Institute of Mental Health, National Science Foundation, U.S. Army Medical Research and Development Command, and Department of Transportation. While some of the agencies initially do not seem to have anything in common with a tutoring facility, an enterprising director can usually find some area of commonality.

Funds from all these agencies must be accepted with a caveat, however: these monies will not always be available. Assuming that the given agency looks favorably and generously on the director's proposal, the funding will nevertheless continue only for a relatively short time and will be restricted in its use. Once these monies are depleted, the director is again faced with the necessity of keeping the program going. So the philosophy of accepting federal support should be the same as that employed for local external support: enjoy the benefits, but do not commit the care of the core program to "soft money."

The Key to Funds: The Center Director

We have now come full circle. While the notion of offering tutorial assistance to academically disadvantaged students is as old as formal education itself, the methods of providing this service have changed. The earliest service was paid for by the student being tutored, a basic case of exchanging capital for service. This exchange still supports tutoring facilities, but now the recipient of the service is not necessarily the source of the funds. A successful director is one who can convince administrations and granting agencies that the center is providing a service that will ultimately benefit them and that supporting the center financially is indeed cost effective.

Today few deny the need for a tutoring facility, nor does anyone deny the high cost of providing this service. Fortunately for the center director, there are many funding sources. Finding these sources is one of the most important aspects of the director's multifaceted job.

Notes

1. Frederick Rudolph, *The American College and University* (New York: Vintage, 1982), 281.

2. Thomas Griffin, "One Point of View: The Expanding Future of Developmental Education," *Journal of Developmental and Remedial Education* 5 (Fall 1981): 10.

3. Martha Maxwell, *Improving Student Learning Skills* (San Francisco: Jossey-Bass, 1980), 58.

4. Rudolph, 486.

5. Maxwell, 61.

6. Maxwell, 122.

7. Stephen Walsh, "Institutional Support: A President's View," *Journal of Developmental and Remedial Education* 3 (Fall 1979): 22–23.

8. Donald Rippey, "I Never Get No Respect . . . Or Support Either," *Journal of Developmental and Remedial Education* 4 (Fall 1980): 12–13.

9. Andrea Lunsford, "Preparing for a Writing Workshop: Some Crucial Considerations," in *Tutoring Writing: A Sourcebook for Writing Labs,* ed. Muriel Harris (Chicago: Scott, Foresman, 1982), 165–7.

10. Nancy Vandett, "So You Want to Be a Developmental Educator?!" *Journal of Developmental and Remedial Education* 4 (Spring 1981): 20.

11. Vandett, 20.

12. Rippey, 12.

13. Rippey, 12.

14. Maxwell, 128.

15. Maxwell, 136.

10 Efficiency and Insecurity: A Case Study in Form Design and Records Management

C. Michael Smith
Winthrop College

Smith discusses the administrative problem of managing the paper flow. Using a case study, he draws on the expertise of business communication specialists and applies principles of information management to discuss how to streamline writing center forms and recordkeeping.

Most of us who teach writing prefer to ignore issues such as administrative efficiency. We have a higher calling. We may, in fact, boast that we never have had a course in business administration and would not take one under any circumstances. We probably have had no experience managing an office. But if we end up directing a writing center, we find ourselves faced with a rather complex task; we have the responsibility to see that a busy office runs efficiently, that services are delivered to students and faculty as effortlessly as possible. We also must keep records and worry about justifying ourselves, and our budgets, each year.

Our dilemma is like that of a physician who, though skilled in diagnosing and treating the ills of patients, is befuddled by the workings of a medical office. Perhaps the doctor will go back to school at night to take office management courses. Perhaps he or she will forgo the latest issue of the *Journal of the American Medical Association* for Terry and Stallard's text, *Office Management and Control,* or Zane Quible's *Introduction to Administrative Office Management.*[1] Or perhaps the doctor will join with any number of fellow physicians, who, according to one commentator on the paper glut, "adjust their fees upward just to compensate for their paperwork time."[2]

Perhaps our doctor has already been alerted by cries from the business world. Statistics on mushrooming paper and shrinking office efficiency are plentiful. Clerical workers are growing at some two and a half times the rate of the rest of the work force. They spend three-quarters of their time on paperwork—much of it in tasks that are nonessential. Instead of reducing this problem, the new technologies of duplication and computing have only magnified it. Paper is easier to generate than ever. More forms are needed; more information is stored.[3]

A Case Study

My own rude introduction to the problem of forms and record retention came shortly after I began directing a writing center. The college where I taught had adopted a policy requiring that students transferring credit to the college for freshman English pass a writing proficiency examination. The reason was simple. Our own freshman writing course was sufficiently rigorous that poorly prepared students avoided it by taking composition at other schools and transferring back the credit. They would fail or drop or avoid our course, yet return, smugly I always thought, at the end of the summer, certified competent in writing. When we finally initiated our proficiency test—an argumentative writing sample—we found that some 40 percent of these students could not write the equivalent of a D essay by our standards.[4]

The examination turned out to be successful in several ways: we encouraged students to stick with our own courses, and we were able to identify those weak students who transferred composition credit and provide them the individual tutorial assistance which they obviously needed. Most of the students who failed the test were, with writing center help and some hard work, later able to pass the examination.

This digression makes a point about forms. As the new writing center director, I faced the task of devising ways to administer the test and to keep accurate records. I worked out procedural details with the director of records and registration, an individual wily in these matters. Consider the form that she and I devised (see Sample Form 1). It looked official, despite the spelling error that escaped my proofreading efforts. It had an impressive number of blanks and boxes and lines. Indeed, it was a miniature file of information for any student who might be eligible to take the test. I did not know enough about form design to realize the problems with the form and the lines of responsibility it established. I did not even know enough to object when the form was funded through my own budget.

One of the problems with the form was the number of entries that had to be made and who would have to make them. The procedure was as follows. We—a writing center without a full-time secretary—were to receive a computer list of students thought to be eligible to take the test. As many as 400 names would be included, and for each we filled out a separate form, diligently entering social security number, name, enrollment date, and notification date. We then sent a notice to the students, at

Sample Form 1
Original

UNDERGRADUATE WRITING COMPOSITION PROFICIENCY EXAMINATION

| | | | | | | | | | | | | | | | | | | | | | | | | | | | | | | | | [   ]   [   ]

Student No.   Name (Last, First, Middle Initial)

| | | | | |

Date of
Enrollment

[   ]   Notification of times when the Undergraduate Writing Composition Proficiency
Examination will be administered.

_____
Date

FIRST TESTING–Test No. _____

Check one of the following two boxes:
☐ I want my Proficiency Examination to be graded for teacher certification requirements.
☐ I do not want my Proficiency Examination to be graded for teacher certification requirements.

_____   _____
Student's Signature   Date

[   ]   Score. Student notified on _____
                                                    Date

SECOND TESTING–Test No. _____

Check one of the following two boxes:
☐ I want my Proficiency Examination to be graded for teacher certification requirements.
☐ I do not want my Proficiency Examination to be graded for teacher certification requirements.

_____   _____
Student's Signature   Date

[   ]   Score. Student notified on _____
                                                    Date

THIRD TESTING–Test No. _____

Check one of the following two boxes:
☐ I want my Proficiency Examination to be graded for teacher certification requirements.
☐ I do not want my Proficiency Examination to be graded for teacher certification requirements.

_____   _____
Student's Signature   Date

[   ]   Score. Student notified on _____
                                                    Date

FINAL DETERMINATION OF WRITING PROFICIENCY

☐ Passed Proficiency Examination.   ☐ Score of C or better meets teacher
                                                                  certification requirements.
                                                       ☐ Score below C does not meet teacher
                                                                  certification requirements.
☐ Failed for the third time the Proficiency Examination. Student must pass WRI 102 at
Winthrop College and is encouraged to enroll for the course as soon as possible.
☐ Did not take Proficiency Examination during first semester enrolled at Winthrop College.
Student must enroll in and complete WRI 102 at next enrollment at Winthrop.

	Writing Center	Date
Information entered on		
permanent record.	Academic Records	Date

our expense, informing them of the policy, test dates, and procedures. Those students who showed up to take the test signed the form and entered some additional information, a task that required our shuffling through stacks of forms to locate the proper one.

Our handling of the forms did not stop there. We recorded a score each time the student took the test. After the student either passed the test or failed it for the third time, we filled in the bottom portion of the form, entered a code in the box in the upper righthand corner, pulled the four copies of each form apart, extracted the appropriately color-coded third sheet for our own records, and sent the others on to the central records office. The entire procedure, to say the least, was cumbersome. It produced useless paper flow, imposed upon both students and writing center instructors, and contributed nothing to the real purpose of the center. Instead of helping students learn to write better, the writing center staff was spending its time filling out forms and maintaining records. Only the administrators in the office of records and registration were happy—at least as happy as those unappreciated people can be. For once *they* did not have to do all the paperwork.

Three years later, after a summer of administrative haggling, we finally changed this system and the form that caused it. The changes were not effected easily. The problem with forms is that, once in place, they become chiseled in granite. As one executive in a leading business forms company remarked, much of the waste in forms "comes from mere precedent. A company president asks for a report on something once and it becomes a fixture in the company for the next 10–20 years, until somebody realizes it's useless."[5] We had neither precedent nor president to blame. We created the form ourselves; yet to change the form meant to change the procedures and the responsibilities that extended beyond our office. That posed a problem.

The new form we devised (see Sample Form 2) was short and simple, as forms should be. It had just one copy. It was generated by a computer in the records office, where it was stuffed in a window envelope and mailed to the student at the central administration's expense. We in the writing center had nothing to do with the form until the student showed up for the test. We collected the forms at the door, recorded the test results on them, and returned them to the records office. We kept no copies in the writing center because it was not the business of the center to store official college records. We did keep the examination so that we could go over it with the student.

Thus one piece of paper, computer generated, served as notice of examination, ticket to the test, and means of recording the test results and transferring them to the appropriate administrative office. An added benefit to us was that we were not bothered by numerous requests from advisors and others that we check the student's proficiency examination records. Those requests were directed to the central records office.

Rules for Records

Why didn't we think of this simple system three years earlier? One reason was ignorance. We just had not thought about recordkeeping and form design before. Our revision of the original form resulted from our gradual

---

Sample Form 2
Revised Version

WRITING PROFICIENCY EXAMINATION FORM

THE POLICY: ALL WINTHROP STUDENTS MUST DEMONSTRATE WRITING
PROFICIENCY AT WINTHROP COLLEGE. IF YOU ARE
TRANSFERRING CREDIT TO WINTHROP FOR A COURSE
EQUIVALENT TO WRI 102, YOU MUST, IN YOUR FIRST
SEMESTER, TAKE THE WRITING PROFICIENCY
EXAMINATION OR REPEAT WRI 102.

THIS FORM WILL ADMIT YOU TO THE TEST ONLY AT THE TIME AND
PLACE INDICATED BELOW.

TIME: DATE:
PLACE: 318 KINARD BUILDING

```
*****************************************
*              *  YOU MUST HAVE THIS    *
*              *                        *
*              *  FORM, YOUR ID CARD, AND *
*              *                        *
*              *  A PENCIL IN ORDER TO  *
*              *                        *
*              *  TAKE THE EXAMINATION. *
*              *                        *
*****************************************
```

THIS FORM DOES NOT INSURE THAT TRANSFER CREDIT FOR WRI 102 HAS
BEEN ACCEPTED. IF YOU HAVE QUESTIONS, CHECK WITH THE OFFICE
OF RECORDS AND REGISTRATION.

realization of some simple steps and concepts which most management texts suggest:

1. Before designing forms, make flow charts of where the records go.
2. Recognize that a form is itself a blueprint for an entire record-keeping system.
3. Make a list of purposes for storing information, and avoid collecting information that does not meet these purposes.
4. Reduce the number of forms, number of copies of them, and number of times a form is handled.
5. Keep to a minimum both the size of forms and the amount of detail on them.

Our earlier form, with its needless complexity, multiple copies, and repeated handlings, flew in the face of this basic advice.

Another reason for our poor original form, as well as our tendency generally to get bogged down in needless records, was our insecurity. We were a relatively new writing center, with a totally new director. We needed to justify ourselves to ourselves and to others. We were fearful we would be caught without sufficient data or that we would not have enough cross checks in our testing procedures. The extra recordkeeping grew out of a psychological cause, a tendency in insecure companies as well as in insecure writing centers.

The changes we made from the cumbersome, data-heavy form to the slimmed-down one reflect what seems to be a trend among writing centers. As we became more confident in our examination procedures, we reduced paperwork. Likewise, a number of other writing centers have, as they have become better established, moved from overly involved record-keeping designed to provide detailed justification for funding to a more simplified system that retains less data and which is more easily managed.

Even now, some center administrators advocate an oversupply of information and elaborate recordkeeping. Joyce Steward and Mary Croft admonish directors to "have at their finger tips wide-ranging statistics and facts on which to base surveys, requests, and studies and to begin research."[6] Such information might be useful, but I am reminded of what a writing center director once told me about the vast quantities of information he used to maintain in his office: "There's enough information for three dissertations." No dissertations were written, however, and much of the information was collected for no purpose. His experience reinforces the advice of Jon Jonz and Jeanette Harris in their contribution to *Tutoring Writing: A Sourcebook for Writing Labs:* "Keeping elaborate records and generating mountains of impenetrable statistics to prove the merit of a writing center is self-defensive records keeping; it leads to claims that cannot be substantiated and to arguments that should never be joined."[7]

Single Form Systems

The director with three dissertations worth of statistics subsequently simplified his recordkeeping. Now most of his information is contained on one form printed on the inside of the student's writing center folder. The form is keyed to materials in the center so that it serves also as an index of resources. The student's instructor can use this form to indicate what sort of work the student should undertake. The student uses the same form to indicate what she or he has done. One form, kept in the lab, replaces several different ones, each of which would have required handling, filling in, storing, and delivering.

Other colleges use an even less formal system. The student simply comes by the writing center and signs up for an open time slot; formal scheduling of appointments is not necessary. Records are kept in a log that summarizes the student's work and the tutor's impressions and suggestions. A system such as this requires almost no forms and relatively little recordkeeping. It can work well, especially at a small college.

Referral Based Systems

More typical is a recordkeeping system built around a referral form. A referring instructor fills out the form, which calls for basic information about the student and his or her needs. This form becomes the basis for the writing center records. Modifications to this system include maintaining a detailed appointment book recording attendance and missed appointments. For a center that needs to be able to produce statistics on use at the end of the year, the appointment book, with a column for weekly totals, can be helpful. Another modification is sending progress reports to referring instructors. In this way, the writing center tutor can indicate the student's attendance, establish a dialogue with the student's instructor, and encourage future referrals. Here the advantage of better communication with referring instructors must be balanced against the disadvantage of increased paperwork.

Remember: Stay Lean and Trim

Of course, each writing center has to develop its own forms and systems consistent with its own needs. Sample forms from other writing centers are of little help. More useful is a realization of the principles that lie behind form and information system design. Those principles, as already indicated, are simple enough. It's just that center directors often fail to think of them.

I remember my surprise when a professor of business communications reminded me that there are only four ways in which we can use information. He ticked them off on four fingers as he peered at me. We can measure it, store it, retrieve it, and deliver it. As I listened I thought of all the information our writing center stored that was never retrieved or measured or delivered. With that thought came another realization of what should have been obvious. Data should not be stored indefinitely. I thought of all those writing proficiency examinations our transferring students had written in past years. Their essays were still stored, unused, in our cabinets. . . . Since then, I have found the following advice in more than one guide to recordkeeping: never add a file cabinet.

From our experience with the proficiency examination forms, we learned to guard against excess recordkeeping and to be aware of some basic principles of form design and record retention. We also got over some of our initial insecurity. In the process, we discovered that the best advice for recordkeeping is the same advice that our hard-working physician studying business administration texts might give patients: keep lean and trim. Do not glut yourself on forms and records and administrative procedures.

A writing center, like a person, can be slowed down by excesses. After all, the purpose of a writing center is to tutor students, to help them improve their writing. Let's hope a "spare tire" of forms and information does not prevent us from bending to their needs.

Notes

1. George R. Terry and John J. Stallard, *Office Management and Control: The Administrative Managing of Information,* 8th ed. (Homewood, Ill.: Irwin, 1980); Zane Quible, *Introduction to Administrative Office Management* (Cambridge, Mass.: Winthrop, 1977).

2. Lee Grossman, *Fat Paper: Diets for Trimming Paperwork* (New York: McGraw, 1976), 6.

3. In addition to Grossman (above), see discussions in Carl Osteen, *Forms Analysis: A Management Tool for Design and Control* (Stamford, Conn.: Office Publications, 1969), and Frank M. Knox, *The Knox Guide to Design and Control of Business Forms* (New York: McGraw, 1965).

4. The test was a holistically scored writing sample.

5. As quoted in Grossman, 3.

6. Joyce Steward and Mary K. Croft, *The Writing Laboratory: Organization, Management, and Methods* (Glenview, Ill.: Scott, Foresman, 1982), 89.

7. Jon Jonz and Jeanette Harris, "Decisions, Records, and the Writing Lab," in *Tutoring Writing: A Sourcebook for Writing Labs,* ed. Muriel Harris (Glenview, Ill.: Scott, Foresman, 1982), 217.

11 Undergraduate Staffing in the Writing Center

Loretta Cobb
Elaine Kilgore Elledge
University of Montevallo

Adequate staffing is essential to the effectiveness of any writing center. Cobb and Elledge outline in this essay a staffing program utilizing peer tutors. Primarily intended for directors of new centers, their essay touches upon such matters as recruitment, payment, training, and evaluation of tutors.

With the shift from product- to process-oriented teaching in composition classes across the country, many writing center directors are turning more to what Muriel Harris has called "an almost unexplored goldmine": undergraduate staffing of their centers.[1] Peer tutors can serve as excellent staff, provided that the program is effectively implemented. The director must determine carefully how to establish a peer tutoring program and anticipate exactly what training measures must be undertaken. Such issues as the need for peer tutors, selection, tutor training, funding, types of services, evaluation, and public relations must be considered.

Assessing the Need for Peer Tutors

First, one must determine if there is a need for peer staffing. By surveying faculty and by studying final grades earned in freshmen English, one can project the need for individual assistance. Charting the schedule for freshman classes can assist the director in determining times when assistance needs to be available. This kind of information, coupled with students' request for tutoring, provides an estimation of the need for tutorial assistance. This is particularly true at institutions where a process approach to composition and the importance of one-on-one instruction have become accepted.

Any assessment of the need for peer tutoring should also take into account the comments of professionals with experience in the field. Many

123

directors of established tutorial programs feel that peers can be in some ways more effective than classroom teachers. For instance, Paula Beck thinks that tutors change the learning environment because they are likely to share the ideas and experiences of the tutees.[2] Thom Hawkins points out that peer tutors are both "insiders" and "outsiders" and can provide a vital writer-audience link often missing when students write only for teachers. Tutors facilitate the transition to insider: "Students want to have power over their environment, to be in control of what happens to them and they sense that they must learn to manipulate language the way their teachers do before they will be able to play the academic game the way insiders do."[3]

Deborah Arfken provides further support for the effectiveness of peer tutoring. She points out, "Peer tutoring is especially effective because it creates a personalized learning situation for students who often feel anonymous in classrooms with increased student-teacher ratios."[4] Undergraduate tutors often have the patience to *listen* to each individual because their interests are closer to their peers'. Also, students usually talk more freely to a peer, who is not the authority figure a professor is.

It is imperative to recognize the importance of training peer tutors to teach basic writers. Tutors need to be knowledgeable and helpful. The training process should develop knowledge, give insight, make the tutor aware of various helping styles, and provide for practice in the interpersonal aspects of tutoring.[5] Tutors must be trained to recognize the importance of affective as well as cognitive skills. Marvin P. Garrett points out that one must be cognizant of the "delicate balance" between peer-dominant and tutor-dominant tutoring.[6] The current professional literature encourages the inclusion of research-based content in training sessions. For example, Gary A. Olson and John Alton published an article in *The Writing Center Journal* concerning their study of the use of a formal heuristic at the University of Alabama writing center.[7] If tutors are trained to use heuristics, it is difficult to stray into lengthy conversations about last night's rock concert. On the other hand, it is necessary to adhere to Kenneth Bruffee's advice: "If tutors are too well-trained or too much older, tutees don't perceive them as peers but as little teachers, and the collaborative effect of peers working together is lost."[8]

Selecting Tutors

Once directors are convinced that there is a need for peer tutors, they need to establish immediately the combination of tutors and professors working together. When designing the selection process, the director should consult faculty concerning desirable characteristics of a good tutor. This consultation provides a tactful way to remind faculty that excellent scholarship is not necessarily an indication that a person can tutor effectively.

One of the most important attributes is being a good listener. The director can determine if the tutor listens well in an interview—a screening device used by most directors. During the interview the director must stress the importance of patience and true concern for helping basic writers. The tutor should be warned that working in the center can be frustrating as well as rewarding.

Leonard Podis reports that at Oberlin College peer tutors are expected, in addition to the interview, to correct ten sentences and to analyze a paragraph, making written statements to the student concerning strengths and weaknesses. He makes the point that he is not looking for expertise, but promise.[9] Often tutors know *how* but not *why*. Usually, tutors have an intuitive command of language, but the rules have long ago escaped them. However, they will learn quickly as part of their training. William Miller reports in *The Writing Lab Newsletter* that he requires his tutors at Ball State University to meet these prerequisites:

1. Have a 2.75 overall grade average
2. Pass tutor qualification tests, including both grammar and usage examinations and a 500-word theme
3. Secure recommendations from at least two members of the English faculty who are familiar with the candidate's writing[10]

Perhaps the most important prerequisite is faculty recommendation. If faculty are encouraged to assist in selecting and training the staff in a center, they will naturally feel that the writing center is theirs—a part of the English Department. Faculty support is, for many reasons, crucial to the success of a center.

Olson says that professors who fail to provide support are sending harmful messages to the staff and to the students they refer to the center.[11] One method of preventing these harmful messages is to include faculty in the recruitment of tutors for the writing center. One method for accomplishing this is to establish a workshop for faculty and English honor students to familiarize them with what happens in the writing center. The aim is to recruit more volunteers with the assistance of the faculty. During the workshop, faculty and experienced tutors can be paired with honor students for mock tutoring sessions. Arfken suggests that the following be monitored during a mock tutoring session: the tutors' (or mock tutors') ability to explain information accurately and clearly, ability to develop rapport, patience, and listening skills.[12] The workshop system is an excellent way of screening tutors, and it should also provide lively, provocative discussion—even for those who are uninterested in tutoring—concerning the teaching of composition skills. Such faculty-student communication is important for undergraduates, and it also can be enjoyable.

Although faculty assistance and involvement are important, the final selection of tutors should be made by the director. With the increasing number of students using writing centers, directors' responsibilities for supervising tutors increase, and they have no time to supervise students who are not effective tutors.

Funding a Center Staff

When staffing a writing center, directors must consider every possibility. The issue of funding is especially critical during difficult economic times. A director with limited resources might look for private donors. For example, at the University of Montevallo, a private benefactor contributes funds to make tutoring in composition skills possible. He does so because he believes in the importance of communication in the world of business and is a supporter of education. Persons establishing new centers should be especially enthusiastic about pursuing private funding.

An obvious way of overcoming the money shortage is to recruit volunteer tutors. The workshop method is one means, but there are other ways of obtaining volunteer services. Often upper division students will respond positively to a favorite professor's request that they serve as tutors. Professors who stress the process approach and individual instruction can appoint a first-year student as an honor tutor for each class. These tutors work only with their classmates, serving more as good listeners than as editors. Honor tutors can assist their classmates with prewriting discussions and offer feedback during the composing process. The obvious advantage of class tutors is that they are totally familiar with the professor's assignment.

The director also can appeal to honor societies, stressing the importance of volunteer work on vita sheets and the practical benefits of experience in teaching. (Many businesses look for people who have tutored because that interaction indicates good interpersonal skills.) And some excellent students serve as volunteers simply out of dedication to others. In addition, senior citizens frequently are dedicated people with talents to share in the center. At the Southeastern Writing Center Conference in 1982, Lloyd Mulraine reported great success using senior citizens as tutors at Jacksonville State University.

Many schools have the advantage of offering a course for tutors, who may count their work in the center as a practicum. While there are many advantages to this arrangement, at a small school it can be difficult to establish such a course. Also, this arrangement could weaken the director's role in the selection process if all students are allowed to take the course; thus admission to the course might be limited to those students who meet the director's prerequisites and have completed favorable interviews. Teaching tutors about basic writers and the theories of composition lays the foundation for sophisticated tutoring, and the incentive of earning a grade increases motivation. Undoubtedly, a center director who also teaches tutors can demand more from them than a director who staffs only with volunteers. In a tutoring course, students can keep journals, do case studies, acquaint themselves with tagmemics and heuristics from current research, and participate in sharing sessions with other tutors during class time. Every director should at least explore these possibilities.

Some writing center directors may never have to consider staffing through volunteer tutors or students enrolled in a composition class. Those directors who have adequate budgets will find that money is an excellent incentive. Most tutors seem quite content with minimum wage; in fact, many will volunteer one hour for every hour they are paid. When students work four hours a week, they can accumulate a decent sum in a month's time. A less expensive approach is to hire students who qualify for work-study.

Cost-effective staffing *is* possible. At the University of Montevallo last fall, 256.5 hours of tutoring were paid for, but 1,312 hours of tutoring were actually delivered. The unpaid hours are explained by two factors: some tutors were volunteers and group tutoring was encouraged.

Determining Center Services

One of the most important decisions the director will need to make involves types of services offered. The following alternatives should be considered: drop-in tutoring, group tutoring, and appointment tutoring. The convictions (and personality) of the director will largely determine the choices, but one must keep in mind that students have different needs and learning styles. Actually, if the center is large enough and the director is flexible enough, all of these services can be offered simultaneously, though perhaps not quite as efficiently as offering each service at separate hours. Each type of service has advantages, and what works with one student may fail with another; a center should therefore attempt to offer all three.

Drop-in vs. Appointment Tutoring

During the drop-in time, a student who needs occasional help can seek assistance. The kind of student who uses this service ranges from the A student who has one quick question to the less motivated student who never wants to work in the center until the day an essay is due. This service is appreciated by the student who feels an urgent need for help and does not want to schedule a later appointment. For example, the assignment may be due in two hours; thus an appointment two days later would not be helpful.

When appropriate, tutors can encourage those students who need more help to set up a regular appointment with the same tutor for certain hours during the week. It is easier for the students to commit them-selves if they are assured that their progress will be assessed weekly and that they may no longer need assistance after several appointments. This short-term commitment seems to make tutees feel less trapped; conse-quently they often continue until the end of the semester. The director must remember that basic writers often need this kind of structure and discipline.

Group Tutoring

Many basic writers also benefit from group support and will choose group tutoring. This can be very productive, rewarding, and cost effec-tive. The director and a tutor can easily work with eight to twelve stu-dents, allowing a portion of the hour for individual work and then bringing the group together for mechanics drills, sentence combining, or other group activities. Again it is important to remember that different students need different services, and tutors, as well as directors, must be sensitive to those differences.

Evaluating the Results

Directors cannot relax in the knowledge that they are doing well; they must be aware of their accountability.

Evaluating Students

Hunter Boylan suggests that evaluation of student progress be focused on the following measures:

> Student grade point averages
> Gain scores from pretest to post-test on standardized or locally developed achievement measures

Ratings of student satisfaction with program services
Student retention[13]

It is quite difficult to find a standardized test that suits all directors and all faculty, but one must face the fact that figures impress administrators. Most faculty, however, tend to be more impressed by improvement in writing samples. This is especially true when a group of faculty holistically evaluates the initial and final compositions of students who work in the center.

Directors and tutors should not be discouraged when the student's final composition does not reflect the staff's estimation of the growth. Even pre- and post-tests may show only a few points of progress, whereas the grade in the composition class may increase by two letter grades. On the other hand, a student may show significant progress between the pre- and post-test and fail to improve in composition skills.

The staff and the students should be cognizant of the many variables involved. A conference with each individual after the final evaluation is helpful. Staff members may point out areas where more improvement is needed, while stressing the areas where progress has been made. Such variables as ability, determination, and the number of hours spent in the center need to be acknowledged during the conference.

Student Evaluations of Tutors

A director must also recognize the importance of evaluation of the tutors' performance by the tutee. At one university, English tutors are rated in eight areas. For example, in the fall of 1981, thirty-three students responded confidentially to the following questions. A five-point scale was used, with five indicating a frequency of *almost always* and one being *almost never*. The averages are indicated below.

Tutor Evaluation Summary, Fall 1981

1. Did the tutor really seem to care whether your skills improved or not? **4.6**
2. Do you feel that the tutor is competent? **4.8**
3. Did you feel free to come to the director with questions about your individual problems? **4.6**
4. Do you feel that the tutor gave you personal attention? **4.6**
5. Did the tutor give you adequate information concerning your academic problems? **4.5**
6. Was the tutor available during the times he/she was scheduled to work? **4.7**
7. Was the tutor accessible, friendly, and approachable? **4.9**
8. Did the tutor seem to understand your difficulties with the material? **4.6**

This evaluation enables tutors to see how they are perceived; directors may wish to address these perceptions in individual conferences.

Director Evaluation of Tutors

In addition to gathering data from tutees, the director should supervise and regularly evaluate the progress of each tutor. This is done most effectively on an ongoing basis through informal conversations and staff meetings. It is always helpful to point out positive strategies that a tutor has used in a difficult situation; often tutors themselves will then volunteer the problems that need to be discussed. Regular staff meetings enable students to express negative feelings—a process vital for writing center staff who are not permitted to discuss students and their work outside the professional setting. The meetings also enable them to share successes and positive feelings about their work. Most importantly, the director and the tutors need to use all the evaluative data to determine how to improve tutor training and ultimately all the services offered in the center.

When reporting the results of tutor evaluation to faculty and administrators, a director might also point out further evidence of the effectiveness of peer tutors from the professional literature. For example, American College Testing recently conducted a survey of 179 institutions and reported, "Peer Staff (tutors, paraprofessionals) were singled out most frequently by program staff as an element which had great impact on the success and/or retention of students."[14] Also, Podis reports that tutees have consistently evaluated tutors favorably.[15] Such information would be an effective supplement to the director's own findings.

Undergraduate staffing is becoming more widely used across the country. It demands more from the director than supervising graduate students or professional staff members, but it is less expensive and often more beneficial to tutees, who, after all, should be our primary concern.

Notes

1. Muriel Harris, Letter to Southeastern Writing Center Conference, February 7, 1981, in *Proceedings of the Southeastern Writing Center Conference: 1980* (Tuscaloosa, Alabama: Gary A. Olson, 1981).

2. Paula Beck, Thom Hawkins, and Marcia Silver, "Training and Using Peer Tutors," *College English* 40 (December 1978): 432.

3. Thom Hawkins, "Intimacy and Audience: The Relationship between Revision and the Social Dimensions of Peer Tutoring," *College English* 42 (September 1980): 64.

4. Deborah Arfken, "A Peer Tutor Staff: Four Crucial Aspects," in *Tutoring Writing: A Sourcebook for Writing Labs,* ed. Muriel Harris (Glenview, Ill.: Scott, Foresman, 1982), 111.

5. Leonard A. Podis, "Training Peer Tutors for the Writing Lab," *College Composition and Communication* 31 (February 1980): 70.

6. Marvin P. Garrett, "Toward a Delicate Balance: The Importance of Role Playing and Peer Criticism in Peer-Tutor Training," in *Tutoring Writing,* ed. Harris (Glenview, Ill.: Scott, Foresman, 1982), 95.

7. Gary A. Olson and John Alton, "Heuristics: Out of the Pulpit and into the Writing Center," *Writing Center Journal* 2 (Fall/Winter 1982): 49–56.

8. As quoted in Beck, Hawkins, and Silver, 446.

9. Podis, 71.

10. William V. Miller, "Now and Later at Ball State," *Writing Lab Newletter* 6 (February 1982): 1.

11. Gary A. Olson, "Attitudinal Problems and the Writing Center," *Liberal Education* 67 (1981): 310.

12. Arfken, 110.

13. Hunter R. Boylan, "Program Evaluation: Issues, Needs, and Realities," in *Assessment of Learning Assistance Services,* ed. Carol C. Walvekar (San Francisco: Jossey-Bass, 1981), 14.

14. Lee Noel, Randi Levitz, and Juliet Kaufman, *Serving Academically Underprepared Students: A Report of a National Survey* (ACT National Center for the Advancement of Educational Practices, 1982), 1–18.

15. Podis, 75.

12 Developing a Peer Tutor Program

Linda Bannister-Wills
Loyola Marymount University, Los Angeles

Bannister-Wills reviews several well-known tutoring training programs in centers across the country. She goes on to describe a detailed training model consisting of both formal and informal methods.

Perhaps the most important and certainly one of the most popular techniques for teaching writing today is the use of peer tutors. Writing centers and learning laboratories are the primary places where peer tutors are trained to do their work. The growing pedagogical importance of peer tutors and writing centers has influenced the development of peer tutor training, a methodological shift that has been both speedy and revolutionary.

A writing center is a learning-by-doing environment where students examine their writing and the writing of their peers without the threat of teacher evaluation or the fear of being unable to compete. The sense of place in a writing center is one of welcome and comfort where challenges can be met with decreased apprehension and where work is accomplished in a spirit of community. Undeniably, this environment has shaped peer tutor training, but peer tutoring as a method can be linked to a revolution in thinking about writing.

The paradigm shift in composition theory from product- to process-based models has resulted in a corresponding methodological revolution. Rather than focus on written products, composition instruction now concentrates on the "process of getting there." A focus on process demands that attention be given to discourse as it evolves, a process that research has shown does not take place linearly, but recursively.[1] Pedagogy accompanying this theoretical shift incorporates the following concepts: meaning is created and discovered by means of drafts written in response to feedback; instructors are resources, models, facilitators, and learners; students collaborate with each other and the instructor; there is little "preteaching," that is, instruction occurs during composing in response

132

to inquiry; revision is an ongoing process at each stage of composing.[2] The above approaches are at the heart of writing center methodology and peer tutoring. Peer tutors are not teacher-evaluators but peer collaborators, and the writing center environment is ideally suited for such a methodology.

Peer tutoring and peer tutor training have evolved for only a short period. Most of the research on "collaborative learning" is relatively recent,[3] and scholarly discussions of peer tutors as employed in writing centers have appeared only within the last five to ten years. It is clear, however, that allowing tutors to discover how to tutor on their own through trial and error no longer suffices. Rapid growth and the ensuing need for intercenter communication have resulted in a drive toward more sophisticated training procedures. An examination of several well-known tutor training programs reveals some important trends in these procedures.

Review of Programs

There are essentially two types of training programs: those that take place within a college course and those that exist outside a classroom framework. A survey of the available literature shows that most tutor training programs include coursework. At the University of Michigan–Flint, Patrick Hartwell and Robert Bentley established one of the earliest writing centers reported on in the professional literature and one of the most extensive coursework training programs. They trained their tutors by requiring a nine-credit-hour program: an introductory course in linguistics, an upper division composition course (Rhetoric and the Writing Process), and a course of directed readings in urban education and the nontraditional student.[4]

The "Brooklyn Plan"

Structured within a credit-bearing course, Kenneth Bruffee's "Brooklyn Plan" is well known as a method of training peer tutors and has influenced the training programs of many writing centers. Bruffee's method is based on the idea that good writing tutors are created by focusing on the writing and thinking processes. The Brooklyn Plan "creates conditions in which students can learn something which lies close to the center of traditional liberal education, analytical and evaluative judgment of ideas and their expression in symbolic form."[5] The conditions Bruffee mentions result from a progressive series of collaborative judgmental tasks including peer critiques and evaluation of the critiques themselves. Bruffee's tutors write often (four papers, eight peer critiques, and two author's replies), completing the following writing-criticism tasks: (1) an objective rhetorical description, (2) an evaluative rhetorical description, (3) an examination of content, and (4) an examination of issues in peer tutoring and a judgmental evaluation. These four stages may be expressed in the form of the following questions that peer tutors are encouraged to ask themselves while tutoring:

> What form does the writing sample take?
>
> How well is it written?
>
> What does it have to say?
>
> How well have we responded?

Bruffee's work represents not only the first but one of the most important methods of tutor training because through collaborative peer criticism, tutors refine their own writing abilities as well as learn to help others develop their writing skills. The Brooklyn Plan also includes reading and discussing articles on the teaching of composition and keeping a log where tutors record, in journal form, tutorial experiences.[6] Several schools have added to or modified the Brooklyn Plan. A case in point is Nassau Community College, which, in addition to Bruffee's emphasis on peer criticism, includes analysis of professional writing and discussion of grammatical principles in light of style.[7]

Training as a Developmental Process

The program at the University of California also takes place within a course. Thom Hawkins and Rondi Gilbert's tutors at Berkeley earn credit through the school of education and rely on journal writing and "practical guidelines from material resources" found in a "tutor headquarters." These resources form a modular text that is the core of the Berkeley program. In addition, Berkeley holds weekly seminars that respond to tutor concerns. The directors frequently observe tutors, tutors observe one another, and tutors observe themselves on videotape in order to identify strengths and weaknesses. The Berkeley writing center is thus based on learning tutoring techniques, including how to respond to student writing, and adds another important ingredient to Bruffee's peer criticism foundation. Individual tutor methodology, which draws on a growing stockpile of modular exercises and is regularly evaluated, is the focus of this program. Tutors constantly assess and reassess their effectiveness and their modular exercise "tools." Tutors develop skills by becoming aware of their effectiveness or lack of effectiveness.

Another program that envisions training as a developmental process is at Oberlin College, where Leonard Podis divides his training course into two parts. The first half of the semester is spent in preparation, while the second half includes actual tutoring. Tutors discuss and read about the relative values of languages and dialects and the arbitrariness of standards of usage. Students then review a number of articles about individualized instruction and small group interaction and experiment with mimetic writing exercises. Tutor trainees then read one chapter a week from Gary Tate's *Teaching Composition: Ten Bibliographical Essays.* Podis's tutors also review a standard handbook and are taught a set of paper grading guidelines. Trainees grade a series of writing samples in two ways: an objective analysis followed by a comment they would make to a student, illustrating the difference between what is possible to say about a paper and what is useful to say. The significant addition here is an emphasis on discussion of current research in fields related to peer tutoring and the teaching of composition.

At Saint Mary's College, the tutor training course is designed to make the tutor intimately aware of the composing process itself. The focus here is not on composition research but on "research" on the self while composing. Tutors write a history of their education in composition, a narrative account of their most recent composing of an academic paper, and a typical academic essay for peer criticism. Tutors read and discuss a number of approaches to composition such as Peter Elbow's *Writing without Teachers.* However, the most interesting training technique is a required study of some aspect of composition by tutors using recorded or recalled conferences with students and tutors' own writing experiences. These extensive projects on a feature of the composing process are kept on reserve for future tutors.

Training by Doing

Tutor training programs that invent hypothetical tutoring sessions for "practice runs" are also popular. Marvin Garrett's tutor training program at the University of Cincinnati emphasizes two techniques: peer criticism and role playing.[8] Peer tutors experience the writing process from the perspectives of author, critic, and observer-commentator while focusing on a particular kind of writing or attitudinal problem during a mock tutoring session. Garrett's aim is to train "balanced" peer tutors who are neither tutor nor peer dominant. Phyllis Sherwood, also of the University of Cincinnati, adds that peer tutors should be trained through gaming to deal with affective factors like self-perception and that tutors need to be informed about learning styles (audio, visual, tactile).[9]

Communication Theory and Handbooks

Thinking about the interaction between tutor and tutee has caused the development of programs based on communication theory. At New York

University, Lil Brannon focuses on interpersonal communications techniques in her training program, discussing the value (or lack thereof) of four basic peer tutor roles: facilitator, supporter, leader, resister. Tutor as facilitator is tutor as audience. The tutor in this role raises questions that help the writer discover what needs revision. The tutor in the supporter role is tutor as coach, rewarding the writer for what he or she has done well. Tutors as leaders prod or pressure tutees to focus on an assignment, but when tutors are resisters, communication is blocked. Brannon concentrates on awareness in both tutor and tutee, instructing tutors to ask themselves these questions constantly:

1. What do I think the tutee is sensing?
2. What do I think the tutee is thinking?
3. What do I think the tutee is feeling?
4. Why do I think the tutee is here? What are the tutee's expectations?
5. What is the tutee doing? What are the tutee's actions? [10]

Tutor handbooks are also a popular and easy way to orient new tutors. At the University of Tennessee–Chattanooga and East Texas State University, for example, staff handbooks, which include program philosophy, policies, procedures, materials and methods, are used to save time and to make information easily accessible. (For more on handbooks, see Chapter 13 in this collection.) Periodic staff meetings where problems can be solved as they arise complement handbooks.

Many of the concerns addressed by the aforementioned training programs are included in the training course syllabus devised by Joyce Steward and Mary K. Croft in *The Writing Laboratory*.[11] Their syllabus provides a progressive discussion plan for tutors that appears, in various forms, in many training courses. The sessions are titled: (1) The Composing Process and the Lab Process, (2) The State of the Lab, (3) Housekeeping, (4) Discussion of Typical Student Papers, (5) Grammar, Dialect, and Syntax, (6) Prewriting. Steward and Crofts' six major discussion units are designed to acquaint tutors with the day-to-day operation of writing centers, including recordkeeping, the notion of composing as process, the art of peer criticism (here matters of grammar and syntax are discussed), and the thinking process that is the foundation of the writing process. Their program gives a director a formalized training plan that is easily followed.

A Tutor Training Model

An examination of the training methodologies reveals a number of usable techniques: peer criticism, the use of handouts, a discussion of current literature on composing and tutoring, self-evaluation, study of the composing process, role playing, investigation of interpersonal skills and learning styles, the use of handbooks, and staff meetings. Although the types of training in use and the emphases of that training may differ from center to center, directors usually train their tutors with a major concern in mind: helping tutors discover what is appropriate and necessary to help a student be a more able, "at-ease" writer-thinker.

Smooth center operation is dependent upon a tutorial staff that is capable of handling situations they perhaps have never before encountered. Still, training peer tutors is, in some writing centers, little more than assigning working hours and showing tutors where the exercise file is. In this type of center, directors choose tutors for their writing ability and assure them all they have to do is what their instincts tell them. This "sink or swim" approach may produce good tutors, but a higher proportion of good tutors, and some excellent ones, are produced by a training program that is an integral part of day-to-day center operation.

Most center directors agree it is important for tutors to establish a rapport with students that lessens anxiety and increases confidence. The experiences of basic writers with composition generally have been disastrous, and just like other disaster victims, they don't need officiousness at the aid station. They need practical advice—writing counseling as well as instruction. Helping a tutor become an effective counselor and writing audience is a delicate matter. Tutors, too, have anxieties, not only about writing, but about their ability to tutor. Experience *is* a good teacher, but tutors can operate with considerably more ease when given strategic instruction and counseling. Without day-to-day guidance, it is easy for a tutor to become merely a walking grammar text or a speedy proofreader, dependent on handbooks and grammatical terminology. Of course, tutors should be well acquainted with the printed resources the center has available (texts, workbooks, exercises, etc.), but tutors must be trained to make use of their own natural resources; they must be flexible enough to respond to a situation rather than become locked into a method.

A combination of formal and informal training procedures is, in part, a response to a new responsibility posed for writing centers by the recent wave of competency testing.[12] Where the original focus in centers had been on matters involving the actual process of composing essays, many schools are now faced with a situation in which tutors must function in a dual capacity: teaching students to recognize errors on a test as well as acting as a writing audience. Proper tutor training is all the more important in light of this dual role. The following is a six-part tutor training program that directors can adopt or adapt.

Formal Tutor Training

There are at least three means of formal training, each of which is employed in one or more of the programs reviewed earlier. These means are the practicum, assigned readings and discussion of them, and staff meetings.

The Practicum

Center directors can institute a practicum in tutorial methods, a training course for center tutors that exposes them to rhetorical and linguistic concepts. For example, the practicum can be a two-unit English elective offered every semester to students interested in tutoring in the writing center. Students can be recommended by their English professors, but they need not be English majors or minors. (Literacy is not, or should not be, discipline conscious. One of the best ways to demonstrate that to the doubting student is to have a center tutor reveal that he or she is a geography major.) Such a course is about the business of writers writing—tutors examine their own writing, one another's writing, and student writing samples to educate themselves. Tutors attempt to make what they do instinctively and intuitively *concrete,* to understand how composing processes work and what makes them go awry. In other words, the practicum tries to activate in tutors a consciousness of the composing process.

The practicum can meet for an hour once a week and can require the tutor, for example, to write two papers, four peer critiques, and two author's replies, and to create and prepare handouts for one to two writing exercises suitable for use in the center. These exercises may address matters ranging from writing a good introduction to inflectional ending difficulties. In addition, each tutor enrolled in such a practicum can be required to spend three to four hours per week tutoring in the writing center. And directors can institute an optional series of grammar seminars that teach tutors how to convey grammatical information (minus terminology) to students who must pass an error recognition competency test.

In this "theory in practice" course, practicum students write and examine writing (their own and that of others). In a session on evaluation, for example, tutors might learn about different types of grading: holistic, primary trait scoring, and peer evaluation. They then can apply these various procedures to a set of anonymous student written texts. Typically, one tutor will give a paper a B and another will give it an F. This could be a case of "I felt sorry for him!" versus "God, it had four comma splices!" Usually it is far from that simple. Tutors, like instructors, react in different ways to writing problems and tend to emphasize certain elements of an essay over others. Working toward a balanced evaluation where tutors learn to focus on those aspects that are most significant in a given writing situation is a tension-filled process. Old and new writing prejudices are raised and discussed, making these sessions both heated and valuable. Soon tutors will begin to understand how varying reactions to a text are possible and the difficulty of arriving at grading standards.

Tutors also can participate in role playing exercises. One tutor might play an irate student who visited the writing center for help on a paper which was returned bearing a D. Another tutor might play the three-time competency test loser who *has* to get out of freshman English this semester, who wants to graduate by 1990, but who never seems to know exactly what his or her writing assignments are. These role playing situations give tutors an opportunity to experience a problematic tutoring session in a nonthreatening setting.

The practicum is also a forum for tutors to debate the virtues of grammar instruction and the five-paragraph theme, to learn how to increase a student's fluency through freewriting and generative heuristics, and to learn what rhetoricians have to say about activating a student's sense of audience. The writing center practicum encourages students to investigate and discuss composition theory—in the center their discoveries are put into practice. Students can bring problems that arise back to the practicum for discussion. The center and the practicum thus complement and reinforce one another.

Assigned Articles

A second formal approach to tutor training is the reading and discussion of assigned articles on current research in the teaching of writing, the operation of a writing laboratory, and interpersonal communication. In such a program, tutors have a week to read an assigned article and prepare for a general review session. The director can assign articles, like "Is Teaching Grammar Immoral?" "Their To Many Kids Who Can't Rite Good," and "The Ethics of Literacy,"[13] that challenge preconceived notions tutors may have about writing. Since writing for most writers is an activity shrouded in mystery, articles that induce self-questioning and introspective examination are most useful. For example, tutors who read the NCTE publication *Students' Right to Their Own Language* can debate the legitimacy of competency testing, the distinction between substandard and nonstandard English, and the practicality of acquiring fluency in the standard dialect.

Staff Meetings

Center staff meetings are the third formal approach to training tutors. Practicum students, tutors on work-study, graduate assistants, and center faculty can be asked to attend weekly or biweekly staff meetings. The early staff meetings should introduce tutors to one another and to the center. Tutors can discuss how to handle a student's first visit to the center and should be led to discover that the key to a good tutorial session is the open-ended question. It is not the tutor's job to focus on errors and their explanations. The tutor learns to help the student discover when a message did not get through by using the student's own intuitions about audience and rhetorical effect. The student must be the actor in the session—not a receiver of a tutor's explanation.

Tutors also should learn the importance of assembling a "writing profile" on each new student. The profile is a combination of the students' responses to a self-evaluation form, a diagnostic theme they write, their instructors' comments or recommendations, and, perhaps most important, the students' oral descriptions of their experiences with and feelings toward writing. In addition, tutors should receive suggestions from the director that will encourage tutees' future center attendance and facilitate a progressive skills program. These suggestions might include:

1. Tell a student something good about her or his writing.

2. Don't try to deal with too much in one session—one or two problems at most at a time.

3. Don't edit a student's paper.

4. Try to give a student a success experience each time he or she comes to the lab.

5. Don't let a student stay in a workbook too long; individual attention from another human being is essential.

Staff meetings are an ideal time for tutors to discuss problem clients. Some of the liveliest and most beneficial sessions can occur when tutors help one another by sharing how they have dealt with particular situations. For example, a tutor at the University of Central Arkansas named Jill had had difficulty dealing with a student who spent most of his writing center time complaining about his teacher. Another tutor, Ted, suggested she "get tough" with the student. Ted advised, "Tell your student: 'Look you're stuck with this teacher; let's focus on something we can do something about—your writing.'" Jill tried the approach and it worked. At the close of each session, the director should solicit suggestions that will streamline center operation or contribute to its progress.

During the course of formal training procedures, tutors will recognize that a writing center is made up of several levels of expertise that can filter down and up to the benefit of all. The center director is one level, the composition faculty another, the tutors, graduate assistants, and students still others. Just as tutors and students build one another's confidence and skills, so do directors and tutors. This interdependence is responsible for much of a center's success, but the key to a successful center is an ongoing training program that is part of day-to-day operation and in which tutors learn and grow constantly rather than rely on a bag of tricks they have picked up at the beginning of the semester.

Informal Tutor Training

The formal approaches I have described are essential, but some of the most exciting learning in a writing center goes on spontaneously, informally. Informal training programs are not conducted; they are allowed to happen. Most informal tutor training is not controlled by the director, but is the result of interaction between tutors. Of course directors can manipulate scheduling so that tutors complement one another's strengths and weaknesses, but it is most important to create an atmosphere of community and sharing. Without the proper atmosphere, informal training cannot progress.

"Floating Tutors"

One informal training technique a director can implement is the use of the "floating tutor."[14] Floating tutors are tutors who have grown to know and love the center well. Floating tutors may be former tutors, veterans who no longer tutor formally, or they may be currently employed tutors who come in above and beyond their scheduled hours. These role models for new tutors drop in often to lend a hand in a tough tutoring session or simply to talk with new tutors about working in a writing center—a challenging and sometimes frightening situation for the uninitiated. Floating tutors are the experienced hands that provide proof that good tutoring is a skill that can be acquired and enjoyed. Floating tutors are not paid to "float"; they take their coffee breaks and spend their spare time in the center rather than in the student union. Floating tutors are not commissioned to do any specific tasks, but their presence is unmistakably felt. If a center has the proper environment (one of fellowship as well as learning), floating tutors will develop on their own.

Team Tutoring

Team tutoring, a second informal training technique, dispels the notion that one-on-one is the only acceptable method of tutoring. Most experienced tutors can recall a time when they did not have an answer or when they were ready to admit defeat when facing the blank stare of a tutee. Tutors should be advised of the acceptability and value of bringing in a coworker to help tackle the problem. In the course of the weekly staff meetings and the practicum discussions, each tutor's interests and specialties can be made known, facilitating team tutoring. But, of course, even when the resident expert is unavailable, a fresh opinion is usually enough to get the tutoring session rolling again.

Apprentice Tutors

The third approach, tutor apprenticeship, can exist only in a center that has been in operation at least one semester. New tutors may be apprenticed to a veteran and learn by observation how to make a tutorial session work. It is best, because of the pressure accompanying a formal appointment, not to schedule tutor apprentice sessions, but to have the veteran tutor request spontaneously that a new tutor sit in on a session. After the session the experienced tutor can ask for an evaluation and comments. This discussion reinforces what the new tutor has seen and aids the veterans in improving their communication skills as well. Experienced tutors, like experienced teachers, are distinguished by their constant search for better information and methods. It is not useful to rank tutors formally since that fosters separation, but the role of master tutor with tutor apprentices to teach and learn from is one which all dedicated tutors should expect to fill at some time in their tutoring career.

Training as Continuing Education

These formal and informal approaches can be used in the writing center to educate the tutorial staff in a progressive, ongoing fashion. Training techniques should be initiated and incorporated from the first day of the semester to the last. This "continuing education" approach to the instruction of writing center tutors can be highly successful in producing skilled tutors who are capable of meeting and dealing with the idiosyncratic composing processes and problems that each tutee brings with him or her. Under such circumstances, the tutor training program and the writing center share the common premise of adaptability.

Notes

1. See, for example, Nancy Sommers, "Revision Strategies of Student Writers and Experienced Adult Writers," *College Composition and Communication* 31 (December 1980): 378–388; Sondra Perl's "Understanding Composing," *College Composition and Communication* 31 (December 1980): 363–369; Sharon Pianko's "Reflection: A Critical Component of the Composing Process," *College Composition and Communication* 30 (October 1979): 275–278.

2. The techniques listed are based on the research of John Clifford who created an experimental course at Queens College, reflecting the changes in composition philosophy. See his "Composing in Stages," *Research in the Teaching of English* (February 1981): 37–54.

3. Almost all of the work examining the effects of peer tutoring has been done within the past twenty years; the term "collaborative learning" was coined by Edwin Mason in 1972, but Bruffee, in an excellent discussion of the growth of peer tutoring in higher education ("The Brooklyn Plan: Attaining Intellectual Growth through Peer Group Tutoring," *Liberal Education* 64 [December 1978]: 447–68), mentions earlier accounts of the importance of collaborative learning.

4. Patrick Hartwell, "A Writing Laboratory Model," in *Basic Writing,* ed. L. M. Kasden and D. R. Hoeber (Urbana, Ill.: National Council of Teachers of English, 1980), 63–73.

5. Kenneth A. Bruffee, "The Brooklyn Plan: Attaining Intellectual Growth through Peer Group Tutoring," *Liberal Education* 64 (December 1978): 450.

6. One of the best examples of a tutor log is Jackie Goldsby, *Peer Tutoring in Basic Writing: A Tutor's Journal,* Classroom Research Study No. 4 (Berkeley: University of California, Bay Area Writing Project, 1981).

7. Paula Beck, "Peer Tutoring at a Community College," *College English* 40 (December 1978): 438.

8. Marvin P. Garrett, "Toward a Delicate Balance: The Importance of Role Playing and Peer Criticism in Peer-Tutor Training," in *Tutoring Writing: A Sourcebook for Writing Labs,* ed. Muriel Harris (Glenview, Ill.: Scott, Foresman, 1982), 94–100.

9. Phyllis Sherwood, "What Should Tutors Know," in *Tutoring Writing,* ed. Harris (Glenview, Ill.: Scott, Foresman, 1982), 101–4.

10. Lil Brannon, "On Becoming a More Effective Tutor," in *Tutoring Writing,* ed. Harris (Glenview, Ill.: Scott, Foresman, 1982), 108.

11. Joyce Steward and Mary K. Croft, *The Writing Laboratory: Organization, Management, and Methods* (Glenview, Ill.: Scott, Foresman, 1982), 40–44.

12. The tutor training program at the University of Central Arkansas was developed in light of the Freshman Competency Examination which was instituted in the fall of 1981. This examination, a computer-scored, multiple-choice error recognition test, must be passed before a student receives credit for the first semester of English Composition.

13. Barbara Dodds Stanford, "Is Teaching Grammar Immoral?" in *Juxtaposition: Encore* (Chicago: SRA, 1975), 50; "Their To Many Kids Who Can't Rite Good," *US News and World Report,* January 26, 1981, 10; James E. Tanner, "The Ethics of Literacy Training," *College English* 44 (January 1982): 18–24.

14. The terminology and many of the ideas presented in this "informal" training method section were first articulated by Bob Child, a "floating tutor" at the University of Central Arkansas.

13 The Handbook as a Supplement to a Tutor Training Program

Jeanette Harris
Texas Tech University

In this practical essay, Harris presents the fundamentals of creating an in-house tutor manual. Cautioning that a handbook should be a supplement to and not a replacement for a formal tutor training program, the author discusses various types of handbooks, gives advice on style and content, and provides an outline of major handbook sections.

As both teachers and administrators, writing center directors must balance two roles. Although instructing students is their primary responsibility, they must also attend daily to the myriad details associated with the administration of a writing center program. Added to these roles is a third and complementary one—that of training tutors. The preparation of tutors is a responsibility that encompasses the administrative and instructive functions of a director and is crucial to both.

Even though directors may reason, not entirely fallaciously, that their tutors learn from observing their own tutoring behaviors and attitudes, they know that tutors need more than good models. They also need explicit instruction—instruction in the dynamics of student-tutor relationships, in the policies and procedures of the center, in the types and uses of instructional materials, and, most importantly, in the recursive nature of the composing process and the appropriate points of intervention in that process. As Marian Arkin notes, a formal tutor training program is now considered a necessity by most writing center administrators.[1]

Although tutor training programs vary, depending primarily on who staffs the center, a preliminary orientation during which tutors are given basic information is essential. This initial orientation session may consist of a single meeting or an intensive series of meetings, may focus on only the essentials or encompass all aspects of the program, may be informal and casual or formal and highly structured. In any event, certain information basic to the program must be communicated. One of the most effective supplemental tools for this purpose is an in-house tutor manual, or handbook.

A Handbook as a Supplement to Training

The key word in considering what a handbook can do is the word *supplement*. It cannot, nor should it, replace the training program. Used in the larger context of a formal training program, however, a handbook can serve as an extension of a director, reaching tutors at times when the director is not available, communicating information in another medium, adding a new dimension to the training process. Developing an in-house tutoring manual also forces directors to define their programs, to establish objectives and articulate policy that might otherwise be left assumed or vague and, therefore, misunderstood. Thus a handbook serves not only as a resource for tutors but also as a definition and description of the writing center program. As such, it supplements not just training but the program itself.

One of the primary reasons for developing a tutor handbook is a practical one. A handbook can assist a director in communicating to tutors those routine, mundane matters that require time better devoted to other, more important aspects of training. Tutoring involves not only writing and tutoring skills but also a certain amount of practical information about how a center operates daily. What kinds of records must be kept on each student? What materials are available and where are they located? Can tutors proofread ungraded papers? Questions such as these can be answered easily and conveniently in a handbook, leaving more time in the training program for the substantive issues of tutoring and writing.

A handbook also solves some of the problems associated with the constant turnover of tutors that directors face each term. Most writing center programs begin each term with a new, or partially new, staff. Spending valuable training time on mundane operational details when some of the staff is already thoroughly familiar with these matters presents a problem. A handbook can serve as an equalizer, assisting the new, less experienced tutors to learn quickly information that the more experienced tutors take for granted.

A handbook is also an asset when tutors are assigned to a writing center after the initial orientation session has been held. Rather than spending unnecessary hours briefing late arrivals, the writing center director can provide them with a copy of the handbook and schedule a conference with them after they have studied it. In such cases, the handbook does replace the formal orientation session—not an ideal situation but a better solution than omitting the training entirely.

Directors cannot expect their tutors, who are also students and instructors facing another busy term, to take time initially to study a handbook as thoroughly as they might like. Although conscientious tutors may read and digest every word, it is more reasonable to expect the tutors to use the handbook as a reference. In fact, one of the advantages of having a handbook is that it can be referred to repeatedly until the information it contains is assimilated. The handbook, of course, is available to tutors at all times, whereas directors are not.

Producing a Handbook

Because each writing center program is unique, a handbook should be a reflection of the program for which it is developed. For example, Rondi Gilbert and Thom Hawkins, directors of the University of California at Berkeley Writing Center, supplement their training program with a journal written by a student tutor during the first semester that she or he has served as a tutor.[2] And Nancy Wood of the University of Texas at El Paso has developed a handbook that consists of a series of questions and answers.[3] Most handbooks have more conventional formats, but each of them is distinct, reflecting the program it serves. However, some basic issues are common to the development of any handbook.

An initial, and basic, consideration is what kind of handbook to produce. How should it look? Who will print or duplicate it? How elaborate or simple should it be? The answers to these questions depend largely on the financial resources available to a director and on the size of the program. If money is not an issue—a rare but conceivable situation—the handbook can be as elaborate in design and format as the director's imagination and time allow. Most directors, however, are rather severely constrained by their budgets. Thus, they must produce a handbook that is relatively simple and inexpensive, one that can be duplicated within a department or by a university print shop at a minimum of expense. Producing a modest handbook should not be considered a compromise. In fact, two good reasons, in addition to the rather compelling one of cost, exist for developing a simple handbook.

First, handbooks should be inexpensive enough to use freely. Tutors should be able to ask for replacements if they lose or damage their copies of the handbook, and directors should feel free to share their handbooks with other directors as well as with interested faculty members and administrators. The handbook can even be used for public relations purposes since it usually defines a program and gives pertinent information about policies and procedures. For example, students who are assigned as part of a practicum requirement to visit or actually spend time working in a center can benefit from having a copy of the handbook. And visiting faculty members and administrators who are interested enough to request additional information can be given copies. A costly handbook only insures a constrained attitude toward the book and its uses.

Second, handbooks should be inexpensive so that they can be revised frequently. Since writing center programs should be flexible enough to change and grow, the handbooks that reflect them should be able to be revised easily and economically. If a program handbook does not require frequent revision, the writing center director probably should question whether the program is as dynamic as it should, or could, be.

Style and Content of the Handbook

A handbook, like any operation manual (which, in essence, it is), should be written in clear, direct language. As Steven Pauley advises in his text on technical writing, a manual should be written so that it "defies misunderstanding."[4] Tutors read handbooks because they need information; that information should be readily available to them in straightforward, unambiguous prose. Such a writing style need not be graceless, nor should it be condescendingly coy or pompous, in Walker Gibson's terms, neither "sweet" nor "stuffy."[5]

Furthermore, since the primary goal in writing a handbook is to inform, directors should include in the handbook organizational features that make it easier to read. For example, a handbook should begin with a well-organized table of contents, and the text should be divided into sections that are clearly labeled with headings and subheadings. Numbered paragraphs also can be helpful, especially if the book is to be used to supplement meetings and discussions during which it will be necessary to refer to specific sections. In fact, in determining style and format, readability should be a primary consideration.

Because the content of a handbook is largely dictated by the role it is to play in the total training program, the content varies as widely as the ways in which a handbook may be used. Most handbooks, however, include the following sections:

Philosophy, Objectives, and Policies

Primarily, the purpose of a handbook is to supply information to tutors in a convenient, readily accessible form; but it is important to begin even this type of practical, no-nonsense document with a statement of philosophy and purpose. Such a statement need not be lengthy nor involved but should provide a framework for the information that follows. Because it gives the reader an overview, this statement serves as an introduction to the handbook, giving the tutors who read it some insight into not only *what* they will be doing but also *why*.

Although the philosophy, objectives, and policies can be treated in separate sections of the manual, they work well as one section because they are integrally related. Such a section should begin with a clear, concise statement of the philosophical rationale on which the writing center program is based and the goals that the program hopes to attain: Is the program dedicated to autotutorial methods or to personal, individualized instruction? Does it seek to supply students with information about the formal conventions of language, or is it designed to help students understand and improve their own composing processes? Only then should directors outline the policies that evolve out of this philosophical orientation, for they cannot expect tutors to accept policies that are not supported by a thoughtful philosophy. For example, if directors inform tutors that they must not proofread papers, the tutors should understand that the reason behind this policy is that the center is more interested in improving a student's ability to write than in helping him or her achieve a higher grade on a specific assignment. If the handbook instructs tutors not to criticize instructors or the grades they give, tutors should realize that the rationale for this policy is that the center's function is a supportive, supplementary one. And once tutors understand the center's philosophy, they will be able to explain its policies and practices to students.

Routine Procedures

This section should contain the information essential to the daily operation of a center, for instance, the kinds of records that are kept on each student, the routine procedures that are followed in working with a student, a detailed agenda for the initial interview, and an explanation of how this first interview differs from later student-tutor conferences.

Information of this type can be assimilated more readily if it is supplemented by such aids to readability as lists, outlines, and illustrations. A dense text does not provide tutors with the quick answer they often require, especially during their first few days of tutoring. The routine procedures outlined in this section will be among the most frequently consulted of all those included in the handbook. Directors should be as comprehensive, as concise, and as clear as possible in describing these practical matters. Although such information may be routine to a director, it constitutes new information to the novice tutor.

Students and Content-specific Programs

A writing center is often used to supplement a specific course. For example, a basic writing course may have a lab component that requires students to spend a certain amount of time or to complete certain assignments in the writing center. Or an English education course may require students to spend a specified number of hours in the writing center as a practicum experience. Any required work of this sort must be supervised closely and recorded accurately. A handbook can outline the special procedures tutors should follow in working with these students.

Whereas writing centers were once involved almost exclusively with students enrolled in composition courses, especially basic writing courses, today increasing numbers of centers are moving beyond both remediation and composition courses. This across-the-curriculum movement has brought to writing centers a diversity of student groups for which special content-specific programs have been created. Tutors need to know about these special programs and the students who are enrolled in them. They also need to know about other special categories of students who may be represented in a center's clientele. For example, since handicapped students and ESL students need special materials and instructional approaches, the handbook should provide this information. If graduate students are offered assistance with theses and dissertations, tutors need to be aware of any special procedures involved in working with these students.

Materials

Perhaps nothing confuses an inexperienced tutor quite so much as the wealth of materials that most centers provide to supplement their instruction. These materials can be a valuable resource if the tutors know what is available and where it can be found. Becoming familiar with materials is time consuming and is best accomplished by actual experience. A handbook, however, can hasten this process by providing lists of materials to which the tutors can refer. These lists should be comprehensive, and, if possible, special attention should be given to those materials that are most frequently used or most likely to be helpful.

The lists of materials can be organized very simply according to the different types of materials: audio cassette programs, slide-tape or filmstrip-tape programs, programmed texts, general textbooks, workbooks, and handouts. Or the lists can be categorized according to certain instructional categories, such as punctuation, sentence structure, or paragraph structure and development. These general categories in turn can be subdivided. For example, punctuation can be subdivided into the different marks of punctuation, and sentence structure can be subdivided into the different parts of speech. The organization of the lists should, however, correspond as closely as possible to the way in which the materials are organized in the center.

Additional Resources

In addition to detailing the instructional materials found in a writing center, a handbook can introduce to tutors other resources available to them. One of the most important of these auxiliary resources is the reading or learning center. Unlike the materials available in the writing center itself, the reading or learning center is usually located outside the writing center, often across campus or at least in a different building or room; in fact, many tutors and students may be unaware of its existence. These auxiliary centers not only offer students instruction that is closely related to the development of their writing skills, but also provide assistance with study skills such as note taking, test taking, outlining, and summarizing. Because of the growing interest in reading-writing relationships, it is likely that future programs may combine reading and writing instruction. Until this efficient and economical integration of resources occurs, however, writing center tutors need to be aware of the existence of auxiliary centers and to be knowledgeable about the instruction that they provide.

A second resource that a handbook can explain to tutors is computer-assisted instruction. Many colleges and universities provide a lab where students can work with various computer programs, some of which may be related to the development of writing skills. These programs can be an effective means of providing students with drill and skills reinforcement. If word processors are available, students can learn to revise and edit by using these increasingly popular programs. A handbook not only should describe this resource so that the tutors are aware of its existence, but it also should list the available computer programs related to writing.

A handbook can list other resources that might be available on a particular campus. Frequently, there are other tutorial programs that can supplement the instruction students receive at the writing center. Or private tutors can be listed. (If the handbook does mention other programs or tutors, their credentials should be carefully checked since any person or program included in a handbook is assumed to have the endorsement of the writing center.)

Appendix

A final, often helpful, section is an appendix containing items somehow not appropriate to other sections of the handbook. For example, copies of various attendance, record, and referral forms can be included in the appendix. Some directors include copies of previous yearly reports. Others use the appendix to provide tutors with a list of the symbols that are typically used in grading and proofreading papers.

Conclusion

A handbook is only one part of a good training program for tutors, but it is an effective and increasingly essential part. As a writing center grows and a director's time becomes more limited, a handbook can play an important role in the total program. In an article on tutor training, Susan Glassman summarizes the advantages a handbook provides a writing center director:

> Compiling . . . material into a handbook saves time, saves endless repetition of the same materials as each new tutor arrives, provides each tutor with the same information . . . , gives tutors an overview of the program before they begin tutoring, and furnishes tutors with a guide that they can refer to throughout the semester.[6]

In addition to these practical reasons for developing a handbook, there is a less practical but no less valid one. It seems particularly appropriate that writing centers should have written documents that define their procedures and policies since they are, above all, proponents of writing. A handbook affirms this confidence in written discourse as a medium of communication. As directors present tutors with copies of their handbooks, they are saying to them that they believe in writing.

Notes

1. Marian Arkin, "Training Writing Center Tutors: Issues and Approaches," in *Improving Writing Skills,* ed. Thom Hawkins and Phyllis Brooks (San Francisco: Jossey-Bass, 1981), 25.

2. Jackie Goldsby, *Peer Tutoring in Basic Writing: A Tutor's Journal,* Classroom Research Study No. 4 (Berkeley: University of California, Bay Area Writing Project, 1981).

3. Nancy Wood, "Handbook for Writing Tutors" (University of Texas at El Paso, typescript).

4. Steven E. Pauley, *Technical Report Writing Today,* 2nd ed. (Boston: Houghton Mifflin, 1979), 222.

5. Walker Gibson, *Tough, Sweet, and Stuffy: An Essay on Modern American Prose Styles* (Bloomington: Indiana University Press, 1966).

6. Susan Glassman, "Tutor Training on a Shoestring," in *Tutoring Writing: A Sourcebook for Writing Labs,* ed. Muriel Harris (Glenview, Ill.: Scott, Foresman, 1982), 125.

III Special Concerns

14 The Problem of Attitudes in Writing Center Relationships

Gary A. Olson
University of North Carolina, Wilmington

Olson examines attitudinal problems of outside instructors, tutors, and students with respect to the writing center. The author also suggests practical solutions for these problems. The final section of the essay is a report on a survey of referral methods and student attitudes conducted at a large state university.

There are significant obstacles to the effective operation of a writing center, many of them concerning logistics. But there are more important, or at least more immediate, difficulties that writing center directors must tackle if they wish the center to operate as effectively as possible. Among the most prominent of these are attitudinal problems arising from teachers, tutors, and students.

Teacher Attitude

The attitude of teachers who refer their students to the writing center for mandatory weekly conferences is seldom thought to have an effect on the writing center, but it does. Underestimating the significance of the teacher's attitude is understandable because he or she is usually far removed from the writing center. Aside from making the initial referral of the student and perhaps some cursory "checkups" throughout the semester, the average instructor is not much involved with the center. This is unfortunate for a number of reasons.

By not taking the center seriously, the professor fails to provide support to those students who most need it, and by revealing to the staff that he or she does not value their work, the teacher sends them a harmful message. I have had colleagues admit to me that they have no regard for the writing center and the type of student who is sent there. Such negativism, especially if it is widespread, can be very damaging. Staff members, especially undergraduates, cannot be expected to take themselves seriously and strive for professionalism if faculty members themselves shrug off the importance of the writing center. It is absolutely essential that faculty members exhibit concern for what the center is doing and *can* do.

But more insidious than faculty neglect of the writing center is the actual adverse relationships instructors can have with students whom they refer there. Often, teachers *threaten* their students with a referral to the center: "Johnny, if you don't show *some* improvement, I'm just going to *have* to send you to the writing center." Frequently, this statement is made before the entire class, embarassing the student and causing other class members to perceive the center as something to be ashamed of and therefore to avoid.

I will illustrate the problem with the cases of two very different faculty members, both experienced professors at a real university. The first, Dr. A, discovers that one of his students needs tutoring; this student is, in Dr. A's words, a "basket case." Like any other teacher, Dr. A can choose either to send students on their own to the center with a referral slip or to accompany them in order to introduce them to the tutors. Dr. A chooses the latter. His entrance into the center is dramatic. Storming into the room tightly grasping the bewildered student's elbow, Dr. A calls loudly, "I have a student for you. He needs so much help I don't know *where* to begin. I do hope you can do *something* with him." (When Dr. A makes one of these entrances, it is as if he were escorting the student by an ear rather than an elbow.) Of course, this uproar disrupts the entire operation of the usually quiet room, and the tutors and tutees turn around and stare at the by now frantic student at Dr. A's side. Dr. A surrenders his "basket case" and leaves the room shaking his head, probably wondering why God ever created such illiterate people.

This description is *not* exaggerated for rhetorical purposes; it is an accurate account of how this professor (and some of his colleagues) behaves. The consequences are a serious problem. The student's relationship with composition can be impaired permanently by this behavior. Student embarrassment can easily translate into increased diffidence and even into a hate for writing.

And what about those students in the center who witnessed Dr. A's entrance? They might not have had the misfortune of having such a callous teacher, but the chances are good that they will begin to think of themselves in the same light as that poor student of Dr. A. They may start thinking: "So that's why Dr. so-and-so asked me to come here; she must think I'm a horrible writer like that other kid."

Fortunately, most faculties are not peopled solely with Dr. A's; there are also Dr. B's. She is extremely sensitive to student needs, spends more time with her students than perhaps anyone else on the faculty, and sends three times as many students to the writing center as any single faculty member. The difference between Drs. A and B is largely attitudinal. Like Dr. A, Dr. B frequently escorts students to the center for initial scheduling, but her manner is refreshingly different from A's. She enters the room inconspicuously and quietly introduces her student. Dr. B is always offering positive reinforcement to students. She will say, "Elizabeth here has the makings of a good writer but needs much work. She realizes this but knows that she has no problem that cannot be overcome within the semester if she works at it. We've discussed it and she wishes me to refer her to the writing center. I'm confident that she can write well if she works at it." Dr. B reiterates for Elizabeth's benefit that she needs much work, but she does so in a positive and encouraging manner.

Dr. B's Elizabeth and Dr. A's Johnny inevitably have identical writing problems and are writers of equal quality (or lack of quality). However, by accentuating his student's difficulties, Dr. A probably has undermined the motivation and confidence of his student. In contrast, Dr. B, by offering positive reinforcement, has encouraged Elizabeth to do better. By creating a positive environment through a positive attitude, Dr. B has created the best opportunity for her student to help herself. This is not to say that she "babies" her students—far from it. But she does not alienate them by a thoughtless and insensitive attitude as Dr. A does.

Faculty insensitivity need not be as blatant as Dr. A's. It could take the form of sending to the center compositions literally covered with red marks. This is like exposing students in public, rendering them naked for all to see. One student handed a tutor several papers—corrected, by the way, by the very same Dr. A—covered with exaggerated marks made in red crayon—not a pen but a crayon. The student looked at the tutor sheepishly and said, "I guess you don't have to read them; you can tell already how bad I am." Discussion of the psychological effects of correcting papers with red ink has become a hackneyed subject, but it is not the ink that is objectionable; it is the *manner* in which these papers are marked, the *attitude* of the evaluator. The flourish of the pen and the long, exaggerated marks spotlight students' difficulties and further embarrass them. Dr. B has students who make the same mistakes as Dr. A's but prefers, especially if she intends to send the student's papers to the writing center, subdued comments in an unobtrusive color or even in pencil. And when she finds that the student has comma splices throughout the paper, she does not mark all ten; she stops after number four and writes a short note about what to look for.

Of course, the writing center director has no control over the evaluative procedures of colleagues. However, a director can control what tutors work on with each student. Many directors now believe that it is better to avoid working with papers students have had graded and probably have forgotten and instead work on papers that are in progress. These are fresh in each writer's mind, and students are more likely to remember help they receive on them than on themes written weeks before. This practice is also in keeping with the current trend to emphasize "process" rather than "product." Not only is working on papers that are in progress more helpful to students, but it eliminates the need to work with papers covered with red marks—in ink or crayon.

There are other steps a director can take to counter unproductive faculty attitudes. Directors certainly cannot cure frustration or force colleagues to enjoy teaching writing, but they *can* make faculty aware of how attitudinal problems affect center effectiveness, and this is a great step forward. The director's major problem is one of communication: finding ways to raise faculty consciousness. One effective tool is a concise but personal-sounding faculty memo. The memo can be used to tell colleagues exactly how they can help the center. It can remind them, for example, that it is easy to threaten students with the writing center and that instructors can better serve all concerned if they *encourage* their students instead. Obviously, these memos must be diplomatic and succinct if they are to be effective, or even read. But if they are written more as friendly pleas for assistance than as dry impersonal memos, the response should be good. Also, the director should communicate orally with colleagues at every opportunity. A final suggestion for helping to alleviate negativism among the faculty involves positive reinforcement. The director should praise publicly those who work with the center staff during the term and who exhibit a constructive and positive attitude. This can be done with final and mid-semester progress reports to the faculty in which the director thanks by name those professors who have worked in this way with the center.

Tutor Attitude

Faculty negativism (or perhaps more accurately, insensitivity) is integrally related to tutor attitude. As mentioned previously, if faculty members disparage the writing center, tutors are likely to perceive their job as unimportant and to lower their standards as a result. An equally subtle problem—almost the opposite of the one just mentioned—is a condescending attitude toward students. Condescension is as damaging as diffidence in the tutor. First, it is neither positive nor supportive. Also, it interferes with the tutorial process because it is distracting to the student. Fortunately, the center director has adequate control over this problem.

Frequent staff meetings in which a proper attitude is stressed can be effective. Tutors should be shown that they themselves are learning as they teach and that condescension can make them less effective.

The most serious attitudinal problem with tutors is animosity toward the methods or personalities of certain teachers who send students to the center. Invariably, it is Dr. A who alienates the tutors. They will object to his attitude, the way he teaches (or fails to teach) composition, his method or manner of evaluation, or a number of other traits. The tutors cannot help comparing the methods and attitudes of various faculty members and forming opinions and prejudices. Nevertheless, it is absolutely essential that the tutor not criticize a student's teacher. Obviously, it could be extremely damaging for students to hear a tutor criticize the methods their instructors are using because it will interfere with the learning process; they will begin to make excuses for their own faults and blame the teacher for their own lack of progress. The director can head off this problem easily at the beginning of the term by a stiff warning that no tutor is to criticize publicly any faculty member or teaching methods. If the standing rule is reiterated at staff meetings, this rather sensitive problem should not arise. It is not necessary to be authoritarian about the issue; the director can show tutors that he or she understands their predicament and that he or she might even agree with them in particular instances, but that it is essential to be diplomatic and professional for the well being of the students and the writing center.

Student Attitude

Whether the subject is faculty negativism or tutor attitude, the center is most concerned with how the *student* is affected. When a teacher belittles a student in the writing center or publicly threatens a student with a referral to the center, the student is hurt; when a tutor is condescending toward a student or critical of an instructor, the student is hurt. Ultimately, the center staff is most concerned with proper *student* attitude, because it determines whether or not the center is truly effective. Some directors claim that almost half of the tutor's job involves counseling students so that they can *begin* to learn to write. The three types of negative attitude most frequently encountered are hostility, indifference, and diffidence.

Hostility

Hostility in students sent to the writing center is most often directly related to teacher insensitivity. If the student believes that being sent to the center is punitive, the chances are good that the student's reaction will be hostile. Some students are so hostile toward being sent to the center that they develop an acute aversion to writing and an emotion bordering on hatred toward their English teacher. Indeed, I have had to counsel several students who were certain that they were sent to the center simply because their teacher either disliked them or was prejudiced against them.

Sometimes students develop a hostility toward the writing center not because of some aversion, real or imagined, on the part of their teacher, but because of misconceptions among their peers as to exactly what the center is. Evidently, it is all too easy for the center to acquire the reputation of existing solely for instruction in so-called "bonehead English." Admittedly, a large portion of center work involves remediation, but the fact is that many writing centers tutor a high percentage of excellent students who come to polish their writing skills. It is a myth that the writing center is merely for remediation; however, the myth is widely believed by students and some faculty. One of the greatest perpetuators of this myth can be the name some tutorial services have: writing clinic, writing lab, composition clinic, and the like. It has become a cliché in writing center circles to scorn these names—and for good reason. (Most directors believe it is necessary to change the name of the medical sounding "composition clinic" to the more neutral and more accurate "writing center.") I have heard a student ask indignantly, "Clinic! What am I, diseased or something?" With names like "clinic" and "lab," it is no wonder that students believe that those who go there are diseased. It is understandable that freshmen become hostile when they are *threatened* with being sent to a *clinic,* as if they were unfit to study among healthy individuals.

Indifference

The writing center staff is just as likely to find in freshmen an attitude of indifference as one of hostility. Actually, the two seem to be closely related. The indifferent student is the one who asks, "What do I need English for anyway? I'll never need it because I'll never have to write anything." The indifferent and hostile students are alike in that both wish to avoid the writing center and resent being sent there; but the indifferent student, rather than being openly defiant, shrugs off center attendance as one of those distasteful tasks one must perform in order to survive in school. From the perspective of the tutor, it is probably easier to work with the indifferent student than with the openly hostile one. Nonetheless, both students are equally handicapped by their negative attitudes and will learn little from their tutors until this negativism is eliminated.

Diffidence

But by far the most common attitudinal problem encountered among writing center clients is diffidence coupled with a sense of insecurity. What distinguishes the diffident student from the hostile or indifferent one is that diffidence is not really negative and can be transformed easily into a positive attitude. The chances are excellent that freshmen, absent from home for an extended period in a strange environment, will lack self-assurance about their writing abilities, especially if they have written as infrequently as do most students in high school. In fact, it seems that many freshmen can sense all too well their own deficiencies and are harder on themselves than teachers and tutors often are. The diffident student is a bit frightened because of these deficiencies and new surroundings, and finds it difficult to progress as a writer. Most teachers have had students occasionally cry over the seeming hopelessness of their situations. What seems to be happening in many of these cases is that these students concentrate on their deficiencies rather than on writing. Instead of investing their energy in an attempt to correct their various composition problems, these students focus on the problems and on how formidable they seem, thereby plunging themselves deeper into diffidence and dismay.

Positive Reinforcement

Of all the attitudinal problems exhibited by teachers, tutors, and students, the latter are probably the easiest to correct. The key is proper training of tutors. The single most important technique to teach tutors is the ability to offer the student positive reinforcement. It is impossible to overemphasize how important this is. It is the tutors who work closely with the students and provide the *atmosphere* of the tutorial situation; if that atmosphere is positive, friendly, and supportive, the opportunity for correcting poor student attitude is greatly enhanced. The following are six guidelines the director can give tutors to help them emphasize positive reinforcement:

1. Always begin an encounter with students on a positive note by pointing out something good in their papers—a good thesis statement or conclusion, an interesting use of imagery or metaphor, even good handwriting if nothing else can be found. There is always *something* in a student's paper worthy of a compliment. This initial positive note will "break the ice" with the student and help diminish anxiety, especially if the problem is lack of confidence.

2. Always indicate improvements and build on them. If a student has only two sentence fragments this week where there were six last week, do not stress the two but show the student how he or she has improved in recognizing fragments and that working on the problem will soon enable the student to control it completely.

3. In fact, do not merely point out improvements, but try to get students also to *say* they have improved. For example: "I notice an improvement in your sense of organization. Do you? Do you feel that you are mastering it?" Often students are improving but fail to notice it. Encouraging students to say they have improved is a practical method of building writers' confidence, thereby increasing the likelihood that they will experiment and take risks with their writing.

4. Encourage students to discover their mistakes as well as to recognize improvements; not only is it psychologically better for students to find their own mistakes rather than to have someone point them out, but it is the first step on the road to becoming a good writer.

5. Minimize the seriousness of a student's particular writing problem; the world will not end simply because the student has not yet learned to recognize a comma splice. The tutor can either emphasize the wrongness of comma splices, or can describe how easy it is, once the student knows what they are, to avoid them. The latter is the most effective method.

6. When concluding an interview with students, always provide a summary of what was discussed, emphasizing where they have made progress and where they should continue to work. Too often the former is neglected and the latter overemphasized. In fact, if there is time, provide each student with a written list of strengths and a shorter list of needed changes; this method, which is borrowed from social work theory where it is called "goal planning," can increase a student's confidence and provide the student with specific goals to work toward.

If tutors are trained not only to provide the student with accurate advice about composition but to make the learning environment pleasant and painless, the effectiveness of writing centers in overcoming many attitudinal obstacles will be increased significantly. If tutors learn to provide positive reinforcement, not only will they be doing students a service, but they will learn to treat the tutorial situation in a much more professional way, thus helping to eliminate any unprofessional and petty attitudinal problems that they themselves might possess.

Research into Student Negativism

To investigate the issue of student attitudes, I distributed a survey to 260 students referred to the University of Alabama writing center. (Referral students were required by their instructors to attend the center for one-half hour per week.) Altogether, these students visited the center 990 times during the semester for a total of 522 hours, an average of four half-hour conferences per student during the semester. This substantial attendance rate increases the reliability of the survey data because the survey is meant to study attitudes over a span of time: from the time of initial referral to at least the third or fourth visit. It is important to note, however, that while 260 students constitute a high percentage of the University of Alabama's referral students during one semester, such a number may not represent a large percentage for other universities. This study is therefore meant to examine attitudes at one university only and to suggest general trends. More comprehensive studies must be conducted in order to prove unequivocally the existence of these trends.

The Questionnaire

The specific purpose of the study was to elicit precise information from students: exactly what about center referral concerns them most strongly and how their teachers' methods of referral affect the students' attendance and performance. In administering the questionnaire, the center secretary explained to the respondents that the survey could help the center improve services, but she did not inform them that the questionnaire specifically concerned their teachers. Such emphasis helped to divert the respondents' attention from the fact that they, in effect, were evaluating their teachers. In addition, students were asked not to supply their names. The anonymity helped to insure the accuracy of responses, since many students would hesitate to discuss their teachers and their own feelings with complete frankness if they had to sign their names to the statement. The questionnaire follows.

Questionnaire

We are trying to improve our service. Please answer these questions as honestly as possible. Circle the appropriate letter or supply the requested information. Thank you. (No names please.)

1. How many times have you attended the Writing Center?

   _____

2. Exactly how many hours have you spent there? _____
3. Has the center helped you become a better writer?
   Yes   No
4. If so, how much?   (a) A great deal   (b) A fair amount
   (c) A little   (d) Not much

5. When your instructor first referred you to the center, did he/she do so   (a) During class, so that several classmates could hear   (b) In the presence of one or a few other people   (c) Privately, so that no one else could hear   (d) By a note on your paper or test

6. Do you feel that your teacher <u>threatened</u> you with coming to the writing center?   Yes   No

7. Did you, at first, feel resentful about being sent to the center? Yes   No

8. If so, do you still feel resentful?   Yes   No

9. If you do or did feel resentful, please tell us why. _____
   _____
   _____

10. Did the way in which your teacher referred you to the center have any effect on your attitude about coming here?
    Yes   No
    Please explain. _____
    _____
    _____

11. Before coming to your first center appointment, did you experience anxiety or fear?   Yes   No

12. After attending your first appointment, did your attitude change? How? Please explain. _____
    _____
    _____

13. Did your tutor help you feel comfortable about coming to the writing center?   Yes   No

14. If so, how? _____
    _____
    _____

15. What makes you feel most comfortable about the writing center? _____
    _____
    _____

16. What makes you feel least comfortable? _____
    _____
    _____

The objective of studying instructors' referral methods was to discover what percentage of teachers still referred publicly despite a semester-long campaign against the practice. This campaign took the form of several visits to the required graduate practicum in the teaching of college English and memos to the faculty as a whole.

Results

If the campaign had been completely successful, all respondents would
have been referred in private or at least by notes on their papers. However, as Table 1 shows, 23 percent of the respondents were referred in the
presence of other students, 11 percent in the presence of the class. This is
a significantly high percentage of public referrals, especially considering
the consciousness-raising campaign.

Most writing center directors agree that the ideal method of referral is
to speak with the student personally. Nevertheless, of the 77 percent who
were referred privately, only 23 percent claimed that their teachers discussed their referral with them personally; the others were referred by
notes on their papers. Despite the publicity campaign, the extremes were
equally represented: 23 percent of the respondents were referred in the
ideal fashion and another 23 percent were referred in the least desirable
manner. It is reasonable to assume that had the teaching staff not been
encouraged to refer personally rather than publicly, the percentages
would have been weighted much more toward public referral.

Interestingly, of the respondents who claimed that their teachers' mode
of referral did have an effect on their attitudes, 27 percent said they were

Table 1
Modes of Student Referral

Referrals		N and %
Publicly	Referred during class	29 (11%)
	Referred in presence of others	31 (12%)
Privately	Referred personally	60 (23%)
	Referred by a note	140 (54%)
Total		260 (100%)

resentful about attending the center because their instuctors had not explained well what was involved in center attendance, while 73 percent stated that they felt good about coming to the center because their teachers had encouraged them. These results reinforce the general belief that it is best to speak privately and positively with students when referring them to the center.

A large number of students registered various negative attitudes. Over one-third of the respondents claimed that at first they had felt "anxiety or fear" about attending the writing center (see Table 2). In addition, 18 percent of the respondents felt "threatened" by being referred to the center; interestingly, 42 percent of those who felt threatened were referred publicly by their instructors. Furthermore, 25 percent felt "resentful" about attending the center on a mandatory basis; of those feeling resentful, 42 percent had been referred publicly. While much of the anxiety about attending the center can be attributed to simple fear of the unknown, it is certainly safe to assume that there is some relationship between students' feelings and the circumstances of their referrals.

Table 2
Student Attitudes Concerning Center Attendance

Feelings	N and %
Anxious	91 (35%)
Threatened	47 (18%) (20 referred publicly)
Resentful	65 (25%) (27 referred publicly)
Attitudes changed for better after first or second conference	195 (75%)
Total	260 (100 %)

Although many respondents registered a great deal of anxiety and negative emotions upon first being referred to the center, 75 percent said their attitudes changed for the better after attending their first or second tutorial conference. Sixty-two percent of these students said that the reason for this positive change was that they began to feel "relaxed" in the center, and 38 percent claimed their attitudes had changed because they had received valuable practical assistance. However, the most encouraging statistic of all is that 99 percent of the respondents (258 of 260) felt that the tutors made them feel comfortable in the writing center setting. Obviously, the personal quality of the one-on-one relationship is effective in gaining the confidence and trust of tutees. When asked what made them *most* comfortable and why, 60 percent singled out the attitude of the tutor; 42 percent pointed to the fact that they were overcoming their writing difficulties; and 37 percent claimed that the tutorial arrangement itself made them most comfortable. (These totals exceed 100 percent because many students offered more than one reason.)

Most students overcame their original attitudinal problems after attending a few conferences, and most could cite specific reasons why they began to feel more comfortable about attending the center. These data strongly suggest that while a student may initially enter the center with negative perceptions and reactions, the tutor can help alter these feelings.

While most respondents were able to articulate aspects of their center experience that made them more comfortable, only a small number— 37 percent—answered the question "What makes you feel least comfortable?" Of this 37 percent, 12 percent felt that their teachers made them uncomfortable; 17 percent complained of being required to attend the center at a specific time during the week; 29 percent mentioned the physical surroundings (a large room containing other students and tutors); and 42 percent felt insecure about being seen in the center by other classmates. These data more than any other underline a specific and widespread problem among students on most campuses: the writing center is often perceived as a place for rejects. This perception is so strong that it still affects many students even after they have found the center to be helpful and pleasant. As mentioned previously, this perception is perpetuated by students who ridicule their classmates being tutored in the center and by instructors who seem to threaten their students with center attendance.

It is worthwhile to examine this feeling of insecurity on the part of tutees more closely. As with most questionnaires, the most revealing data are often the written answers to the questions. In answer to the question "What makes you feel least comfortable?" students wrote, "I feel that I may be made fun of for not knowing something or for doing it wrong"; "Being in the same room with other students who could see me"; "When there are other people in the room"; "The fact that it's just one big room with other people who can hear us talk"; "Maybe some of my friends see me coming here." These tutees obviously feel insecure about attending the writing center and are ashamed of being seen there; even after three or four visits, they perceive the center as a place for "sick" students.

A variation of this attitude is apparent from answers to the question "What makes you feel most comfortable about the writing center?" Consider these answers: "I no longer feel so ignorant because I found out I wasn't the only freshman needing help"; "My tutor let me know that my mistakes are common and that I am not stupid"; "I felt stupid but my tutor didn't treat me like I was"; "My tutor did not try to embarrass me and discussed things in private." Similarly, other students wrote that they felt most comfortable because "nobody put you down just because you have a writing problem"; "Nobody makes a big deal out of it"; "The tutor treated me as a person instead of a grammatical problem"; "He talked to me like I am a person. He doesn't talk down to me." The import of these statements is clear. Many students fear being labeled stupid or inferior. They wish to be treated as persons who just happen to have a few writing difficulties. When the tutor is friendly, not condescending, and explains that writing problems are common, he or she helps raise the self-esteem and confidence of students who enter the center feeling that they are there only because they are ignorant.

Survey Conclusions

The survey reveals several facts about the attitudes of students referred to the writing center: (1) the instructor's method of referral *can* have a positive or negative effect on student attitudes; (2) many students feel resentful and threatened with center attendance at first, but it is likely that this feeling will dissipate if the tutor is professional and amiable; (3) while some students may not feel resentful or threatened, they may be anxious or fearful when first attending the center; (4) students are likely to feel more comfortable about attending the writing center, thus increasing the possibility that they will learn something there, if both their teacher and tutor treat them in a positive fashion; (5) tutees worry most about being labeled stupid or inferior because they attend the center; (6) students feel most comfortable about attending the center when they are made to feel that their writing problems are not uncommon and that they are not different from their peers.

The tutorial situation is likely to be most effective (1) when the referring instructor quietly and privately explains to the student that the writing center is not a place for "basket cases," but a place where students can seek professional help for common problems and (2) when it is clear that the center does not stigmatize anyone as stupid or inferior. Thus, for the writing center to be effective, both teachers and tutors must do their part. Teachers who refer their students must do so in a diplomatic manner and must remain sensitive to the concerns of the students they send there. Tutors have a complementary role: they must win the trust of tutees.

15 "I Would Prefer Not To": A Consideration of the Reluctant Student

Mary K. Croft
University of Wisconsin, Stevens Point

Croft, coauthor of one of the few books about writing centers, considers in this essay a problem of all tutorial programs: the student reluctant to accept assistance. Croft uses a set of five questions to probe the sources of student resistance; drawing on research and other materials, including her own considerable experience, Croft sketches as well many methods of dealing with reluctant students.

> . . . A motionless young man one morning stood upon my office threshold.
> . . . I called to him, rapidly stating what it was I wanted him to do—namely, to examine a small paper with me. Imagine my surprise, nay, my consternation, when, without moving from his privacy, Bartleby, in a singularly mild, firm voice, replied, "I would prefer not to."
> I sat awhile in perfect silence, rallying my stunned faculties. Immediately it occurred to me that my ears had deceived me, or Bartleby had entirely misunderstood my meaning. I repeated my request in the clearest tone I could assume; but in quite as clear a one came the previous reply, "I would prefer not to."

Herman Melville's Bartleby, a copyist (surely an occupation requiring only the most mechanical aspect of writing), avoided responsibility or suggestions, orders, involvement, or even life itself, responding instead with a flutelike "I would prefer not to." He epitomizes the student that writing centers are sometimes heir to: the student who does not want to be there; the student for whom the triumvirate of prewriting, writing, and rewriting is preceded by antiwriting. To alter that state of affairs, to bring about a behavior change, is often an unavoidable mission of the writing center.

As Gary A. Olson notes in Chapter 14 of this collection, students often come to the writing center exhibiting various degrees of defeatism, apprehension, resistance. They bring the sum of past experiences, behaviors, values, expectations. What are writing centers to do? Carl Rogers, in a 1958 speech, suggests a direction: "If I can listen to what he tells me, if I can understand how it seems to him, if I can sense the emotional flavor which it has for him, then I will be releasing potent forces of change within him."[1]

Therefore, to bring about meaningful change, we must look closely at our practices; we must give attention to questions such as the following:

1. *How are we meeting the reluctant student?* What face, what atmosphere are we presenting in the writing center?

2. *How are we offering information?* Is the information new? Is it needed? Can we create or encourage need? Are we using appropriate strategies, taxonomies?

3. *Are we leading our students to value the new information?* Do they need it? Do they know they need it? Do they want to get it?

4. *Are we offering opportunities to practice?* Is practice in the writing center adequate and appropriate? Is the center a place that encourages risk taking, error making?

5. *Are we preparing our students to continue working in the new pattern of improved writing skills?* Are we giving the students the emotional and analytic support, the ability to face new situations, the ability to adapt newly acquired skills? What happens when the students are back in the classroom, with real assignments—away from the supportive and encouraging atmosphere of the center? What happens later when the students are in the "real world"? In other words, have we produced the change we wanted—to keep our students writing and learning and succeeding?

Like the steps in the composing process, these questions are not distinct and sequential. Instead, their order and treatment depend, as always, on the specific student and the specific situation. In this essay I shall address these five areas, though various concerns and strategies will, of necessity, overlap and merge at times just as they do in the reality of the writing center situation.

How Are We Meeting the Reluctant Student?

The need for a nonthreatening, tension-free, friendly, personal atmosphere in writing centers has often been stressed. Indeed, the very nature, the very existence, of a writing center implies a nurturing environment, one that is conducive to work and productivity, one that follows Kenneth Koch's lead: "Raise your hand if you need help or praise." Because such an atmosphere is more important than ever with resistant students, efforts to create and maintain that milieu must be constant.

How Are We Offering Information?

Our greatest asset is the fact that the conference method is the heart of writing center teaching—and the individualization provided by the conference holds the key to success with reluctant writers. Joyce Steward and I have defined conferences according to the purpose of the session: (1) for diagnosis, (2) for problem solving, (3) to teach revising and editing skills, and (4) as program, as ongoing workshop. All of these apply to the resistant learner, but the diagnostic conference is essential, certainly at the onset.[2]

Theories of learning bear out what we see manifested daily in the writing center. Consistency theories suggest that whenever persons are placed in an unbalanced situation, they will experience tension and attempt to reduce it. Inconsistency can provide the motivating force to bring about changes in behavior. Leon Festinger has extended this theory to include "cognitive elements" such as knowledge, attitudes, and perceptions. Dissonance can be reduced by changing one or more of the cognitive elements; by adding new elements to either side of the tension; by coming to see the elements as less important; by seeking consonant information; or even by distorting or misinterpreting.[3] Thus, by changing the circumstances under which learning is carried out, writing centers can alter learning achievement. Centers can do so because they are open and open-minded, not affected by labels or grades or test scores, not convinced some students are better learners than others—permanently.

Are We Leading Students to Value New Information?

Central to diagnosis is information about students' attitudes toward their writing and their habits of writing. The first function, then, is to elicit and deal with such information because resistance to writing is frequently the basis for resistance to the center. The following are strategies that some teachers have found successful.

Tests, Autobiography, and Protocols

Whether the apprehension the student feels is self- or teacher-generated, the apprehension itself is real, as many researchers have demonstrated, particularly in the past decade.[4] The Daly-Miller Apprehension Test, a self-rating instrument requesting responses on a scale of 1 (strongly agree) to 5 (strongly disagree), helps to identify the student's level of apprehension:

1. I avoid writing.
2. I have no fear of my writing being evaluated.
3. I look forward to writing down my ideas.
4. I am afraid of writing essays when I know they will be evaluated.
5. Taking a composition course is a very frightening experience.
6. Handing in a composition makes me feel good.
7. My mind seems to go blank when I start to work on a composition.
8. Expressing ideas through writing seems to be a waste of time.
9. I would enjoy submitting my writing to magazines for evaluation and publication.
10. I like to write my ideas down.
11. I feel confident in my ability to clearly express my ideas in writing.
12. I like to have my friends read what I have written.
13. I'm nervous about writing.
14. People seem to enjoy what I write.
15. I enjoy writing.
16. I never seem to be able to clearly write down my ideas.
17. Writing is a lot of fun.
18. I expect to do poorly in composition classes even before I enter them.
19. I like seeing my thoughts on paper.
20. Discussing my writing with others is an enjoyable experience.
21. I have a terrible time organizing my ideas in a composition course.
22. When I hand in a composition, I know I'm going to do poorly.
23. It's easy for me to write good compositions.
24. I don't think I write as well as most other people.
25. I don't like my compositions to be evaluated.
26. I'm no good at writing.[5]

When administered in a center, this kind of test can provide information about high or low apprehension; it can also serve as a starting point for a discussion of the writer's attitudes. Student and tutor can talk over the survey, compare reactions, establish a basis for rapport.

Janet Emig pioneered the use of a writing autobiography. Such an assignment, used with or without the Writing Apprehension Test, will provide additional information as well as writing practice and a sample. Students can be given such directions as

> Write freely for ten minutes or so about either the pleasure or value, or lack of it, which you find in writing. Before you start writing, try to recall how your feelings toward writing have devel-

oped during your education. Use specific instances of your experience with particular teachers, classes, subjects, assignments, grades, books, or whatever. Think back. How did you come to feel about writing the way you do?

Lou Kelly approaches the reluctant student with

> Forget the list of stupid subjects you couldn't write about on the exam. Forget about organization and spelling and grammar. Just try to put on paper what you're feeling and thinking right now. No matter how confused and angry it sounds. Use the words other English teachers might mark inappropriate or offensive, if you want to. Your paper will not be marked or graded. I really want to know what you think and feel about being here. And about failing the exam. Why did you? After all those years in English classes. Did you fail or did somebody along the way fail you? Whatever you think, whatever you feel, say it—on paper.[6]

John Hayes and Linda Flower propose the use of a protocol, "a description of the activities ordered in time, which a subject engages in while performing a task."[7] Students cite, usually orally, everything that comes to mind as they prepare a paper. In what is a fragmentary and jumbled commentary, students can then look closely at the process of writing as well as examine their particular thoughts and actions. Talking or writing out their processes and problems, they can achieve distance and even develop their own solutions. Moreover, this technique illustrates the complexities of writing far better than any lecture could, and it demonstrates the convolutions and choices involved in what Steinbeck called "that strange and mystic business."

Many writing centers have developed questionnaires or forms to assist students with the analysis of their writing habits. Students are asked to analyze a specific writing experience. Questions on one such experience, "What Is Your Write Way?" might include:

1. How did you go about collecting information?
2. When did you start actually writing the paper?
3. How did you get started writing?
4. What changes or revisions did you make?
5. How long did it take you? Break this down into collecting, connecting, writing, rewriting.
6. What was most difficult about the assignment?
7. What was most enjoyable?
8. Are you satisfied?

9. What would you do differently another time?
10. What will be easier another time?
11. What did you teach yourself? What hints do you have for others?

The Writing Journal

To encourage keeping a writing journal or log, the center teacher can share the writing journals of professional and student writers, thus emphasizing the commonality of problems and illustrating the writers' involvement with their work. For example, in *Getting the Facts,* Jerome Murphy develops an entire chapter on "Analyzing and Writing" by describing how it was written. At one point he discusses his process of reflecting on his notes:

> What I've done this morning is review my notes and make notes on my notes—groping toward a tentative design or group of categories for organizing the data. I've made the analytic decision to deal with the analytic process in time sequence (could have done differently). Now I want to move toward a rough outline of various sections of the chapter and then group various things to include in the outline. . . . Then, with that in hand, I am prepared to write a very rough draft, I think.[8]

Another example for the tutor's repertoire is the joint effort of Donald Graves and Donald Murray. Murray kept a journal while he was revising a novel and several pieces of nonfiction. Graves, in a second column on each page, commented on the writer's journal and pointed out the implications of the writer's testimony, as in:

> Murray has a different pace than that permitted in most school situations. He waits, listens, suspends judgement. He is surprised by his characters and information. The waiting is the best aid to redrafting. "Oh, this is missing. I forgot to say why he was upset." Papers due within the same class period, or even in the short space of a few days, do not aid listening or that important sense of ownership of the writing.[9]

In similar fashion the tutor can comment on a student's writing log. (And, not so incidentally, Graves' conclusions are particularly applicable to writing centers. We can provide the luxury of time and listening. We can accommodate individual rates of learning.)

Acknowledging Writing Blocks

Students in general, not just reluctant writers, do not know how writers behave. They often feel inadequate and are convinced writing will merely expose those inadequacies. But the tutor should help the student acknowledge the existence of writer's block. Karin Mack and Eric Skjei offer three reasons for blocking: (1) writing is hard work, (2) writing evokes our internal critic, who constricts our writing progress, and (3) writing is exposure: "Justly or unjustly, most of us tend to think, 'I *am* what I write' and 'I am how I write.' We know whomever we're writing for will be responding not only to *what* we say, but also to how we say it—and as a consequence, we think, to what kind of human being we seem to be."[10] To emphasize the universality of writing blocks further, tutor and student can read and laugh over Robert Bernardi's poem "I Can't Write Today Because" and can add to Bernardi's list of excuses.[11] Tutors will also want to have on hand quotations from professional writers, like Red Smith's anguished, "Writing is easy. All you do is sit staring at a blank sheet of paper until the drops of blood form on your forehead."

Questions

Donald Murray asks questions at the beginning of a conference:

> What did you learn from this piece of writing?
> What do you intend to do in the next draft?
> What surprised you in the draft?
> Where is the piece of writing taking you?
> What do you like best in the piece of writing?
> What questions do you have of me?

but then—

> And now that I have my questions, they quickly become unnecessary. My students ask these questions of themselves before they come to me. They have taken my conferences away from me. They come in and tell me what has gone well, what has gone wrong, and what they intend to do about it. . . . I listen and they learn.[12]

The students Murray describes have made the change writing centers seek. As the work proceeds, students require less feedback; they not only learn more, they also become more proficient at learning.

Any and all of these approaches help students become more reflective writers, broadening their understanding of the composing process. Some strategies work with some students, some with others. Through slow, patient, joint exploration, with humor and tenacity, the writing center tutor can initiate and reinforce the essential process of change. The reluctant writer at this point, it is hoped, will have espoused a willing suspension of disbelief. For some students this can come about during the first visit. More likely, though, several visits will be needed to establish a climate of trust, a willingness to move ahead.

Are We Offering Opportunities to Practice?

And such a climate means practice. The practice will serve as part of the learning process, reinforcing needed skills. But it will do more: "the greater the amount of effort one puts into a task, the more he will rationalize the value of that task."[13] The practice can take many forms, and indeed it should, but it need not be grim or prescriptively academic. Errors should be seen as attempts to learn; they should not be interpreted by either tutor or student as dangerous to self-esteem. This is especially true for the basic writer who becomes so concerned over mechanics and usage that the writing is very slow and halting. Attention to mechanics, under most circumstances, should be withheld until the final draft has been completed. Tutors should encourage experimentation, risk taking, playing with language. Students should learn to be conscious of their language, but not to be self-conscious about it. They should learn that writing can lead them to what they did not know they knew, and, inversely, writing can help them discover what they do *not* think. That, too, is important. They should learn to silence their internal critic during early phases of writing. In later drafts, when a pattern has emerged, when concepts and development are clear—that is the time for the internal critic.

A writing center is especially suitable for practice sessions. Here the tutor can engage in the gentle art of shoving: urging the student to return and write. As one nontraditional student said of her tutor, "So many times I would become discouraged, and she would pick me up and dust me off and say, 'Well, let's get going.'" In such sessions tutors can select from a number of useful devices.

Free Writing

When you freewrite, you are under no obligation to produce a well thought out, well-supported, properly punctuated piece of writing. Freewriting is a method of encouraging students to *practice* writing.

Brainstorming and Other Writing Activities

This is a form of force-feeding and probing—fast, free, nonjudgmental. The student records whatever ideas or details come to mind on the topic at hand. Sometimes the tutor can choose to be the scribe, thus freeing the student from the physical act of writing, itself a block for some basic writers. Other writing exercises include summarizing, an especially valuable exercise and skill which is often neglected; composing a private draft (a form of "write before writing," it can serve as catharsis or rehearsal); and a reading log (this log is a record of reactions, connections, insights, musings—a way to get more deeply involved in a reading assignment as well as a way to practice writing).

Bio-poem

The delightful creation of Michael Wendt of Lake Oswego, Oregon, this exercise has the students (and the tutors) writing about their favorite subject: themselves. It provides a structure, demands specificity and conciseness, even teaches parallelism—and does so painlessly. The setup of the bio-poem is:

Line 1: Your first name only,

Line 2: Four traits that describe you,

Line 3: Sibling of . . . ,

Line 4: Lover of . . . (3 people or ideas),

Line 5: Who feels . . . (3 items),

Line 6: Who needs . . . (3 items),

Line 7: Who gives . . . (3 items),

Line 8: Who fears . . . (3 items),

Line 9: Who would like to see . . . (3 items),

Line 10: Resident of (your city),

Line 11: Your last name only.

Are We Preparing Students to Continue in the New Pattern?

There are several issues at stake here. Center teachers must avoid allowing the initial reluctance of students to become dependence. Tutors have a responsibility to wean students away from the center and must avoid superimposing their ideas and editing on the student. Editing students' papers for them is easy and fast, but it sanctions continued dependence. As one colleague said, "If you think what you're told to think, you don't have to give it a second thought."

Tutors must avoid identifying too many problems in a student's paper. When students are confronted with too many issues at once, overkill results. Tutors must select one or at the most two areas that are important to a student at a particular juncture, keeping in mind the goals that were previously set.[14] Tutors also must avoid interfering or intervening too soon. Instead of initiating the critique, they must draw more about the process out of students or encourage them to expand on their opinions of their texts. In other words, listen.

Finally, centers must not let concern for good writing develop the attitude that one student expressed recently: "Yes, I learned from my teacher, but he did not foster a love for writing." William Powers, John Cook and Russell Meyer warn that "to continue traditional instructional practices and ignore the propensity for increased negativism regarding writing will likely add to the growing number of students who lack basic writing skills."[15] And Suzette Haden Elgin states the problem even more strongly, "Literacy is the ability to read with sufficient pleasure and write with sufficient ease so that both activities become a part of one's daily life that one would be unwilling to give up." She continues:

> By the terms of this new definition, do we have a literacy crisis? You can bet your mortarboard we do, though it's not the one we've been reading about. We are systematically, with the most incredible dedication and energy, putting all of our considerable expertise and resources into the creation and maintenance of a very real crisis. A student cannot pick up a newspaper today, cannot open a magazine, cannot turn on a radio or a television set, cannot enter a classroom without hearing yet again how second-rate he is. He doesn't have to read the *Harvard Educational Review;* he can read *TV Guide* or simply listen to us.
>
> We are creating a generation of young people with a deep and abiding hatred for everything associated in even the most peripheral way with reading or writing.[16]

Even though many center directors do not share her deep pessimism, they do admit to concern. Lee Odell thinks students should enjoy the satisfaction that comes with discovery: "The very process of learning, which can make writing so difficult and unpleasant, is also our most compelling motivation for writing. . . . Our problem as teachers is to do what we can to help students negotiate this uncertainty and again *increase their chances* of arriving at insights or hypotheses that they will find rewarding."[17] With this understanding and satisfaction, students can meet new challenges and can come to value writing as a learning tool. Mary Edel Denman, reporting on her pilot study at the Study Skills Center of San Diego State University, concludes: "But in addition to learning to write more effectively, students instructed by humanistic processes apparently undergo changes in attitude toward writing, developing satisfaction and a measure of joy in written expression. Even more important and more significant, students report experiencing generalized personal growth and increased ability to function effectively."[18] The teachers cited throughout this essay, in seeking and achieving the cooperation of reluctant writers, are doing what good teachers have always done—treating students individually, humanely, knowledgeably, effectively.

The scrivener Bartleby provoked much consternation in the mind of his superior: "Poor fellow, poor fellow! thought I, he don't mean anything; and besides, he has seen hard times, and ought to be indulged. . . . Others may have loftier parts to enact; but my mission in this world, Bartleby, is to furnish you with office-room for such period as you may see fit to remain." Melville's narrator could not bring himself to dismiss Bartleby or to give up on him. Similarly, when it comes to reluctant students, writing centers too would prefer not to.

Notes

1. Carl Rogers, *On Becoming a Person* (Boston: Houghton Mifflin, 1961), 332.

2. Joyce S. Steward and Mary K. Croft, *The Writing Laboratory: Organization, Management, and Methods* (Glenview, Ill.: Scott, Foresman, 1982). See pp. 63–66 for detailed suggestions for structuring the four types of conferences.

3. Stephen W. Littlejohn, *Theories of Human Communication* (Columbus, Ohio: Charles E. Merrill, 1978), 180–183.

4. See William G. Powers, John A. Cook, and Russell Meyer, "The Effect of Compulsory Writing on Writing Apprehension," *Research in the Teaching of English* 13 (October 1979): 225–26, for a concise review of this research; see Helen Heaton, "A Study of Writing Anxiety among High School Students Including Case Histories of Three High and Three Low Anxiety Students" (Dissertation, University of Wisconsin–Madison, 1980), 1–8, for a more detailed review.

5. J.A. Daly and M.D. Miller, "The Empirical Development of an Instrument to Measure Writing Apprehension," *Research in the Teaching of English* 9 (Spring 1975): 246.

6. Kelly, 8.

7. John R. Hayes and Linda S. Flower, "Identifying the Organization of Writing Process," *Cognitive Processes in Writing,* ed. Lee W. Gregg and Erwin R. Steinberg (Hillsdale, N.J.: Lawrence Erlbaum, 1980), 4.

8. Jerome T. Murphy, *Getting the Facts* (Santa Monica, Calif.: Goodyear Publishing, 1980), 146.

9. Donald H. Graves and Donald M. Murray, "Revision: In the Writer's Workshop and in the Classroom," *Journal of Education* 162 (Spring 1980): 39.

10. Karin Mack and Eric Skjei, *Overcoming Writing Blocks* (Los Angeles: J. P. Tarcher, 1979), 30–31.

11. As quoted in Bill Bernhardt, *Just Writing* (New York: Teachers and Writers Collaborative, 1977), 3.

12. Donald M. Murray, "The Listening Eye: Reflections on the Writing Conference," *College English* 41 (September 1979): 15–16.

13. Littlejohn, 183.

14. See Linda S. Flower and John R. Hayes, "The Dynamics of Composing: Making Plans and Juggling Constraints," *Cognitive Processes,* ed. Gregg and Steinberg, 41–44, for strategies that reduce constraints.

15. Powers, Cook, and Meyer, 230.

16. Suzette Haden Elgin, "The Real Literacy Crisis," *Change* 10 (November 1978): 11.

17. Lee Odell, "Teaching Writing by Teaching the Process of Discovery: An Interdisciplinary Enterprise," *Cognitive Processes,* ed. Gregg and Steinberg, 142.

18. Mary Edel Denman, "Personality Changes Concomitant with Learning Writing," *Research in the Teaching of English* 15 (May 1981): 171.

16 Derrida's "Play" and Prewriting for the Laboratory

Thomas Nash
Southern Oregon State College

Known for his research on teaching invention in writing centers, Nash provides a thorough discussion of prewriting in the tutorial setting. This essay is an interesting combination of theoretical speculation about the process of invention and practical applications of heuristic devices in the center. It concludes with an answer to the question, "Why a writing center?"

What is "familiarly known" is not properly known, just for the reason that it is "familiar." When engaged in the process of knowing, it is the commonest form of self-deception, and a deception of other people as well, to assume something to be familiar, and to let it pass. . . .

Hegel, *The Phenomenology of Mind*

I do not know of any other way of associating with great ideas than *play*.

Nietzche, *Ecce Homo*

In the decade of the 80s it is remarkably unfashionable for teachers of writing to show ignorance of terms like *tagmemics* and the *dramatistic pentad*. By now, most composition specialists have learned at least the jargon of invention and prewriting. However, for many teachers, "prewriting" is a troublesome reminder of a nagging obligation; and for many, it is an overly formal and mechanistic exercise that works better in the pages of journals than in the classroom. Similarly, writing center directors often speak eloquently of prewriting exercises at conferences and in the pages of *The Writing Lab Newsletter;* but, as researchers for the Southeastern Writing Centers Association recently discovered, "few writing center directors (or their tutors) actually use invention techniques in the writing center, and they rarely use a formal heuristic."[1]

Even though it is clear that informed tutors and teachers believe that prewriting is essential to the composing process, it is equally clear that these practical people are having problems with the application of formal heuristics and prewriting models. Perhaps, as Sabina Thorne Johnson says, these invention strategies are too seldom student centered. Johnson complains that "whenever I read articles or hear presentations on one approach to prewriting or another, I am bewildered, amidst my marvelling at their cleverness, by the growing sense that I am in a factory, an invention factory, where efficiency of output is the chief concern and the student of value only as raw material."[2] In fact, a great many formal heuristics remain ineffectual because they are designed more for teachers than for tutors and students. Such prewriting plans are often too rigid, applicable only in cases where the student has a reasonable grasp of the material at the level of consciousness; unfortunately, most students need help to uncover ideas that linger in the subconscious or unconscious realms of the mind.[3]

In the wake of scholarship based on composition as process, few writing center directors today would deny the need for effective invention strategies, both in the classroom and as part of writing center instruction. Our students, for the most part, are paralyzed by the need to dwell on the familiar, safe ideas that reaffirm their unexamined values. And their academic training has rarely challenged those values. As Janet Emig says, "The major kind of essay too many students have been taught to write is algorithmic, or so mechanical that a computer could readily be programmed to produce it: when a student is hurried or anxious, he simply reverts or regresses to the only program he knows, as if inserting a single card into his brain."[4] To overcome those mechanistic responses, the writing center director must provide prewriting tasks that unleash the powers of the mind, rather than those that hasten the retreat to safe harbors. Aristotle's *topoi*, for example, tend to overwhelm students, forcing them even farther into familiar havens. Tagmemics, for all its virtue, is confusing even to teachers and tutors when the heuristic is considered in its original form. And yet, should the center director abandon entirely the great promise of these heuristics, retreating finally to the seemingly "anarchistic" freewriting methods of Peter Elbow's *Writing without Teachers* or Ken Macrorie's *Telling Writing?* Although freewriting and brainstorming and other loosely organized methods have great virtue for the writing center tutor, we also need to look toward ways of distilling the "playful" elements from the more systematic prewriting approaches. For best use in the laboratory setting, a prewriting plan should combine the frivolous elements of freewriting with the organization of the formal heuristic. In fact, the students who frequent the writing center today are most often students "who have not yet learned the pleasure of *playing with ideas* and of bringing their intellectual experiences to bear on their lives."[5] Consequently, the first obligation of the center is to stress *play,* a complex term that transcends its simple and frivolous connotations. The word *play* has many meanings and associations, most of them suggested by the French *jeu,* a word central to the deconstructionist language theories of Jacques Derrida.

Derrida, in his treatises on language, writing, and literature, conducts "a sustained argument against the possibility of anything pure and simple which can serve as the foundation for the meaning of signs."[6] He says that the history of writing is the search for "a past that has never been present."[7] That is, according to Derrida, Western culture and its literature are based on a series of fictions, erroneous assumptions about God, Being, and other concepts that did not ever exist but which humankind has fabricated and perpetuated through a series of linguistic signs. Language, including written prose, is therefore merely an artificial system of arbitrary markers that have meanings only in relation to one another, not as symbolic units relating to some higher plane of existence or to some actual object in this world. As Derrida says, "the signified concept is never present in itself, in an adequate presence that would refer only to itself. Every concept is necessarily and essentially inscribed in a chain or a system, within which it refers to another and to other concepts, by the systematic play of differences."[8] For Derrida, "the play of differences," or *differance* as he call it, is a measure of the relationships between words, sounds, and concepts within the chain. William A. Covino, in a recent article in *Freshman English News,* says that the terms *differance* and *invention* are synonymous, both involving a playful investigation of graphemic, semantic, and syntactic distinctions.[9] Therefore, in the process of invention, it is the "play of differences" that makes the tagmeme interesting, the *pentad* challenging, and the *topoi* stimulating; each of these heuristics has at its heart the concept of "play."

Play (jeu) immediately suggests a frivolous activity, sometimes irrational, perhaps a flight of fancy beyond the barriers of logic and physics that so often characterizes the games of children. But *play* also means the interplay of objects or ideas, as in the "play" of two musical strains or the "play of light upon a windowpane." Furthermore, the word *play* is a synonym for the dramatic performance, with emphasis on actor, scene, conflict, and purpose. There are other associations as well, including the frolic of sports and the risk of gambling. By whatever definition, *play* should retain something of the frivolous, the ethereal, and the dramatic, for it is a way of uncovering associations that lie beyond the realm of conscious knowing. For Derrida, this interplay of ideas is always a kind of gamble. As he says in *Speech and Phenomena,* "In marking out *differance,* everything is a matter of strategy and risk."[10]

Playing with Perspective

The gambling interplay of strategy and risk lies at the center of all creative thought. In the search for writing center materials, the risk involved in free interplay must of course be balanced by the security of a structured heuristic. Among the most interesting prewriting exercises available in current textbooks is Gregory and Elizabeth Cowan's "cubing," a simple adaptation of the Aristotelian *topoi.*[11] In "cubing," the student imagines a cube (or die) with something different written on each of its six sides:

> One side of the cube says: *Describe it.*
> Another side of the cube says: *Compare it.*
> A third side says: *Associate it.*
> The fourth says: *Analyze it.*
> The fifth says: *Apply it.*
> The sixth side says: *Argue for or against it.*

In this plan, the student proceeds through each step in order, taking no more than three to five minutes for each task:

1. *Describe it.* Look at the subject closely and describe what you see. Colors, shapes, sizes, and so forth.

2. *Compare it.* What is it similar to? What is it different from?

3. *Associate it.* What does it make you think of? What comes into your mind? It can be similar things, or you can think of different times, places, people. Just let your mind go and see what associations you have for this subject.

4. *Analyze it.* Tell how it is made. (You don't have to know; you can make it up.)

5. *Apply it.* Tell what you can do with it, how it can be used.

6. *Argue for or against it.* Go ahead and take a stand. Use any kind of reason you want to—rational, silly, or anywhere in between.

Cowan and Cowan seem to recognize the playful aspects of cubing, because they instruct the student to look for one of these tasks "that made you smile, something that caused your pen to move faster, something you felt some interest in and even some excitement about."[12] In a sample cubing exercise printed in the textbook, the student writer, after describing, comparing, associating, and analyzing the subject (a chocolate-covered cherry), "started getting playful and putting things down even if he didn't know whether they were right or not. He probaby has never been in a chocolate-covered cherry factory, but he had fun pretending he knew about it. And who knows what those fantasies might bring into his mind and what thoughts they might lead to."[13] After proceeding routinely through the first four steps of cubing, the student wrote:

5. APPLY IT. The cherry can be used for anything but usually is used for parties or things like that. It sets a festive mood when used at Christmas time because it seems to be a natural association with Christmas. It can be used to put in chairs for practical jokes. It makes a nice looking mess on somebody's clothes. It can also. . . .

6. ARGUE FOR OR AGAINST IT. The cherry is definitely a needed thing in our society and without the chocolate cherry where would America be. It's like the old tradition—Christmas is not Christmas without a chocolate-covered cherry. After all, the father of our country, George Washington, brought our awareness of the cherry in his childhood, even before he was president and he was elected by the people so it is evident that Americans are totally aware of the cherry's heritage and as. . . .

Of course, there are limitations to the prewriting plan called "cubing." Janice Lauer, seeking a metatheory of heuristic procedures, says that a first test for models of invention is *transcendency*. She asks, "Can the writer transfer this model's questions or operations from one subject to another?"[14] Well, no. Not always. However, most of those heuristics that would satisfy Lauer are too difficult, too formal, too lengthy, or too ambitious for writing center students who bring with them only vague, untested notions about their topics. Limited methods such as cubing are actually preferable in many ways, partly because such approaches are simple and easy to administer and partly because they facilitate "the play of differences" in a systematic manner.

Dramatistic Play

Another variety of prewriting approach with great potential for the writing center is a variation on the *dramatistic pentad,* first explained by Kenneth Burke in *A Grammar of Motives.*[15] For Burke and his followers, invention begins with a look at five essential relationships in the human drama of any action: Act, Scene, Agent (Actor), Means, and Purpose. Burke's assumption—"all the world's a stage"—invokes another meaning for the term *play,* as it is used to refer to invention. Burke's pentad is based on the notion that any action, idea, proposal, or concept involves the questions "What are people doing? How are they doing it? Why are they doing it?" In order to expand these basic questions, the studious writer looks for "perspective by incongruity," a rearranging of conventions in ways that create tension, paradox, and originality. The goal of the dramatistic pentad is the rearrangement of details until conventions and expectations are violated, forcing the writer to take a fresh, risk-filled perspective on the topic. "The writer is eloquent," says Covino, "only insofar as he invents something that creates new categories which complement and advance the old ones."[16]

Although Burke admits that creating new categories may take some practice for the beginning writer, the basic form of the pentad has the virtue of simplicity. Increasingly the pentad, in one form or another, is appearing in the "prewriting" sections of freshman English textbooks. For example, in the latest edition of *The Holt Guide to English,* William Irmscher has broken the pentad into its usual categories, adding a series of more specific questions to each section:[17]

1. ACTION
   What happened?
   What is happening?
   What could happen?
   What is it?

2. ACTOR-AGENT
   Who did it?
   Who is doing it?
   What did it?
   What kind of agent is it?

3. SCENE
   Where did it happen?
   Where is it happening?
   Where will it happen?
   When did it happen?
   What is the background?

4. MEANS
   How did the agent do it?
   What means were used?

5. PURPOSE
   Why?

Irmscher's version of the pentad is an effective and systematic method for uncovering *differance.* Further, the model can be applied to most writing tasks with ease; it even fits Janice Lauer's standards of transcendency, flexible order, and generative capacity.[18] The model, not at all complex in this form, can be expanded in two ways. First, the tutor can ask the negative form of each question: "Which ones of the likely actors did *not* do it?" "What means did the actor *not* use that were available to him?" Second, any two of the five elements of the pentad can be viewed together. (Burke calls these "ratios.") For instance, the writer may wish to compare the actor and scene in the question of Nixon's role in the Watergate affair: "In what way was the President (actor) influenced by the protective curtain of office (scene) during the Watergate investigation?"

In using the pentad, the student writer engages in a less frivolous sort of play than during cubing exercises. Rather, the play is dramatic, with character, conflict, setting, and motivation central to the method of invention. For tutors in the writing center, Irmscher's application of the pentad might be made more meaningful if students practice the model as they describe a complicated photograph or an action-filled painting. While speculating about the five major considerations of the pentad, the student should gain useful practice. Also, the tutor could use a prescribed scenario for introducing the ratios and a series of negative questions. For instance, an impressionist painting of a Paris street scene or a crowded cafe might give the young writer an interesting topic for analysis. This playful comparison and rearrangement of details provides the most basic kind of help for the beginning writer, especially one fighting the question "Where do I begin?" As Irmscher says, "Playing with the combinations, seeing what they imply, and forming an opinion become a way of finding a thesis, the focus that in the final analysis makes a subject manageable and permits you to write about it."[19]

Tagmemic Play

Richard E. Young, Alton L. Becker, and Kenneth L. Pike, borrowing from the fields of linguistics and physics, created the investigation procedure known as tagmemics. In *Rhetoric: Discovery and Change,* these authors describe a system of great complexity that asks the writer to consider each subject as a particle, a wave, or a field: "That is, the writer can choose to view any element of his experience as if it were static, as if it were dynamic, or as if it were a network of relationships or part of a larger network."[20] In addition, the authors ask the writer to consider *contrast* (how the subject differs from others), *variation* (how much the subject can change and still be itself), and *distribution* (where and when the subject occurs). Of all the established heuristics, tagmemics may best exemplify Derrida's concept of "the play of differences." The entire multi-dimensional system of invention is based on differences in time, space, and type that separate any two objects, ideas, or propositions.[21]

Both Derrida's *differance* and Pike's tagmeme reflect the pioneering linguistic studies of Ferdinand de Saussure, whose work on semiotics established both the arbitrariness of signs and their interdependence.[22] Echoing Saussure, Derrida argues that, in language, a word or sound has no significance except in relation to some past element and some future element. Moreover, all concepts exist within this great chain of time and space, the concepts gaining relevance only through the "play of differences." In terms of tagmemic invention, ideas and concepts may be viewed independently, but they ultimately form part of a system which may be, in itself, part of an expanding circle of systems. Learning where something belongs in the system—and how it functions in relation to other items in the system—is much like the investigation procedures of a child:

> When a very young child finds something that to him is strange and interesting—a telephone, a transistor radio, or a watch—he sets about trying to understand it. He turns it over in his hands, shakes it, drops it, puts it in his mouth, takes it apart, and so on. Whatever adults may think of this, he is actually engaging in the very important activity of rendering the enigmatic world intelligible, and his initial efforts are devoted to accumulating as much relevant information as he can as quickly as possible.
>
> An adult confronted with a problematic situation engages in comparable, if less sticky and destructive, activity; but his effort usually involves mental rather than physical exploration, although it may involve both. Such exploration brings into play at least two distinctly human abilities: the ability to use language and the ability to shift perspectives on a unit deliberately. These abilities enable him to explore problematic data, both tangible and intangible, with astonishing speed and thoroughness by manipulating linguistic symbols and mental images rather than the objects themselves.[23]

Unlike the pentad, which merely takes practice to master and apply, the tagmemic heuristic, as devised by Young, Becker, and Pike, is probably forever beyond the abilities of young writers in a laboratory program. Consequently, for best results, tutors must distill the "playful" elements from the model in one of two ways. First, the tutor may focus on one of the two general approaches, either the particle/wave/field perspective or the contrast/variation/distribution perspective. Second, tutors may employ tagmemic elements in a prewriting questionnaire that they construct for a particular writing assignment.

A good prewriting questionnaire that focuses on only one of the two general approaches of tagmemics is available in the textbook *Writing,* by Cowan and Cowan.[24] This model stresses the linguist's perspectives— contrast, variation, and distribution:

CONTRASTIVE FEATURES
1. How is the subject different from things similar to it?
2. How has this subject been different for me?
3. What would a snapshot of this subject be?
4. How is this subject made?

VARIATION
5. How much can this subject change and still be itself?

6. How is it changing?

7. How does the subject change from day to day?

8. What different varieties of the subject do I know or have I encountered?

9. What particular experiences do I have that illustrate the different kinds of things I know or problems I have in relation to this subject?

10. How do I change in relation to this subject?

DISTRIBUTION

11. Where and when does this subject take place?

12. What is the larger thing of which this subject is a part?

13. What is the function of the subject in this larger thing?

14. How does this subject fit into my life?

15. What other things (experiences) preceded it? followed it? were similar for me?

A student at Auburn University, using this tagmemic model in prewriting exercises at the writing center, discovered some interesting cultural patterns attached to what he considered a shallow subject: the American tradition of the handshake. Below are his responses to questions 11–15 on distribution:

11. Usually men shake hands with other men. Women don't shake very often. It's for introductions, or concluding business deals, or when somebody hits a home run or scores in basketball or some other sport. The handshake can happen anywhere. But in the South you see men shaking hands a lot—not so much in other parts of the country. It's very formal. Kids don't shake hands unless it's with adults.

12. The handshake is part of the act of friendship, but it is also a kind of greeting between strangers. It's like saying "Look, I got nothing in my hand. I'm friendly and harmless." People shake right-handed, even if they are lefties. It's also part of the sports world, but that handshake is entirely different, a slap or a wrist-lock of some kind. And a handshake is also a sign of acceptance. If someone won't shake with you, there's going to be trouble.

13. The handshake is a formal sign of agreement and it means acceptance. In a business deal it means "I agree to these terms." Like when I bought a car from my friend Alex. Before I had the money to pay him, we concluded the deal simply by shaking hands. That meant we were both obligated. When you meet a stranger, it means acceptance. You usually say, "I'm glad to meet you" or "How do you do" while shaking hands. Sometimes it means peace. I saw a baseball game on TV the other day where there was a big brawl, and the umpire made the two players who started it shake hands before the game could start up again. Sometimes the handshake is a special sign. Blacks I know use a slapping kind of shake, and I never know exactly how to do it. Who slaps first? I usually miss anyway. Some people don't shake at all, but they bow or they nod their heads. But it's really the same thing.

14.   A special way the shake fits into my life involves the frat. The Sig Ep handshake is a secret one, but it involves clasping the fingers and wrist in a special way that I can't describe. All the frats have different kinds of shakes. Other times I don't shake hands that much—maybe on a job interview or when I meet my parents' friends. Teenagers don't use the handshake much. My brother just waves his hand when he meets someone his own age. It's a dying convention, and it's too formal for our society.

15.   The handshake follows the signing of a contract or making an agreement, or when two strangers have just been introduced by someone who knows them both. At a sports game, it follows a successful score or good play.

Afterwards, sometimes people just talk. Sometimes they step away from each other, like they don't really want to get any more involved. At the frat, the shake is followed by the password (I also can't tell it).

A kiss is like a shake. Sometimes women kiss each other instead of shaking hands. A hug is like a shake. Also a bow or a curtsee [sic]. And the "high-five" in sports. I imagine it's different in other countries and cultures. People touch their foreheads as a kind of salute. And the salute, of course, is like a shake. It's really pretty complicated.

This student, befuddled at first by the lack of depth to his subject, finally chose to write on the cultural differences he saw in the handshake, interviewing students from other countries and from other regions of the United States. The tagmemic approach allowed this student to see his topic from several perspectives. When he began to write in the center, he suffered no shortage of detail.

A second, more challenging choice for the tutor would be to create a tagmemic questionnaire to fit the assignment. Such a questionnaire could have several kinds of questions, but most should stress playful assumptions about change. For example, a questionnaire originally used in the writing center at Central Michigan University was designed for students writing character sketches. This questionnaire included inquiries such as "Would you be able to have a similar relationship with this person if he/she were (a) changed to the opposite sex, (b) changed to another race of people, or (c) aged by twenty years? Which change would have the most profound effect? Why?" Tagmemically-based prewriting sheets are usually effective because they ask beginning writers to speculate on *differance,* the distance between what things seem to be and what they might be in other contexts and with other variants.

The Play of Analogy

The search for analogies is central to the composing model proposed in 1964 by D. Gordon Rohman and Albert Wlecke.[25] In this prewriting program the experimenters, working with groups of students at Michigan State University, found that writers profited greatly from exercises that revealed unusual links between concepts not previously joined. In one part of the process, the students encounter this exercise:

> Following are two lists of activities common to us all. Choose an activity from the righthand list to explain by describing it in terms of an activity from the lefthand column (or vice versa). Push the application as far as it will go; don't be afraid of being "unusual." Stretch your wits. Try to condense your comparisons in a phrase or a word, rather than in extended actions or clauses.

Activities A	Activities B
Playing cards	Writing essays
Changing a tire	Making love
Selling	Growing up
Walking	Growing old
Carpentry	Rising in the world
Sailing	Studying
Skiing	Meditating
Making match-stick houses	Preaching
Cutting out paper dolls	Swindling
Day dreaming	Teaching
Sewing	Dreaming
Plowing	Reforming
Drafting	Reasoning
Launching rockets	Wooing
Running for office	Chaperoning
Hunting	Failing
Broiling	Eating
Playing baseball	Quarreling
Playing marbles	Making peace
Russian roulette	Negotiating
Hooking a rug	Brawling
Fencing	Revolting
Knitting	Flying
Swimming	Lending
Brushing teeth	Inventing

For Rohman and Wlecke, the creating of analogies is but the third part of the prewriting process, following journalkeeping and meditation. In the full course of these exercises, the student should grasp the notion of "reader-based" writing (Linda Flower's term) as opposed to "writer-based" writing, in which the ideas remain ill formed and valid only esoterically. The investigators promote what Dorothy Sayers calls the "as-if attitude" in which the student writer, filling the role of the child, treats the "familiar world 'as if' it were something else, the rug as if it were a battlefield, the wagon as if it were a stagecoach."[26] Rohman and Wlecke, apparently concerned about the lack of high seriousness in their methods, warn that "play is not merely childish; it is one of the archetypal forms of human activity." They add:

> The pre-writer's play involves the constructive use of illusion, conscious self-deceit, daydreams, associations which imply no immediate benefit, the willingness to manipulate words, concepts, everyday assumptions, toying with apparently irrelevant objects and things. The pre-writer's play, as we tried to instruct our students, was not merely a lighthearted waste of time, but a potentially profound order of constructive effort, corresponding on a conscious level with the unconscious "play" of bisociation within everyone's experience.[27]

In the writing center, this kind of prewriting search for analogies can be highly productive, especially as an aid to a writer who has no idea where to begin. Rohman and Wlecke's prewriting model is simple to use, yet challenging. As an added benefit, it needs no adaptations or additional revision by tutor or director. And, of course, the idea of "play" is built directly into the exercise.

Certainly, these are not the only types of playful prewriting activities available for writing center tutors. Also to be considered are brainstorming, freewriting, and even computer play.[28] Common to the most useful models, however, is a structure for rearranging "reality" so that the known, familiar perspectives fall away and the unusual, "perverse" perspectives become visible. For the best tutors, this kind of approach may soon be internalized so that the tutor can begin extemporaneously the process of "play," even without a heuristic at hand. It is probable that the experienced tutors at a number of schools have been doing just that for many years.

Implications for the Writing Center

All of this emphasis on the play of prewriting tasks is really a prologue to the long-ignored question "Why a writing center?" Although there are many good reasons for the growth of interest in the laboratory movement, the best one may involve prewriting. "In the writing laboratory," says Rudolph Almasy, "students can find someone who will help them discover something to say."[29] Once, in a world less complicated and more bookish, young writers came to college with a well-developed internal model for creating and inventing. But that is not the world of today. In the 80s "the first task of such [writing center] teachers is to help students feel the initial dissonance that will necessitate the process of inquiry and make the assignment a real writing experience."[30]

In truth, despite all its other virtues, the writing center exists and prospers because it is an ideal playground for ideas. Here, the writer can rediscover the child in himself, engaging in a frivolous creative interchange that fills an intellectual void. Kenneth Bruffee, in his best-known essay on peer tutoring, comes close to pinpointing the reason for the writing center movement when he says that "students . . . must deal with ideas not as artificial entities fully formed into an abstract and completed state; they deal with ideas in their fluid, incomplete state of change, as developing emanations of human beings' minds."[31] This playful transformation of incomplete ideas and half-formed impressions occurs not only in peer tutoring dialogues, but whenever the writing center tutor uses questionnaires, heuristics, directed writing, or any other methods to challenge the "familiarly known" values of a student writer. Of course, prewriting could occur in the classroom (but rarely does) and could also be part of the student-teacher conference. But, in practical terms, the laboratory, with its flexible structure, its vast resources, and its nonthreatening reputation, is the logical place for prewriting activities to occur.

Notes

1. Gary A. Olson and John Alton, "Heuristics: Out of the Pulpit and into the Writing Center," *Writing Center Journal* 2 (Fall/Winter 1982): 49. The authors report that only 35 percent of respondents use informal prewriting methods, such as brainstorming and freewriting; only 5 percent employ a formal heuristic.

2. Sabina Thorne Johnson, "The Ant and the Grasshopper," *College English* 43 (March 1981): 240.

3. William Irmscher in *Teaching Expository Writing* (New York: Holt, Rinehart, and Winston, 1979), 31, says that simply "mulling over a project" is productive, "not because it leads anywhere immediately, but because it sets into motion a subconscious or pre-conscious activity that has a way of operating without our awareness of it." See also Johnson, 233.

4. Janet Emig, *The Composing Processes of Twelfth Graders,* National Council of Teachers of English Research Report No. 13 (Urbana, Ill.: NCTE, 1971), 50–51.

5. Aviva Freedman, "A Theoretic Context for the Writing Lab," in *Tutoring Writing: A Sourcebook for Writing Labs,* ed. Muriel Harris (Glenview, Ill.: Scott, Foresman, 1982), 8.

6. David B. Allison and Newton Garver, Preface to *Speech and Phenomena,* by Jacques Derrida, trans. David B. Allison (Evanston, Ill.: Northwestern University Press, 1973), xxii.

7. Derrida, *Speech and Phenomena,* 152. This observation occurs in the essay "Differance," pp. 129–60 of the text. For introducing me to the work of Derrida and for helping me labor with its intricacies, I would like to thank Dan Latimer of Auburn University.

8. *Speech and Phenomena,* 140.

9. William A. Covino, "Making Differences in the Composition Class: A Philosophy of Invention," *Freshman Engish News* 10 (Spring 1981): 2. Covino's article, a brief and general discussion, is nonetheless indispensable as a beginning point for understanding the ties between *differance* and invention.

10. *Speech and Phenomena,* 135. See also Derrida's *Of Grammatology,* ed. Gayatri Spivak (Baltimore, Md.: Johns Hopkins University Press, 1976), first published as *De La Grammatologie* in 1967 by Les Editions de Minuit.

11. Gregory and Elizabeth Cowan, *Writing* (New York: John Wiley, 1980), 20–26. Cubing is loosely structured according to the *topoi* and also bears some resemblance to Burke's pentad.

12. Cowan and Cowan, 22.

13. *Ibid.*

14. Janice Lauer, "Toward a Metatheory of Heuristic Procedures," *College Composition and Communication* 30 (1979): 279.

15. Kenneth Burke, *A Grammar of Motives* (Berkeley: University of California Press, 1969), esp. xv–xxiii.

16. Covino, 3.

17. William Irmscher, *The Holt Guide to English,* 3rd ed. (New York: Holt, Rinehart, and Winston, 1981), 33–34.

18. For Lauer, flexible order means that the model specifies a clear sequence of operations and yet is flexible enough to allow writers a return to previous operations or a leap to subsequent ones. Generative capacity is the structure that allows writers to perform such tasks as visualizing, analogizing, classifying, rearranging, and dividing.

19. Irmscher, 41.

20. Richard E. Young, Alton L. Becker, and Kenneth L. Pike, *Rhetoric: Discovery and Change* (New York: Harcourt Brace Jovanovich, 1970), 122. I have removed italics from the original version.

21. Cf. Derrida, *Speech and Phenomena,* 136ff., where he talks about *differance* as a matter of time and space on the one hand and as a matter of identity on the other.

22. See Ferdinand de Saussure, *Cours de linguistique generale,* ed. C. Bally and A. Sechehaye (Paris: Payot, 1916); English-language edition is *Course in General Linguistics,* trans. Wade Baskin (New York: Philosophical Library, 1959).

23. Young, Becker, and Pike, 121–22.

24. Cowan and Cowan, 43–44.

25. D. Gordon Rohman and Albert Wlecke, *Pre-Writing: The Construction and Application of Models for Concept Formation in Writing* (East Lansing: Michigan State University, 1964).

26. Rohman and Wlecke, 36.

27. *Ibid.*

28. Hugh Burns and George H. Culp have programmed computers to participate in invention dialogues with student writers. See Burns and Culp, "Stimulating Invention in English Composition through Computer-Assisted Instruction," *Educational Technology* (1980): 5–10. The computer programs reflect the methods of Aristotle, Burke, and Young, Becker, and Pike.

29. Rudolph Almasy, "The Nature of Writing Laboratory Instruction for the Developing Student," in *Tutoring Writing,* ed. Harris, 15.

30. Freedman, 5.

31. Kenneth A. Bruffee, "The Brooklyn Plan: Attaining Intellectual Growth through Peer-Group Tutoring," *Liberal Education* 64 (1978): 462.

17 Assessing a New Professional Role: The Writing Center Tutor

Rodney Simard
California State College, Bakersfield

Simard provides a unique perspective of tutoring: that of the tutor. He points out that the role of tutor is quite different from other professional roles. The author treats the basic facets of that role: preparation and attitude, pedagogy, and the types of students the tutor encounters in the center.

I. Attitude and Preparation

Despite their various formats designed to meet the equally various needs of individual institutions, writing centers have been firmly and permanently established in many American colleges and universities. Having increased in numbers perhaps as much as a hundredfold within the last decade,[1] writing centers, as Gary A. Olson observes, have "progressed from the old grammar *lab* model, in which tutors lecture to students, to the modern writing *center,* in which tutors engage in a type of Socratic dialogue with their pupils."[2] Professional attention to the theory and administration of writing centers, however, has been slow to catch up to the proliferation of facilities. Almost entirely absent in existing commentary is substantive discussion of the actual position and role of the tutor, on whom the burden of daily center services generally falls.

Centers are often staffed with tutors who face a bewildering set of challenges and difficulties that bear little resemblance to other pedagogical roles. Even if they are experienced classroom teachers, new tutors face a situation that differs greatly from what they have encountered in the classroom. They often have only their own experience of student conferences (if that) on which to base both their attitudes toward their new jobs and their methods of writing center tutoring, and often the traditional methods of individualized instruction that they have employed in their offices prove to be counterproductive in the center. In fact the accounts of effective training and supervisory situations one encounters in the professional literature (see, for instance, Lou Kelly's description of The Writing Center at the University of Iowa) seem to be the exceptions rather than the rule.[3]

H. Eric Branscomb argues that "teaching the composing process demands experience, a deep background in good writing, and an unusual willingness to listen patiently to students."[4] With the possible exception of experience, these are the same qualities that mark the successful teacher, so new tutors should not be discouraged at the poverty of their tutorial skills, but rather should maximize all the resources at their disposal and consciously build those skills. Generally, new teaching assistants receive some sort of formal guidance before or during their first experiences in the classroom, and these sessions can be an initial source of valuable information about many aspects of pedagogical theory. While each center should supplement these classes with training directed specifically toward the tutorial experience, perceptive tutors early realize that much of the burden of responsibility falls on them for the improvement and review of their basic teaching skills. A review of basic grammar and current composition practice is necessary; this may at first seem redundant, but a tutor often discovers that a large amount of theoretical and pedagogical knowledge has become dormant through disuse. A complete background review is also necessary to avoid compartmentalizing the center into "specialists," a practice that decreases the efficiency and defeats the individualized approach of the center. Branscomb cites the example of the "spelling person," who specializes in this one area, familiarizing him- or herself only with spelling-related equipment and resources; Branscomb warns that "this 'specialist' approach to writing reduces the lab's ability to respond holistically to students and their writing."[5] The tutor must also become familiar with the resources of the writing center—texts, workbooks, tests, programs, and equipment.

As part of the basic review, a tutor might consult with specialists in fields relevant to the functions of the writing center. Better yet, the center director can, as at the University of Iowa, organize these preparatory steps into a formal class or can present them as a series of informal colloquia. For example, a linguist can be enlisted to discuss the application of transformational grammar to composition theory.

Once tutors reach this initial stage of preparation, they face another obstacle: their own attitudes toward the tutorial experience. These attitudes often involve major reevaluations in the way they, as new figures of authority, confront students. In order to disguise their trepidations, new tutors, particularly, may attempt to define their new role rigidly and can become inflexible in both their stance and attitude. But adaptability to each student's needs is a tutor's most important function, and, as Muriel

Harris points out, the traditional paradigm of teacher-pupil is inapplicable to the position of the tutor: "We have an ideal teaching situation. In a non-threatening, non-evaluative setting where we are coaches and helpers, not graders, we work with students more receptive to learning."[6] Each student who comes to the center already has a teacher, and while in some cases teacher and tutor may prove to be the same person, the roles should be different. The student often has fears and anxieties to overcome, and many may involve classroom experience; the tutor can perpetuate these problems inadvertently by reproducing the atmosphere of the class.

Of primary importance is the tutor's willingness to be flexible to meet the individual needs of the student. The undeniable reality of the tutorial situation is that each student's problems are uniquely his or her own and that an effective writing center is founded on one-on-one counseling concerning these unique problems. In practice, tutors will occasionally find that they repeat themselves from student to student, but the personal attention each student receives is crucial. If tutors become rigid in their attitudes or methods, they will become ineffective and perhaps even destructive, reinforcing the student's basic prejudices about the composition process. As Suzanne E. Jacobs and Adela B. Karliner point out, "the stance of the instructor should . . . be variable, depending on what the student and his paper need, anywhere from friendly authoritarian to fellow conversant to recorder."[7]

Self-preparation is only half of what the tutor must anticipate, however. The student approaches the tutorial situation with the same sense of novelty and inadequacy as an inexperienced tutor but also with some very real writing problems. While each student must ultimately be dealt with on an individual basis, the tutor can expect to confront a number of characteristic attitudes. Tilly Eggers points out the common syndrome of the student as an outsider,

> Students see themselves as outsiders: they do not see themselves as writers, not as writers in their future jobs and not even as writers in the classes for which they write papers, exams, and reports. They do not see themselves as part of the literate community, and, consequently, whatever we teach is temporary, superficial, and, at best preparatory.[8]

Similarly, Mina Shaughnessy observes that for the basic writing student, "academic writing is a trap, not a way of saying something to someone."[9] Eggers suggests that tutors must avoid being elitist in their own right. Rather, they should adopt the attitudes that "people who write are writers" and that writing is "a skill to develop, not a natural talent which some have and others have not, not a set of social conventions which they do not understand because they are not in the right group, and not as something buried on a page."[10] Once students begin to view themselves as writers, they begin to see their problems as *writing* problems, not as deficiencies in personality or intelligence. But whatever the cause of students' negative views of themselves and their abilities, the tutor's job is to help alter those views. While Bruffee suggests that students must learn to view their tutors as distinct from their teachers, he notes that "it is important to keep in mind that the [tutor] must see himself differently too," for the tutorial experience is essentially collaborative, and tutors must adapt themselves to the student's needs or they have ceased to fulfill the expectations of their role. The nature of writing is personal and subjective, and the student must never be made to feel enmeshed in the wheels of some depersonalizing machinery; the tutorial, with its basis in one-on-one counseling, affirms the personality of the individual student as a writer, and the shift from writing "lab" to writing "center" is indicative of the rejection of the pathology of error and "bad" writing.

II. Pedagogy

In addition to their own preparation and attitude, tutors must consider pedagogical matters. In the older view of the function of the writing "lab," a student was sent to correct a deficiency, a weakness measurable in terms of rules, typically the rules of grammar and usage. While much can be achieved in writing center-sponsored miniclasses that refresh groups of students on basic grammar, punctuation, and usage conventions, the individual student can seldom be dealt with effectively on a strictly grammatical basis. Rules may underlie the tutorial, but if they become the basis of it, the tutor runs the risk of entrenching the students' prejudices against what they feel may be inaccessible, esoteric knowledge. An emphasis on grammar has at any rate been proved to be ineffective; as Karen I. Spear points out, "abundant research has successfully documented the weak correlation between writing improvement and grammar instruction."[11] Current practice is to admit freely to the student, as does William Strong, "that a technical knowledge of grammar will have little or no impact on . . . ability to use the language with grace and precision. . . ."[12] In a study that helped encourage current practice, Shaughnessy observes that "so absolute is the importance of error in the minds of many writers that 'good writing' to them means 'correct writing,' nothing more," and that "error is more than a mishap; it is a barrier that keeps [students] not only from writing something in formal English but from having something to write."[13] Students must first be made to feel that they are writers and will be writers for the rest of their lives.

They can then learn why rules and conventions exist and how they work, both in theory and in practice. The tutor who presents grammar by fiat only enhances the students' feeling of inability and futility. Unless students understand that writing is a continuing learning *process* rather than something one is able to do after one has learned, they will continue to view themselves as outsiders who are stupid rather than temporarily deficient.

In the one-on-one conference, the tutor is confronted with an array of problems, and no one formula will work for all of them. Shaughnessy correctly observes that "the best programs are developed *in situ,* in response to the needs of individual student populations and as reflections of the particular histories and resources of individual colleges."[14] Tutors have two important immediate responsibilities. Students cannot be told *what* their problems are because they have been given traditional prescriptions many times; they must be led to an understanding of the *nature* of their weaknesses. How to do this, of course, must be formulated in conference with the students, considering their specific problems in conjunction with their own personal anxieties and personalities.

Second, as Jacobs and Karliner emphasize, the tutor must diagnose the student's problems correctly.[15] If the tutor is properly prepared, this should not prove to be an overwhelming task. Tutors seeing students who have been referred to the center for work on specific problems clearly outlined and listed by a teacher have the responsibility of confronting those problems. But what a teacher has marked on a paper may only be a manifestation of more deeply rooted problems. Comprehensive diagnosis is one of the major distinctions between the roles of teachers and tutors. If a student is experiencing trouble with subject/verb agreement, the tutor has the responsibility to seek the causes, which, for example, could very well lie in a basic dialectal difference between the student's speech patterns at home and at school. Similarly, a problem such as illogical reasoning may be the result of a misunderstanding of paragraph organization. The tutor must also be alert for other substantive problems which for some reason have passed undetected, such as speech and hearing disorders, learning disabilities, and the like. A surprising number of what appear to be simple errors are manifestations of quite real but subtle physical and psychological handicaps.

A final warning about tutor pedagogy involves a problem Branscomb identifies: "During the brief history of learning centers in general, their one real weakness has been . . . to substitute individual busy-work for individual teaching and learning."[16] A diffident tutor, confronted with a particularly unresponsive student and surrounded by a library of materials that generally includes exercise sheets and self-paced programs, may be tempted to send the student into a corner to "practice" alone. While exercise programs can be useful tools and produce results, they are seldom effective when divorced from the one-on-one conference. The materials do give students the opportunity to learn for themselves, but when used in isolation, they tend to compound the student's feelings of rejection and sense of being outside the composition process. However strong the temptation to substitute "practice" for instruction, tutors cannot afford to relinquish the role of guide to the student.

III. Special Tutoring Relationships

Since the majority of students who attend writing centers are composition students, I have directed my comments primarily toward the concerns and needs of this specific group, and while a tutor inevitably encounters a variety of types of students with an equally varied range of problems, writing problems are almost inevitably involved in any student's attendance at a writing center. The same standards and procedures tutors apply to composition students can be effectively employed in work with any student, as long as the tutor's response is tailored to specific and personal needs.

Students enrolled in literature courses, for example, are often concerned with their ability to comprehend a text. Many approaches are available to the tutor attempting to build up students' confidence in their reading and critical abilities, fear, rather than any substantive problem, usually being the root of their difficulties. Tutors' methods should be extensions of their work with composition students; as John R. Trimble notes, "a writer isn't self-sufficient until he has learned to think well."[17] Research into programs of heuristics suggests several successful methods for use with the literature student.[18]

Another type of student many tutors can anticipate working with is the graduate student. At the University of Alabama, for example, the Graduate School of Social Work requires its students to take a written competency test; if two or three readers from the English faculty find a student deficient in any area, the student is required to work in the writing center. With graduate students, tutors will often confront problematic attitudinal situations. Graduate students often feel demeaned by having to attend a "lab" normally associated with freshman students for work on deficiencies they may firmly believe they do not possess. Although graduate tutees may initially resent being tutored by a fellow graduate student, that equality is the tutor's best tool, since a level of intimacy is more important in dealing with a sophisticated student whose pride may be in jeopardy than it is with students who are more accustomed to teacher authority. Most graduate students are professional enough to acknowledge the realities of specialization, and once they accept the tutor as a colleague who possesses specialized knowledge that they can benefit from and the proper atmosphere is established, the actual work on the problems for which they were referred can progress smoothly and rapidly. And when their attendance is voluntary, graduate students are often the most delightful and stimulating tutees to work with, if only because their problems are often less severe than those of undergraduates, and counseling them involves more subtle problems and techniques. If tutors create a relationship that is both friendly and professional, they often experience a lively and enlightening discussion of their own field from another perspective.

Tutors may also work with foreign students. The tutor has no real need to be wary of nonnative speakers, but these students may pose problems that will require tutors to do some extra study of their resource materials,[19] perhaps in consultation with an ESL specialist. One can expect foreign students to view their problems quite differently (and for unprepared tutors, quite disconcertingly) from the usual undergraduate. Matters that are seldom problems for native speakers (such as the uses of the prepositions *to* and *of*) may confound foreign students. On the other hand, foreign students often ask challenging questions about grammar that can take tutors by surprise if they are not prepared. Many of the problems the tutor will be asked to address, however, are little different from those faced by the native speaker; therefore, as with all students, the proper rapport with the student is inevitably the most important aspect of the tutorial.

The number of other types of students a tutor can expect to see is directly proportionate to the number of services the writing center provides. Most tutors will confer with students seeking help in writing graduate school applications, preparing for standardized tests, composing letters, writing newspaper articles—the list can be endless. Tutors thus have an opportunity to expand the range of services their centers offer, and, at the same time, increase their own efficiency and gain valuable professional experience for themselves. For example, while the administration of the center is generally the responsibility of the director, the tutor usually has administrative duties. Detailed and conscientious recordkeeping can provide director and teacher with a record of the student progress, but these records can also provide the basis for a tutor's own case study research, an underdeveloped area of exploration in the profession. Also, as organizers of miniclasses or professional symposia, tutors can gain experience that can substantially aid them in their own careers.

The potentials are great for the innovative tutor; through conscientiousness and diligence, the tutor's efforts directly benefit the student, the tutor, the writing center, the sponsoring department, the institution, and ultimately, the profession.

However many tangible rewards of tutoring there may be, none of them competes with the sense of satisfaction a tutor receives by clearly effecting a change in the course of a student's academic career and process of self-discovery. Every teacher who has been in the classroom knows something of the gratification of a student's epiphany or leap in self-confidence, but in the writing center, this satisfaction is intensified by the intimacy and immediacy of the tutor-student relationship. Of all his or her responsibilities, the tutor is likely to find writing center duty to be among the most satisfying and personally rewarding, high on the list of those experiences that bind a teacher to teaching.

Notes

1. Muriel Harris, "Growing Pains: The Coming of Age of Writing Centers," *Writing Center Journal* 2 (Fall/Winter 1982): 1.

2. Gary A. Olson, "Reaffirming: Research, the Humanistic Tradition, and the Modern Writing Center," *CEA Forum* 12 (February 1982): 8.

3. Lou Kelly, "One-on-One, Iowa City Style: Fifty Years of Individualized Writing Instruction," *Writing Center Journal* 1 (Fall/Winter 1980): 11, discusses how tutors take a graduate "seminar/practicum" during their first semester in the center and work under the supervision of experienced tutors.

4. H. Eric Branscomb, "Persons, Places and Things in the Writing Center," *Writing Lab Newsletter* 6 (November 1981): 3.

5. Branscomb, 2.

6. Harris, 6.

7. Suzanne E. Jacobs and Adela B. Karliner, "Helping Writers to Think: The Effect of Speech Roles in Individual Conferences on the Quality of Thought in Student Writing," *College English* 38 (January 1977): 505.

8. Tilly Eggers, "Reassessing the Writing Center: Helping Students See Themselves as Writers," *CEA Forum* 12 (February 1982): 3–4.

9. Mina P. Shaughnessy, *Errors and Expectations: A Guide for the Teacher of Basic Writing* (New York: Oxford University Press, 1977), 7.

10. Eggers, 5.

11. Karen I. Spear, "Toward a Comprehensive Language Curriculum," *Writing Center Journal* 2 (Fall/Winter 1982): 35.

12. William Strong, *Sentence Combining: A Composition Book* (New York: Random House, 1973), xiii.

13. Shaughnessy, 8, 11.

14. Shaughnessy, 6.

15. Jacobs and Karliner, 504.

16. Branscomb, 4.

17. John R. Trimble, *Writing with Style: Conversations on the Art of Writing* (Englewood Cliffs, N.J.: Prentice-Hall, 1975), x.

18. See, for example, Gary A. Olson and John Alton, "Heuristics: Out of the Pulpit and Into the Writing Center," *Writing Center Journal* 2 (Fall/ Winter 1982): 48–56.

19. While many recent texts and guides are available, a valuable tool is Alice Maclin, *Reference Guide to English: A Handbook of English as a Second Language* (New York: Holt, Rinehart and Winston, 1981).

18 Meeting the Needs of Foreign Students in the Writing Center

Alexander Friedlander
University of Alabama

Writing center tutors are frequently ill-equipped to handle the special needs of foreign students. Friedlander, a specialist in English as a Second Language, describes how to incorporate an ESL tutorial program within the framework of the writing center. The essay includes a brief bibliography of ESL materials for writing centers.

While freshman composition teachers have become accustomed to students who appear in urgent need of intensive remediation, they are not always fully equipped to handle the continually growing population of foreign students. All too often, foreign students find themselves lumped with native speakers in freshman English courses. Their teachers soon label them "poor writers," apparently severely deficient in basic writing skills. Unsure of how to handle the situation, those teachers with access to writing centers often dispatch the poor foreigners to such a place. These students, accompanied by papers covered with autumnal shades, arrive at the center to be placed in the care of a tutor whose worst problems may have been football players who at least are native speakers of English. Confronted with a student who appears to have trouble understanding the intricacies of English, the tutor desperately attempts to inform the unhappy foreign student of the correct way to approach each and every one of the numerous errors. A few sessions like this and foreign students are usually little better off than when they first came to the writing center, having consumed but not fully understood a mass of confusing and complex information.

Pessimistic as it may seem, this scenario is often close to reality. Writing centers are not always equipped and tutors not always trained to deal with the special problems of foreign students, especially since the problems these students face are often grammatical and idiomatic rather than rhetorical. While readily able to find developmental workbooks that certainly supply ideas and help, tutors do not necessarily know how to cope with omitted articles and subject pronouns, with a lack of understanding of correct word order or appropriate word choice, or with incorrect preposition and article usage. In addition, most workbooks are not designed for foreign students and contain words, phrases, and ideas that can cause cultural misunderstandings, thus increasing the dilemma of the tutor. For example, foreign students do not always recognize common American first or last names and often do not know whether the name implies male or female. Similarly, the foreigner may not understand the cultural connotations of a certain word.

Some foreign students may be fortunate enough to attend an institution which conducts special sections of freshman English designed exclusively for nonnative speakers. But even if this is the case, many of these students need help that is difficult to provide in the classroom setting. At the University of Alabama, for example, foreign students can enroll in two special sections of freshman composition designed for foreigners; however, many students need to focus on individual problems that are more easily overcome in a tutorial setting, such as can be provided by a writing center. When students in these classes are referred to the center, two problems often arise. First, the students see their referral as punitive; for some, it represents loss of face and an implied inadequacy. Second, tutors are uncertain how to cope with ESL students; frequently tutors have never faced the unique problems encountered with learners of English. To help solve these problems, a tutorial program within the writing center can be established.

The University of Alabama program is quite simple: one writing center tutor is assigned full-time to work with foreign students in freshman English. (Budgetary restrictions have prevented additional tutors.) In addition, all students in the special sections of freshman English are required to attend the center at least thirty minutes a week. This course requirement helps alleviate cultural antagonism. Actually, to avoid overloading the tutor, only those students with the most serious writing difficulties attend the center on a regular basis; the other students visit occasionally to work on specific problems. While this scheme represents one means of getting ESL students into the writing center, what happens once they start to appear? What needs to be done to prepare for foreign students?

Setting Up a Program

Writing center directors need to be prepared for foreign students, particularly in areas of the country attractive to students from outside the United States. While there may be instances in which the influx of foreign students is so great that a separate facility for ESL writers may be the best solution, foreign students usually must be accommodated in the general writing center. In fact, foreign students should not be treated differently from American students. This essay assumes that this is the situation—that the foreign student will be referred by a faculty member or will walk in and be assigned a tutor just as any other student.

Tutors

Ideally, one tutor (or more if the number of students warrants and the budget allow) should be assigned to work with foreign students, either as part or all of his or her center assignment; students thus will make appointments to see that individual exclusively. This tutor, whether a graduate student or a peer tutor, will need training in ESL problems. In addition, the director or a suitably qualified person should be available in a supervisory position, at least at the beginning of the semester.

Materials

Obtaining materials is more problematic. While workbooks designed for writing centers are useful, as mentioned previously, there are cultural problems inherent in such texts, and tutors might spend more time explaining idioms than working on a particular deficiency. The center should stock a number of source materials designed particularly to aid ESL students. (A brief list appears in the bibliography following this chapter.) Aside from these materials, center- and tutor-developed hand-outs, based on student writing, are invaluable; and centers should create their own ESL materials file.

Funding

An ESL writing center program is dependent upon adequate funding. Unfortunately, in many centers funds are limited, and directors may have to allot part of their already strained budget towards ESL. The department within which the center is placed should be the first source of additional funds. Outside of the department, the college administration may prove the best hope for additional funding. A good case for funding can be based on the growing number of foreign students attending American institutions. (A recent *Newsweek* article suggests that the number of foreigners enrolled in American colleges may double by 1990.[1]) Center directors should prepare a thorough feasibility study, based on their own records, college admissions, and projected enrollment. It also may be possible to procure a grant from a government or state agency or from a local company associated with foreign trade.

Tutor Training

Training tutors to work with foreign students is essential because of the specialized needs of nonnative speakers. As Mina Shaughnessy has told us, tutors will find themselves in the position, first, of having "to teach features of English [they have] seldom had to think about, features whose complexity and irregularity or arbitrariness have been masked by habit, and second, of having to search out [their] students' preferences for erroneous forms."[2] For instance, we all know intuitively when to use and when to omit the article; however, when confronted with a student who does not understand why it is acceptable to say "The dogs are in the yard" but not "The dogs are man's best friend," tutors often fumble the fine distinction. (And unless tutors have been trained, terms like *count* and *noncount nouns* may be alien.) We all know that "He gave me the book which it was written by his teacher" contains too many pronouns, and we agree that "Is a pleasant town" lacks a subject. What a tutor may not be aware of is that these errors are indicative of interference from the student's native language. Without training, tutors will find themselves frustrated when dealing with foreign students.

Ideally, one or more tutors should be assigned to work exclusively with ESL students (depending upon the population of foreign students). In addition to the training all tutors receive as part of their orientation to the center, tutors of foreign students should become acquainted with the special problems they will encounter. The starting point should be an analysis of a short essay containing typical errors of ESL students: structural problems, punctuation, spelling, usage, idiom. At this initial stage of the training program, tutors are likely to be overwhelmed by the number and types of errors and, once they have at least a vague understanding of the piece of writing, are likely to undertake a remediation process of laboriously correcting every error. Tutors must not yield to this temptation.

With the resulting awareness of the complexity of the situation, tutors are ready for the next stage: an introduction to error analysis. This aspect of the training program should begin with a discussion of error analysis and first language interference. After reading articles on these topics, tutors should be given a number of typical paragraphs with varying types of errors; successive paragraphs should present increasingly complex situations. They then should group the errors into broad categories: organization and development, sentence structure, punctuation, usage, and idiom. Through their analysis, tutors must decide where to begin with the student. Tutors must become aware of which errors contribute most to the students' difficulties and learn not to correct every single error.

The next stage is to examine strategies that address different error categories. Tutor trainees should be introduced to a number of books which will prove helpful when working with ESL tutees. In addition, the training program should involve material development. Since there are relatively few ESL workbooks suitable for use in the writing center and most developmental texts inhibit foreign student progress, tutors should try to develop materials closely related to the students' writing, thus giving tutees a better perspective of their problems.

Finally, directors should ask tutors to examine an ESL handbook. One that is invaluable is Alice Maclin's *Reference Guide to English: A Handbook of English as a Second Language.* Tutors need to become acquainted with the formal terminology they will be using, as many foreign students have a solid grammar base and use terms that tutors may only distantly be aware of, such as nominative absolutes or pluperfect tense. While native speakers know their language, they cannot always explain it. Through this review, tutors will improve their own understanding and have a source to rely on when faced with awkward situations.

Two admonitions complete the program. The first has already been discussed but bears repeating: it is crucial that tutors not attempt to correct every error. This leads to frustration and confusion as the learner struggles to master a variety of structures. Second, tutors should never fake answers to questions. Tutors will be faced with situations they cannot handle, and they should not be afraid to ask questions of their supervisor. Tutors must be honest in order to retain credibility. With these two subjects in mind, the director should supervise tutors closely during their initial meetings with foreign students.

Tutorial Strategies

The starting point in remediation must be an analysis of the writer's errors. Errors are a natural part of the learning process. In the words of Heidi Dulay and Marina Burt, "You can't learn without goofing."[3] There are many factors leading to student errors, the easy cases being those of carelessness. With many foreign students, however, errors signal a lack of familiarity and competence with English. It is not that nonnative learners are stupid; rather, they write from acquired knowledge that may be based on their first language (L1) or may result from what they have learned in their second language (L2), English. Thus, when Spanish speakers write "theirs books," they are using their L1 structure, where adjectives agree with nouns. Students must be shown that they need not be ashamed of mistakes, that their errors can be seen "as necessary stages in all language-learning, as the product of intelligent cognitive strategies and therefore as potentially useful indicators of what processes they are using."[4] Remediation focuses initially on the *global* errors, those that interfere most with communication, and thereafter with the lesser or *local* errors.[5]

Prior to focusing on a particular remediation strategy, the tutor needs to put the student at ease. Rather than begin with errors, the tutor should ask students to talk about their writing, the topic itself, and what they intended to say about the topic. This discussion helps the tutor avoid the trap of telling students what they should have said and thus obscuring the students' perspective of the topic. Another procedure for the tutor is to ask the students what problems they had in writing the particular assignment. Not only does this help the students, but it also gives the tutor a better perspective on each essay. The next stage is to focus on some of the correct aspects of the paper to show the students that they *can* produce acceptable work. This groundwork prepared, the tutor can begin to analyze the errors in the paper and group them into four broad categories: organization and development, sentence structure, punctuation, and usage.

Organization

A major problem area for many foreign students is organization. This is often culturally based. Many students come from cultures where patterns of organization differ from the typical linear pattern of the English paragraph. English teachers expect to see a topic sentence followed by five or six sentences clearly developing and supporting the central idea. This paragraph is obviously linked to the remainder of the essay, providing (in theory at least) a unified coherent composition. Unfortunately, this mode of development does not necessarily hold true for other languages.

In a thorough examination of this subject, Robert Kaplan notes that paragraphs written by Arabic speakers display a complexity of parallelism and much coordination, with little subordination; however, American English teachers see this as a sign of syntactic immaturity. Some Oriental writing is developed in a circular fashion, showing the subject indirectly "from a variety of tangential views"; Engish instructors see this as lack of coherence. Kaplan also points to Romance languages where writers digress much more freely than in English, again implying incoherence.[6]

An understanding of the existence of such differences in essay development is crucial for the tutor. The realization that a seemingly incoherent piece of writing results from a different cultural perspective leads the tutor to an explanation and discussion of the English paragraph. Typically, the tutor should begin with the central idea of the student's paragraph and help shape it into a topic sentence. Through discussion, the tutor can elicit from the student the key ideas that the writer wishes to express in the paragraph. Then the tutor should instruct the student to write one sentence about each idea. At this stage, with most students, the tutor is able to focus on molding the sentences into a unified paragraph. In those cases where students still have problems in viewing the relationship between sentences, the tutor can work on scrambled paragraphs where the student must organize a group of sentences into a logical structure following clues within each sentence. This procedure resembles work covered in the typical ESL class; in the center, these exercises are done by those students experiencing the greatest difficulty.

Sentence Structure

The area of sentence structure includes sentence errors such as dangling modifiers, fragments, and overuse of simple sentences. One of the most effective pedagogical tools tutors can use is sentence combining.

Developmental workbooks usually include large numbers of traditional sentence writing exercises; with most foreign students these are of limited value. ESL students quickly learn a pattern and regurgitate it in each sentence, but are often unable to transfer this knowledge to their own writing. Sentence combining gives tutors a great deal of freedom to overcome this difficulty. For instance, they can use controlled sentences where students must use a required structure:

He gave me the book.

He enjoyed reading it. [which]

Such exercises help the student with a particular structure as well as an error typical of many foreign students—the retention of a pronoun despite the presence of a relative pronoun performing the same function:

He gave me the book which he enjoyed reading it.

Sentences can be designed to focus on any aspect of sentence structure. Tutors then can move gradually to the other end of the scale: free combining. Given a number of sentences, students may combine them in any coherent fashion they choose. This also helps students understand that sentences may be combined in a number of acceptable forms. Alternatively, the tutor can ask the student to generate a series of simple sentences on a particular topic and then combine them into a number of complex structures. A careful path from controlled to free combining helps the student with individual errors and with a realization of the almost infinite variety of available sentence types. Combining also aids those students whose writing consists primarily of simple and compound sentences. Gains in syntactic maturity are quite marked in some cases.

One problem inherent in using sentences in books published in this country is that they are extremely culture-bound. For example, one passage in William Strong's *Sentence Combining* uses the phrases "littered with refuse," "stained with lipstick," and "to bus their own dishes," all of which either tend to be misunderstood or are not comprehended at all by foreign students. When using such materials, the tutor is likely to spend more time explaining meaning than the student does writing. As a result, tutors should try to use sentences with foreign students that are as culture-free as possible, creating their own materials when necessary.

Punctuation

Sentence combining can be highly effective in helping students overcome punctuation problems as well. Practice with combining leads foreign tutees to an understanding of where punctuation symbols can be used and which are best in a specific sentence. Workbooks are valuable, although exercises based on American culture are again least effective; tutors have better results with materials they themselves have formulated. Tutors also should be aware of punctuation errors that result from L1 interference. For example, the comma in "I enjoyed the book that, you gave me" may be caused by a similar structure in the tutee's first language.

Usage

For the student who has difficulty with usage, whether this be a particular tense or the -*s* morpheme in the present tense, guided writing is invaluable. Simply put, the tutor assigns a passage in which the student must follow a specific direction: "Rewrite this passage changing 'these students' to 'this student'" or "Rewrite changing 'this man' to 'this woman.'" When these changes have been made, the student must in the first passage change the relevant words into singular form, paying attention to the form of the third person singular verbs; in the second instance, the tutee must change all words relevant to gender. The tutor can construct passages to deal with any number of problems, but the student should be asked to attend to one specific area at a time.

There are two areas that cause most foreign students much difficulty: prepositions and article usage. Unfortunately, there are no easy solutions here. It is best to have tutors work through as many examples as possible, supplying the few rules that they can to help the foreign students. A modified cloze exercise can help students with article and preposition usage. The cloze, a passage in which words are systematically omitted (usually every fifth or seventh word), should be modified as follows: instead of simply omitting articles or prepositions, students should be given a choice of three and asked to choose the correct one. The exercise is most effective when the required prepositions fit a particular pattern—all prepositions of place or time, for instance.

A writing center ESL program will not overcome every single problem students have, but it will help students gain a greater awareness of standard written language and go a long way towards alleviating the problems that nonnative speakers of English face in freshman composition courses. If writing center directors are prepared for foreign students and can train tutors who have the patience, interest, and understanding needed in the tutorial situation, they will be able to meet the needs of this rapidly growing writing center population.

A Brief ESL Bibliography for Writing Centers

Azar, Betty. *Understanding and Using English Grammar.* Englewood Cliffs, N.J.: Prentice-Hall, 1981.

Bander, Robert G. *Sentence-Making: A Writing Workbook in English as a Second Language.* New York: Holt, Rinehart and Winston, 1982.

Burt, Marina K., and Carol Kiparsky. *The Gooficon: A Repair Manual for English.* Rowley, Mass.: Newberry House, 1972.

Frank, Marcella. *Modern English: Exercises for Non-native Speakers.* Parts 1 and 2. Englewood Cliffs, N.J.: Prentice-Hall, 1972.

Kunz, Linda. *26 Steps: Controlled Composition for Intermediate and Advanced ESL Students.* Revised ed. New York: Language Innovations, 1979.

Maclin, Alice. *Reference Guide to English: A Handbook of English as a Second Language.* New York: Holt, Rinehart and Winston, 1981.

Paulston, Christina B., and Mary Bruder. *Teaching English as a Second Language: Techniques and Procedures.* Cambridge, Mass.: Winthrop Publishers, 1976.

Notes

1. "A Surge of Foreign Students," *Newsweek,* May 17, 1982, 71.

2. Mina P. Shaughnessy, *Errors and Expectations: A Guide for the Teacher of Basic Writing* (New York: Oxford University Press, 1979), 92.

3. As quoted in Barry M. Kroll and John C. Schafer, "Error Analysis and the Teaching of Composition," *College Composition and Communication* 29 (October 1978): 243.

4. Kroll and Schafer, 244.

5. Marina K. Burt and Carol Kiparsky, *The Gooficon* (Rowley, Mass.: Newberry House, 1972), 6–7.

6. Robert B. Kaplan, "Cultural Thought Patterns in Inter-Cultural Education," in *Readings on English as a Second Language for Teachers and Teacher-Trainees,* ed. Kenneth Croft (Cambridge, Mass.: Winthrop Publishers, 1972), 250–54.

19 Tutoring Business and Technical Writing Students in the Writing Center

Bertie E. Fearing
W. Keats Sparrow
East Carolina University

Fearing and Sparrow discuss how a center director can prepare tutors to work with students in business or technical writing. The major part of the essay is an outline of six skills basic to this type of writing. The authors also supply a list of professional development resources.

I. Introduction

Since business or technical writing differs enough from other types of composition to warrant separate textbooks and courses, this special kind of writing also warrants separate centers to provide supplemental instruction for its students. However, limited budgets usually rule out such a costly accommodation. The result is that the growing number of students in business and technical writing classes must be referred to existing writing centers for tutoring, no matter how unready these centers are to serve this purpose.

In preparing their centers for this purpose, directors face two problems. The first is the scarcity of qualified business and technical writing instructors to serve as tutors. Relatively few English graduate students or faculty members have ever taken a course in business and technical writing, much less taught one; and those who are qualified by education or experience to teach this special kind of writing usually command higher salaries than writing centers can afford. The second problem is the dissatisfaction that results when business and technical writing clients are tutored by instructors prepared only in freshman composition. Students become disgruntled at being inadequately tutored, while instructors become demoralized at being unable to tutor adequately.

The most practicable solution to these staffing problems is to help writing center instructors acquire competency in basic business and technical writing. Preparing instructors can be approached in several ways. One is to arrange for an on-campus business and technical writing specialist to conduct workshops for the writing center staff. Another is to hire (if funds are available) an off-campus authority in business and technical writing to conduct the workshops. A third is to ask the nearest chapter of the Society for Technical Communication for assistance; part of STC's mission is to assist educational institutions plan and carry out programs. (The national office of STC, whose address is given in the second part of this essay, will be happy to provide the address and phone numbers of local chapters.) A fourth option—and perhaps the best for the continued success of the program—is for directors to equip themselves to conduct the workshops.

The purpose of Parts II and III of this essay is to offer guidance for directors who must train themselves to conduct both initial and follow-up workshops. Part II contains brief discussions of six representative writing skills (and sources relevant to them) which should enable directors to conduct initial workshops about key needs of business and technical writing students. Part III, a list of professional development resources, identifies opportunities for directors who wish to conduct follow-up workshops in more advanced business and technical writing skills.

II. Basic Skills

The six fundamental business and technical writing skills explained here are simple diction, economy, appropriate voice, parallelism, emphasis, and paragraph length. Although these subjects are usually taught in freshman composition, the following discussions explain and illustrate how they differ in business and technical writing.

Simple Diction

To achieve its purpose of presenting information "accurately and efficiently," business and technical writing must be as clear, concise, and easy to understand as possible. Yet the ideal is not always the reality. A recent survey reports that technical proposals are seriously and regularly flawed by foggy language and gobbledygook.[1] The chief culprit is word choice. If "absolute clarity at first, rapid reading"[2] is a hallmark of good business and technical writing, as Fred MacIntosh says, then the first step toward that instant clarity is plain and simple language.

Indoctrinated as they are by their disciplines, business and technical students often err in selecting the impressive over the expressive word:

activate for *start, conceptualize* for *think, endeavor* for *try, finalize* for *finish, optimum* for *best, prioritize* for *rank,* and the like. Helping writers convert the complex to the simple is one of the first and easier steps to clear writing. Helping students down the ladder of abstraction is another, but not so easy, step.

Abstract words abound in poorly written business and technical documents, and since students tend to imitate what they read, they assiduously plant abstractions in their writing. Writing center instructors can help students by asking them pointed questions about their word choice: Is a *factor* a "reason" or a "cause" here? Does *formulate* mean "purpose," "state," or "develop" in this sentence? Does the verb *illustrate* ask your reader "to explain," "to give an example," or "to draw a visual aid"? Your instructions tell the reader *to join part A to part B:* should the reader "glue them," "weld them," "solder them," or "screw them" together?

Specificity is a must in effective business and technical writing, yet it brings up the question of when to use technical terms. Writing center instructors can tell students that word choice is a matter of selecting the appropriate level for the intended reader. As Ron Blicq explains, if the reader is an expert, fully knowledgeable in the field, then the writer can use precise technical terms. But if the reader is a layperson, then the writer should use more generally understood terms.[3] Gordon Mills and John Walter put it succinctly: "Just don't use words your reader won't know."[4]

Economy

To write with economy is not to write little but to waste little. Why is economy so important in business and technical writing? Perhaps the chief reason is that particularly in business and industry, where people have much to read and little time, verbose documents may not be read. Since the busy reader always wants each memo, letter, or report to be as concise as possible, the business and technical writer should take pains to make every word count.

The findings of a recent study suggest, however, that despite declarations in favor of directness, general composition teachers are likely to reward papers with inflated prose and to equate prolixity with good writing.[5] In view of these findings, when students from business and technical writing classes seek advice from instructors with traditional training, they are not likely to receive much help. Only if instructors really appreciate economy and are prepared to teach general and specific ways of achieving it can they provide the needed tutorial assistance.

A recent text, *Communicating through Letters and Reports,* provides general guidelines for economical writing: (1) eliminate unnecessary ideas from early drafts, and (2) revise later drafts to remove deadwood phrases.[6] Unnecessary ideas are those the reader already knows:

BEFORE:	In reply to your recent letter in which you request an adjustment for the damaged trees you ordered from us, I am pleased to report that we are refunding fifty percent of the purchase price.
AFTER:	We are refunding fifty percent of the purchase price as an adjustment for the damaged trees. (Reduced 46 percent)

Other unnecessary ideas are those that do not need to be stated if they can be implied:

BEFORE:	I have studied the problem and have concluded that I can solve it.
AFTER:	I can solve the problem. (Reduced 38 percent)

Deadwood phrases are expressions that add nothing to content: *at this point in time, in the judgment of Dr. Maier, costs a total of $5,* and *for the purpose of viewing the.* With the deadwood removed, these ideas can be expressed as *now, Dr. Maier thinks, costs $5,* and *for viewing the.*

Michael Adelstein explains specific ways to achieve economy.[7] Among these are:

1. Reduce adjectival clauses:

WORDY:	Salaries which are paid to teachers comprise 80 percent of the school budget.
REDUCED:	Teachers' salaries comprise 80 percent of the school budget. (Reduced 33 percent)

2. Eliminate expletive sentence openers:

WORDY:	There are many theories to explain stock market fluctuations.
ECONOMICAL:	Many theories explain market fluctuations. (Reduced 33 percent)

3. Simplify sentence structure:

WORDY:	As you realize is natural in these situations, production costs have increased since estimates were prepared.
SIMPLIFIED:	Naturally, production costs have increased since estimates were prepared. (Reduced 44 percent)

4. Factor out repeated or similar words:

WORDY:	The manager was an aggressive, domineering, and caustic person.

      FACTORED: The manager was aggressive, domineering, and caustic. (Reduced 22 percent)

5. Replace *-ion* nouns:
   accusation—charge
   commiseration—pity
   remuneration—pay
   termination—end
   transcription—copy

In teaching economy, however, the writing center instructor should distinguish between brevity and economy. Brevity refers to shortness; a brief document often sacrifices completeness, clarity, vividness, and courtesy. On the other hand, economy refers to eliminating waste. Business and technical writing is not necessarily brief, but to be effective it must be economical.

Appropriate Voice

Conventional textbooks are quick to point out the undesirability of the passive as opposed to the active voice: it distorts proper emphases by inverting normal syntax and emphasizing the receiver instead of the doer of the action; it often detracts from forcefulness, vividness, and clarity by not identifying the actor; and it usually involves more words. Even when books note that the passive has its uses, they often do so only with grudging generalizations. In their panegyric to the active voice, for example, Strunk and White allow that writers need not "entirely discard" the passive, conceding (almost sadly) that it is "sometimes necessary."[8]

Because the passive is overused, these warnings serve a purpose. However, since certain functions justify the passive, business and technical writers should understand that it offers them flexibility. Thus, writing center instructors must be able to develop this understanding in their clients by explaining the special situations when the passive is appropriate.

As *Communicating through Letters and Reports* notes, the passive is often desirable in refusing claim adjustments.[9] When giving the reasons for refusals, letter writers using the active voice may sound as though they are accusing or belittling the reader: "You failed to add the oil before cranking the engine." Using the impersonal passive can reduce the offensiveness: "The oil was not added before the engine was cranked."

Other situations in which the passive may be helpful are, as Kenneth Houp and Thomas Pearsall explain, in emphasizing the result instead of the process ("The hogsheads are transported to the pick-up station by conveyer belt") and in emphasizing the action rather than the actor ("The most symmetrical music was composed by Vivaldi").[10] Moreover, the passive also serves effectively when the subject is obvious or unknown ("The plane was piloted safely through the storm") and when the harshness of imperatives should be avoided ("Time for a coffee break should not be taken until 10:30").[11]

Yet, as several authors have cautioned, using the passive to suggest scientific objectivity may not be appropriate, even though some company officials, journal editors, and dissertation committees insist that writers use it for this purpose.[12] Sound research, defensible facts, and valid inferences—but not the impersonality of the passive voice—result in credible reporting. Business and technical writers should know that the use of the passive to create an air of just-the-facts may result in dull, stilted communications.

Parallelism

Parallelism, or the use of similar grammatical structures for similar ideas, serves the same purposes in business and technical writing that it does in conventional writing: it lends clarity, consistency, and thriftiness to the ideas being expressed. It lends these qualities to outlines, comparisons and contrasts, items in series, and constructions involving correlative conjunctions.

However, as Charles Brusaw, Gerald Alred, and Walter Oliu explain, parallelism serves in a number of special business and technical writing situations as well: it clarifies and regularizes tables of contents, headings and captions, lists or enumerations, and instructions.[13] In fact, its applications in business and technical writing are so numerous that its use may at first seem excessive to writers who have been taught to avoid monotony and prefer structural variety. It is, therefore, a skill that writing center instructors should be able to justify and teach to business and technical writing students.

In tables of contents (and in lists of figures), parallelism serves as it does in outlining. Besides enabling readers to move quickly from one point to another, it points up "the relative value of each item."[14] Textual headings are especially useful in reports and résumés. As Raymond Lesikar observes, parallel textual headings in these documents not only emphasize the relativity of the parts but also, because of their orderliness, improve the appearance of the contents.[15] In a similar vein, keeping visual aid captions parallel with one another helps readers understand the contents of tables or figures without delay and relate them to the appropriate text, as Nell Ann Pickett and Ann Laster suggest.[16] Brusaw, Alred, and Oliu observe that listing or enumerating specific items helps readers comprehend key ideas, as in setting forth criteria for decision making.[17] However, if the relative importance of each point is to be easily understood, all items in the list should have parallel structure.

Success in writing instructions, directions, and procedural manuals—among the principal tasks of technical writers—depends largely upon simplifying and clarifying the process for readers. A proven way of simplifying and clarifying a process is by dividing it into numbered steps, each an imperative: "*Third,* tighten the bolt with the lug wrench." Changing the syntax from one step to another can distract or confuse readers and interfere with comprehension, whereas using parallel structures lets readers move easily, methodically, and quickly through each step of the instructions. In discussing parallelism, Winston Weathers writes: "Style is the art of choosing, and one of our tasks, as writers and teachers of writing, is to identify as many compositional choices as possible. Our comprehension—and practice—of style improves as we organize verbal locutions and constructions into areas of choice and indicate how the choice within any given area is to be made."[18] Because the functions of parallelism in business and technical writing are so numerous, explaining this verbal construction of choice is an important means of improving the style of business and technical prose.

Emphasis

Failure to stress important points and to place those points in emphatic positions are weaknesses in business and technical writing. Writing center instructors can teach two approaches to increase emphasis: rhetorical techniques and mechanical devices.

Rhetorical techniques for emphasizing key points are prominent position, economy, vigorous words, and sentence structure. Busy readers of business and technical documents expect the main points in the most prominent position: the beginning. Therefore, key paragraphs should come first in a report, key sentences first in a paragraph, and key words first in a sentence. However, important points may also be reemphasized last in a report, paragraph, and sentence. Economy is a second technique for emphasis. As suggested earlier, too often important material is obscured by a mass of detail; clear up unnecessary detail—and points will stand out. Short paragraphs, short sentences, and short, concrete words highlight information. Deborah Andrews and Margaret Blickle advise: "Generally, complex matters should be assigned to short sentences; easy matters to longer ones."[19] Finally, along with compact sentences, both parallel structure and active voice help to emphasize key points by presenting these points methodically and forcefully.

Rarely touched upon in freshman composition is the use of mechanical devices for emphasis: typography, textual headings, and enumeration. Writing center personnel can show students how to emphasize key points typographically by using underlining, italics, small capitals, large capitals, italic large capitals, boldface, and large and small capitals. Headings not only highlight important materials, but also visually outline the content of a report and indicate the sequence of its divisions. When differentiated by typography and indentation to show degree, headings and subheadings help readers see the hierarchical relationships among the parts of a report and zero in on needed information. Enumeration, the third mechanical device, gives the writer yet another means for highlighting important material. As Don Testa advises, each item listed should be surrounded by white space and should begin with a bullet (●), a block (■), or a flag (▶) to designate divisions or with a number to indicate order.[20]

The following summary illustrates the principles of emphasis:

> To highlight important points in a technical document, the writer should consider using a combination of rhetorical techniques and mechanical devices:
> 1. Rhetorical techniques
>   * Prominent position
>   * Economy
>   * Vigorous words
>   * Sentence structure
> 2. Mechanical devices
>   * Typography
>   * Headings
>   * Enumeration

Paragraph Length

Lack of paragraph development is one of the most frequent complaints of freshman composition instructors. Almost the opposite is true in business and technical writing classes, where students are urged to chunk information into bite-size, easy-to-read paragraphs. Again, conserving the reader's time and increasing readability are prime considerations. If, as Andrews and Blickle state, complex material should be cast in short sentences and simple material in longer sentences, then the same rule holds true for paragraph development. Short paragraphs stand out; and, by attracting attention, increase readability and emphasis of important material.

There are instances, however, when writers erroneously assume that the nature of the material necessitates longer paragraphs. The following paragraph illustrates how lengthiness obscures clarity:

> Ideally, you want a car dealer who performs reliable service and who offers fair prices. There are several precautions you can take. Look at a dealer's service area. It should be two to three times the size of the showroom. If not, the dealer is not serious about repairs. Check around for diagnostic equipment, such as an engine oscilloscope that can take expensive guesswork out of repairs. You want a

shop the dealer has spent a lot of money to equip properly. Make price comparisons among several dealers. The difference can save you money on repair and maintenance bills. Ask friends and relatives about the service their dealers give. Personal testimony is among the best of guarantees. If a dealer consistently gets a high rating, then buy whatever kind of car that dealer sells. Finally, don't do business with a dealer who misleads you during the selling process. Unethical salesmen usually mean unethical repairmen.

Although not complex in content, the paragraph is cumbersome, burying important material in continuous lines unrelieved by white space. A key service the writing center staff can render is to show basic business and technical writing students how to emphasize important information by "subparagraphing." According to Blicq,[21] subparagraphing "offers a useful way to maintain continuity through a series of points that are only partly related, and to draw attention to specific items." This advice can be used to revise the paragraph:

Ideally, you want a car dealer who performs reliable service and who offers fair prices. There are several precautions you can take:

1. Look at a dealer's service area. It should be two to three times the size of the showroom. If not, the dealer is not serious about repairs.
2. Check around for diagnostic equipment, such as an engine oscilloscope, that can take expensive guesswork out of repairs. You want a shop the dealer has spent a lot of money to equip properly.
3. Make price comparisons among several dealers. The difference can save you money on repair and maintenance bills.
4. Ask friends and relatives about the service of their car dealers. Personal testimony is among the best of guarantees. If a dealer consistently gets a high rating, then buy whatever kind of car that dealer sells.

Finally, don't do business with a dealer who misleads you during the selling process. Unethical salesmen usually mean unethical repairmen.

The revised paragraph illustrates each of the six basic skills of effective business and technical writing. Simple diction, economy, appropriate voice, parallelism, emphasis, and short paragraphs help to present information in a clear, concise, easy-to-understand manner.

III. Professional Development Resources

The following compilation of professional development resources in business and technical writing is divided into three areas: summer institutes, journals, and books. By attending a summer institute and reading journals and books, writing center directors should be able to conduct staff workshops on other special business and technical writing skills as well as on more advanced topics such as special forms and formats, audience analysis and accommodation, and visual aids.

Summer Institutes

Institute in Technical Communication (Southeastern Conference on English in the Two-Year College). Nell Ann Pickett, English Department, Hinds Junior College, Raymond, Mississippi 39154. (1984)

Teaching Technical and Professional Communication. Conference Coordinator, Department of Humanities, College of Engineering, University of Michigan, Ann Arbor, Michigan 48109.

Teaching Technical and Professional Communication. Offices of Continuing Studies and Special Programs, P.O. Box 1892, Rice University, Houston, Texas 77001.

Teaching Technical and Professional Writing. Director, Scientific and Technical Communication, 14 Loew Hall, University of Washington, Seattle, Washington 98195.

Teaching Technical and Professional Writing Workshop. School of Continuing Education, Old Dominion University, Norfolk, Virginia 23508.

Technical Writing Institute for Teachers. Technical Writing Institute, Division of Continuing Education, Rennselaer Polytechnic Institute, Troy, New York 12181.

University of Minnesota Institute in Technical Communication: Advanced Seminar for Teachers. Department of Rhetoric, 1364 Eckles Avenue, University of Minnesota, St. Paul, Minnesota 55108.

Journals

ABCA Bulletin and *Journal of Business Communication,* published by the American Business Communication Association, University of Illinois, 608 South Sixth Street, Urbana, Illinois 61801. Dues, $30.

Journal of Technical Writing and Communication, published by Baywood Publishing Company, Farmingdale, New York 11735. Subscription, $50 (institution), $24 (individual).

Teaching English in the Two-Year College, published by the National Council of Teachers of English, 1111 Kenyon Rd., Urbana, Ill., 61801. Subscription, $15.

Technical Communication, published by the Society for Technical Communication, 815 Fifteenth Street, NW, Washington, D.C., 20005. Dues, $40, nonmember subscription $23.

The Technical Writing Teacher, published by the Rhetoric Department at the University of Minnesota for the Associated Teachers of Technical Writing. Send membership dues to Nell Ann Pickett, English Department, Hinds Junior College, Raymond, Mississippi 39154. Dues, $12.

Books

Anderson, Paul, ed. *Teaching Technical Writing: Teaching Audience Analysis.* Morehead, Ky.: Association of Teachers of Technical Writing, 1980.

Cunningham, Donald H., and Herman A. Estrin, eds. *The Teaching of Technical Writing.* Urbana, Ill.: National Council of Teachers of English, 1975.

Douglas, George H., ed. *The Teaching of Business Communication.* Champaign, Ill.: American Business Communication Association, 1978.

Harris, John S., ed. *Teaching Technical Writing: Training Teachers of Technical Writing.* Morehead, Ky.: Association of Teachers of Technical Writing, forthcoming.

Pearsall, Thomas E. *Teaching Technical Writing: Methods for College Teachers.* Washington, D. C.: Society for Technical Communication, 1977.

Sawyer, Thomas M., ed. *Technical and Professional Communication: Teaching in the Two-year College, Four-year College, Professional School.* Ann Arbor, Mich.: Professional Communication Press, 1977.

Sparrow, W. Keats, and Nell Ann Pickett, eds. *Technical and Business Communication in Two-year Programs.* Urbana, Ill.: National Council of Teachers of English, 1983.

Stevenson, Dwight W., ed. *Courses, Components, and Exercises in Technical Communication.* Urbana, Ill.: National Council of Teachers of English, 1981.

Whitburn, Merrill, ed. *Teaching Technical Writing: First Day in the Technical Writing Course.* Morehead, Ky.: Association of Teachers of Technical Writing, 1980.

Notes

1. Fred H. MacIntosh, "How Good Is Our Product? Feedback from Industry, Government, the Armed Forces, and Research" (Paper delivered to Advanced Composition Section, South Atlantic Modern Language Association Annual Convention, Atlanta, November 1979).

2. Fred H. MacIntosh, "Writing for the World's Work," *Teaching English in the Two-year College* 2 (1975): 9.

3. Ron S. Blicq, *Technically—Write!,* 2nd ed. (Englewood Cliffs, N.J.: Prentice-Hall, 1981), 17. For an excellent analysis of the five levels of audience, see Thomas E. Pearsall, *Audience Analysis for Technical Writing* (Beverly Hills: Glencoe, 1981), xii–xiii.

4. Gordon H. Mills and John A. Walter, *Technical Writing,* 3rd ed. (New York: Holt, Rinehart and Winston, 1970), 25.

5. Rosemary L. Hake and Joseph M. Williams, "Style and Its Consequences: Do as I Do, Not as I Say," *College English* 43 (1981): 433–51.

6. C. W. Wilkinson, Peter B. Clarke, and Dorothy Colby Menning Wilkinson, *Communicating through Letters and Reports,* 7th ed. (Homewood, Ill.: Irwin, 1980), 36–38.

7. Michael E. Adelstein, *Contemporary Business Writing* (New York: Random House, 1971), 139–54.

8. William Strunk, Jr., and E. B. White, *The Elements of Style,* 3rd ed. (New York: Macmillan, 1979), 18.

9. Wilkinson, Clarke, and Wilkinson, 212.

10. Kenneth W. Houp and Thomas E. Pearsall, *Reporting Technical Information,* 4th ed. (Beverly Hills: Glencoe, 1980), 127–28, 171–72.

11. Adelstein, 172–77.

12. See, for example, Houp and Pearsall, 172.

13. Charles T. Brusaw, Gerald J. Alred, and Walter E. Oliu, *The Business Writer's Handbook,* 2nd ed. (New York: St. Martin's, 1982), 411–15, 428–29, 438–39.

14. *Ibid.,* 428–29.

15. Raymond V. Lesikar, *Basic Business Communication,* Revised ed. (Homewood, Ill.: Irwin, 1982), 241–49, 441–43.

16. Nell Ann Pickett and Ann A. Laster. *Technical English: Writing, Reading, and Speaking,* 3rd ed. (New York: Harper and Row, 1980), 433.

17. Brusaw, Alred, and Oliu, 335–36.

18. Winston Weathers, "The Rhetoric of the Series," *College Composition and Communication* 17 (1966): 217.

19. Deborah C. Andrews and Margaret D. Blickle, *Technical Writing: Principles and Forms,* 2nd ed. (New York: Macmillan, 1982), 105.

20. Don L. Testa, *How to Develop a Format for Any Publication* (Washington, D.C.: Society for Technical Communication, 1978), 16.

21. Blicq, 37.

Selected Bibliography

Selected Bibliography

Books, Dissertations, and Unpublished Manuscripts

Arkin, Marian and Barbara Shollar. *The Writing Tutor.* New York: Longman Inc., 1982.

Beach, Richard. "The Effects of Conference Feedback on Student Self-Assessing and Revising." Paper presented at CCCC, Washington, D.C., 1980.

Beaumont, Patricia. "A Descriptive Study of the Role of the Tutor in a Conference on Writing." Diss. University of San Diego, 1978.

Berdie, Douglas R. and John Anderson. *Questionnaires: Design and Use.* Metuchen, N.J.: Scarecrow Press, 1974.

Bloom, Sophie. *Peer and Cross-Age Tutoring in the Schools.* National Institute of Education, HEW, Washington, D.C.: U.S. Government Printing Office, 1976.

Boice, Robert. "Observational Skills." Unpublished manuscript, State University of New York—Albany, 1981.

Bramley, Wyn. *Personal Tutoring Higher Education.* Guilford, Surrey: University of Surrey, 1977.

Bruffee, Kenneth. *A Short Course in Writing.* Second Edition. Cambridge, Mass.: Winthrop, 1980.

Burns, Rex S. and Robert C. Jones. *Two Experimental Approaches to Freshman Composition—Lecture-Tutorial and Team Teaching.* ERIC ED 015 214.

Cooper, Charles. "What College Writers Need to Know." Unpublished manuscript, Third College Composition Program, University of California at San Diego, 1979.

Croft, Mary and Joyce Steward. *The Writing Laboratory: Organization, Methods, and Management.* Glenview, Ill.: Scott, Foresman and Co., 1982.

Davis, Ronald J. *Student-to-Student Tutoring in Selected English Language Skills at the Island Trees Junior High School.* Ann Arbor, Mich. Xerox University Microfilms, n.d., 68–1122.

Dawe, Charles and Edward Dornan. *One to One: Resources for Conference-Centered Writing.* Boston: Little, Brown and Co., 1981.

Delaney, Mary. "A Comparison of a Student-Centered, Free Writing Program with a Teacher-Centered Rhetorical Approach to Teaching College Composition." Diss. Temple University, 1980.

Elias, Kristina. "A Comparison Between Teacher-Centered and Peer-Centered Methods for Creating Voice in Writing." Diss. University of Connecticut, 1981.

Faggett, Harry Lee. *Therapeutic Values in Writing-Laboratory Relationships.* ERIC ED 103 849.

Ford, Robert. "The Effects of Peer Editing/Grading on the Grammar Usage and Theme-Composition Ability of College Freshmen." Diss. University of Oklahoma, 1973.

Garrison, Roger. *One-to-One: Making Writing Instruction Effective.* New York: Harper and Row, 1981.

———. *Teaching Writing: An Approach to Tutorial Instruction in Freshman Composition.* Portland, Maine: Westbrook College, 1973.

Goldsby, Jackie. *Peer Tutoring in Basic Writing: A Tutor's Journal.* Classroom Research Study No. 4, Bay Area Writing Project. Berkeley: University of California, 1981.

Golub, Lester S. *Computer Assisted Instruction in English Teacher Education.* ERIC ED 064 277.

Good, Carter Victor. *Introduction to Educational Research: Methodology of Design in the Behavioral and Social Sciences.* New York: Appleton-Century-Crofts, 1963 (4th ed. Robert M. Travers, 1978, Macmillan).

Harris, Jeanette. "Handbook for Writing Center Tutors." Unpublished manuscript, East Texas State University, 1980.

Harris, Muriel. "Structuring the Supplementing Writing Lab." ERIC ED 124 966, 1976.

———. "The Teacher as Coach, Commentator, and Counsellor." ERIC ED 172 223.

——— ed. *Tutoring Writing: A Sourcebook for Writing Labs.* Glenview, Ill.: Scott, Foresman and Co., 1982.

Hasselquist, Joan. "Learning-Centered Writing as a Teaching Method." Diss. Temple University, 1982.

Hawes, Lorna and Barbara Richards. "A Workshop Approach to Teaching Composition." ERIC ED 155 936.

Hawkins, Thom and Phyllis Brooks, eds. *New Directions for Learning Assistance: Improving Writing Skills.* San Francisco: Jossey-Bass, 1981.

Hayman, John L. *Research in Education.* Columbus, Ohio: Charles E. Merrill Co., 1968.

Henderson, Maurice. "A Study of the Writing Laboratory Programs in Two-Year Community Colleges." Diss. Indiana University of Pennsylvania, 1980.

Hunt, Barbara. "Establishing and Implementing a Writing Center on the College Level." Diss. University of Michigan, 1980.

Karliner, Adela. "Final Report: Conferences with Students About Writing: A Descriptive and Evaluative Study." Unpublished manuscript, Muir Writing Program, Writing Clinic, June 1978.

Kasden, Lawrence N. and Daniel R. Hoeber. *Basic Writing: Essays for Teachers, Researchers, and Administrators.* Urbana, Ill.: NCTE, 1980.

Kelly, Edward F. "To Help Them Learn." Unpublished evaluation of the Tutoring and Special Programs Office of the Academic Support Center, Syracuse University, 1977.

Kelly, Lou. *From Dialogue to Discourse.* Glenview, Ill.: Scott, Foresman and Co., 1972.

Klaus, David J. *Patterns of Peer Tutoring.* ERIC ED 103 356.

Laque, Carol Feiser, and Phyllis A. Sherwood. *A Laboratory Approach to Writing.* Urbana, Ill.: NCTE, 1977.

――――. "A Teaching Monograph: A Co-Designed Laboratory Approach to Writing." Diss. University of Cincinnati, 1975.

Lazar, Gloria. *Peer Teaching Assistants and English Composition in the Community College.* ERIC ED 130 725.

Learning Skills Centers: A CCCC Report. Urbana, Ill.: ERIC and CCCC, 1976.

Lunsford, Andrea. "An Historical, Descriptive, and Evaluative Study of Remedial English in American Colleges and Universities." Diss. Ohio State University, 1977.

MacKenzie, I.C. "The Student-Teacher Writing Conference: The Patterns of Segmenting." Diss. University of New Hampshire, 1978.

Maxwell, Martha. *Improving Student Learning Skills: A Comprehensive Guide to Successful Practices & Programs for Increasing the Performance of Underprepared Students.* San Francisco: Jossey-Bass, 1979.

Metzger, Elizabeth. *Individualizing Remedial Writing at the College Level.* ERIC ED 113 733.

Mills, Helen. *A Do-It-Yourself Kit for Individualized Instruction.* ERIC ED 064 730.

――――. *Individualized Instruction: A Shift in Perspective.* ERIC ED 090 579.

Moore, Will G. *The Tutorial System and Its Future.* Oxford: Permagon Press, 1968.

Murray, Donald M. *A Writer Teaches Writing: A Practical Method of Teaching Composition.* Boston: Houghton Mifflin, 1968.

Neuleib, Janice P. *The Writing Center: How To.* ERIC ED 159 666.

Newman, Sylvia. *The Writing Workshop: Philosophy, Form, and Function in an Elective Composition Program.* ERIC ED 124 965.

Noel, Lee, Randi Levitz and Juliet Kaufman. *Serving Academically Underprepared Students: A Report of a National Survey.* ACT National Center for the Advancement of Educational Practices, 1982.

North, Stephen. "Writing Centers: A Sourcebook." Diss. State University of New York–Albany, 1979.

Olson, Gary A., comp. *Proceedings of the Southeastern Writing Center Conference: 1981.* Tuscaloosa, Al.: University of Alabama, 1981 (ERIC ED 202 041).

――――. comp. *Proceedings of the Southeastern Writing Center Conference: 1982.* Tuscaloosa, Ala.: University of Alabama, 1982 (ERIC ED 214 164).

Perl, Sondra. "Five Writers Writing: Case Studies of the Composing Processes of Unskilled Writers." Diss. New York University, 1978.

Pianko, Sharon H. "The Composing Acts of College Writers: A Description." Diss. Rutgers University, 1977.

Reigstad, Thomas. "Conferencing Practices of Professional Writers: Ten Case Studies." Diss. State Univ. of New York–Buffalo, 1980.

Reigstad, Thomas and Donald A. McAndrew. *Training Tutors for Writing Conferences.* Urbana, Ill.: NCTE and ERIC/RCS, 1984.

Russell, James D. *Modular Instruction: A Guide to the Design, Selection, Utilization, and Evaluation of Modular Materials.* Minneapolis, Minn. Burgess Publishing Co., 1974.

Sadlon, John. "The Effect of an Auxiliary Writing Skills Center Upon the Writing Improvement of Freshman Community College Composition Students." Diss. Indiana University of Pennsylvania, 1978.

Sanders, Sara. "A Comparison of 'Aims' and 'Modes' Approaches to the Teaching of Junior College Freshman Composition Both with and without an Auxiliary Writing Lab." Diss. University of Texas—Austin, 1973.

Scanlon, Bené. "Future Priorities for College and University Writing Centers: A Delphi Study." Diss. George Peabody College for Teachers, 1980.

Schaier, Barbara, ed. *Critical Issues in Tutoring.* New York: Bronx Community College NETWORKS, n.d.

Schiff, Peter M. "The Teacher-Student Writing Conference: New Approaches." ERIC ED 165 190.

Sears, Mary. "Effects of a Student-Centered Procedure on the Self-Concepts and Writing Practice of College Freshmen." Diss. Florida State University, 1970.

See, Sarah G. *Implementing the Learning Resources Center: Who, Where, How, and With What.* ERIC ED 103 830.

Shaughnessy, Mina P. *Errors and Expectations: A Guide for the Teacher of Basic Writing.* New York: Oxford University Press, 1977.

Shouse, Claude. "The Writing Laboratory in Colleges and Universities." Diss. University of Southern California, 1953.

Smith, Mark. *Peer Tutoring in a Writing Workshop.* Ann Arbor, Mich.: Xerox University Microfilms, 76–9320, 1975.

Stafford, William. *Writing the Australian Crawl: Views on the Writer's Vocation.* Ann Arbor: University of Michigan Press, 1978.

Steward, Joyce. *The Writing Laboratory at the University of Wisconsin— Madison: A Handbook.* Madison: University of Wisconsin, 1979.

—— and Mary Croft. *The Writing Laboratory: Organization, Management, and Methods.* Glenview, Ill.: Scott, Foresman and Co., 1982.

Tomlinson, Barbara. *A Study of the Effectiveness of Individualized Writing Lab Instruction for Students in Remedial Freshman Composition.* ERIC ED 108 241.

Van Dalen, D. B. *Understanding Educational Research: An Introduction.* Fourth edition. New York: McGraw Hill, 1978.

Wheeler, Thomas C. *The Great American Writing Block: Causes and Cures of the New Illiteracy.* New York: Penguin, 1980.

Wood, Nancy V. "Handbook for Writing Tutors." Unpublished manuscript, University of Texas at El Paso, n.d.

——. *Selecting Effective Peer Tutors.* ERIC ED 154 372.

Articles in Anthologies, Journals, and Proceedings:

Almasy, Rudolph. "Instructional Materials for the Writing Laboratory." *College Composition and Communication,* 27 (Dec. 1976), 400–403.

———. "The Nature of Writing-Laboratory Instruction for the Developing Student." In *Tutoring Writing: A Sourcebook for Writing Labs.* Ed. Muriel Harris. Glenview, Ill.: Scott, Foresman and Co., 1982, 13–20.

Amigone, Grace. "Writing Lab Tutors: Hidden Messages That Matter." *Writing Center Journal,* 2, No. 2 (1982), 24–29.

Arbur, Rosemarie. "The Student-Teacher Conference." *College Composition and Communication,* 28 (Dec. 1977), 338–342.

Arfken, Deborah. "A Peer-Tutor Staff: Four Crucial Aspects." In *Tutoring Writing: A Sourcebook for Writing Labs.* Ed. Muriel Harris. Glenview, Ill.: Scott, Foresman and Co., 1982, 111–122.

Arkin, Marian. "Training Writing Center Tutors: Issues and Approaches." In *New Directions for Learning Assistance: Improving Writing Skills.* Eds. Thom Hawkins and Phyllis Brooks. San Francisco: Jossey-Bass, 1981.

———. "Using the Journal and Case Study to Train Writing Peer Tutors." *Teaching English in the Two-Year College,* 9, No. 2 (1983), 129–134.

Bamberg, Betty. "The Writing Lab and the Composition Class: A Fruitful Collaboration." In *Tutoring Writing: A Sourcebook for Writing Labs.* Ed. Muriel Harris. Glenview, Ill.: Scott, Foresman and Co., 1982, 179–185.

Bannister, Linda. "Peer Tutor Training: An Ongoing Process." In *Proceedings of the Southeastern Writing Center Conference: 1982.* Comp. Gary A. Olson. Tuscaloosa, Ala.: University of Alabama, 1982 (ERIC ED 214 164).

——— and Robert Child. "The Writing Lab as Group." *Teaching English in the Two-Year College,* 9, No. 2 (1983), 99–103.

Bates, Patricia T. "The Public-Relations Circle." In *Tutoring Writing: A Sourcebook for Writing Labs.* Ed. Muriel Harris. Glenview, Ill.: Scott, Foresman and Co., 1982, 206–215.

———. "The Writing Center Revisited." In *Proceedings of the Southeastern Writing Center Conference: 1982.* Comp. Gary A. Olson. Tuscaloosa, Ala.: University of Alabama, 1982 (ERIC ED 214 164).

Beach, Richard. "Self-Evaluation in an Activity-Oriented English Classroom." *English Journal,* 64, No. 3 (1975), 59–63.

Beaven, Mary H. "Individualized Goal Setting, Self-Evaluation, and Peer Evaluation." In *Evaluating Writing.* Eds. Charles R. Cooper and Lee Odell, Urbana, Ill.: NCTE, 1977, 135–156.

Beck, Paula. "Peer Tutoring at a Community College." *College English,* 40 (1978), 437–439.

———. "The Writing Skills Workshop: Not a Laboratory." *Teaching English in the Two-Year College,* 2 (Winter 1976), 99–100.

———, Thom Hawkins, and Marcia Silver. "Training and Using Peer Tutors." *College English,* 40 (Dec. 1978), 432–449.

Bell, Elizabeth. "The Peer Tutor: The Writing Center's Most Valuable Resource." *Teaching English in the Two-Year College,* 9, No. 2 (1983), 141–144.

Brannon, Lil. "On Becoming a More Effective Tutor." In *Tutoring Writing: A Sourcebook for Writing Labs.* Ed. Muriel Harris. Glenview, Ill.: Scott, Foresman and Co., 1982, 105–110.

Branscome, Eric. "Persons, Places and Things in the Writing Center." *Writing Lab Newsletter,* 6, No. 3 (1981), 3.

Brostoff, Anita. "An Approach to Conferencing." *Writing Lab Newsletter,* 4 (March 1980), 7–8.

——. "The Writing Conference: Foundations." In *Tutoring Writing: A Sourcebook for Writing Labs.* Ed. Muriel Harris. Glenview, Ill.: Scott, Foresman and Co., 1982, 21–26.

Bruffee, Kenneth A. "The Brooklyn Plan: Attaining Intellectual Growth through Peer-Grouping Tutoring." *Liberal Education,* 64 (Dec. 1978), 447–468.

——. "Collaborative Learning: Some Practical Models." *College English,* 34 (Feb. 1973), 634–643.

——. "Staffing and Operating Peer-Tutoring Writing Centers." In *Basic Writing: Essays for Teachers, Researchers, and Administrators.* Eds. Lawrence N. Kasden and Daniel R. Hoeber. Urbana, Ill.: NCTE, 1980, 141–149.

——. "Training and Using Peer Tutors." *College English,* 40 (Dec. 1978), 432–433.

——. "Two Related Issues in Peer Tutoring: Program Structure and Tutoring Training." *College Composition and Communication,* 32 (Feb. 1980), 76–80.

Budz, Judith and Terry Grabar. "Tutorial versus Classroom in Freshman English." *College English,* 37 (March 1976), 654–656.

Butler, John. "Remedial Writers: The Teacher's Job as Corrector of Papers." *College Composition and Communication,* 31 (Oct. 1980), 270–277.

Carnicelli, Thomas A. "The Writing Conference: A One-to-One Conversation." In *Eight Approaches to Teaching Composition.* Eds. Timothy R. Donovan and Ben W. McClelland. Urbana, Ill.: NCTE, 1980, 101–131.

Castlelucci, Marry Ann F. "Some Thoughts and Reminiscences on How a Faculty-Centered Skills Center Became a Peer Tutoring Program." *Writing Lab Newsletter,* 111, No. 3 (November 1983), 1–2.

Clark, Cheryl and Phyllis A. Sherwood. "A Tutoring Dialogue: From Workshop to Session." *Writing Center Journal,* 1, No. 2 (1981), 26–32.

Clark, Irene. "Dialogue in the Lab Conference: Script Writing and the Training of Writing Lab Tutors." *Writing Center Journal,* 2, No. 1 (1982), 21–33.

Clowes, Darrel. "More Than A Definitional Problem: Remedial, Compensatory, and Developmental Education." *Journal of Developmental and Remedial Education,* 4, No. 1 (1980), 8–10.

Cobb, Loretta. "Overcoming a Financial Obstacle: Undergraduate Staffing in the Composition Lab." In *Proceedings of the Southeastern Writing Center Conference: 1981.* Comp. Gary A. Olson. Tuscaloosa, Ala.: University of Alabama, 1981 (ERIC ED 202 041).

Cobb, Loretta and Elaine K. Elledge. "Peer Tutors as a Source of Power for Basic Writers." *Teaching English in the Two-Year College,* 9, No. 2 (1983), 135–139.

——. "A Practical Approach to Countering Student Resistance." In *Proceedings of the Southeastern Writing Center Conference: 1982.* Comp. Gary A. Olson. Tuscaloosa, Ala.: University of Alabama, 1982 (ERIC ED 214 164).

Coffman, Patricia. "There Is a Simple Answer to the Writing Problem." *NASSP Bulletin,* 62 (Feb. 1978), 98–100.

Collins, James and Charles Moran. "The Secondary-Level Writing Laboratory: A Report from the Field." In *Tutoring Writing: A Sourcebook for Writing*

Labs. Ed. Muriel Harris. Glenview, Ill.: Scott, Foresman and Co., 1982, 196–204.

Comins, Suzanne. "To the 'Manner' Born: A Rebuttal." *Writing Lab Newsletter,* 3, No. 3 (November 1983), 3–4.

Cooper, Charles. "Responding to Student Writing." In *The Writing Processes of Students.* Eds. Walter Perry and Patrick Finn. Buffalo: State University of New York, 1975, 31–39.

Croft, Mary. "A Lab for All Reasons." *Wisconsin English Journal,* 21 (Jan. 1979), 2–6.

———. "The Writing Lab: Serving Students and the Community." *Report on Teaching* (July 1976), 46–47. (No. 2 in a series by *Change* magazine.)

Crouch, Mary Lou. "The Writing Place at George Mason University." *Writing Center Journal,* 2, No. 2 (1982), 33–35.

Davis, James E. "The Language Laboratory as Medium and Model in a Talk-Write Composition Course." *NALLD Journal,* 9 (Winter 1975), 16–19.

Devet, Bonnie. "A New Tutor's Role in a College Writing Center." *CEA Forum,* 12, No. 3 (Feb. 1982), 12–13.

Dicks, R. Stanley. "Eight Suggestions to Attract More Students to Labs." *Writing Lab Newsletter,* 2 (April 1978), 1–2.

Dow, Ronald. "The Writer's Laboratory—One Approach to Composition." *Arizona English Bulletin,* 16 (Feb. 1974), 55–66.

Downs, Virginia. "What Do English Teachers Want?" *Writing Center Journal,* 2, No. 2 (1982), 30–32.

Draper, Virginia. "Training Peer Tutors: Respect, Response, Insight." *Writing Lab Newsletter,* 6, No. 7 (March 1982), 6–7.

Dugger, Ronnie. "Cooperative Learning in a Writing Community." *Change,* July 1976, 30–33.

Duke, Charles R. "The Student-Centered Conference and the Writing Process." *English Journal,* 64, No. 9 (1975), 44–47.

Dunn, James. "Review of *One to One: Resources for Conference-Centered Writing.*" *Writing Center Journal,* 2, No. 2 (1982), 40–42.

Edwards, Marcia H. "Expect the Unexpected: A Foreign Student in the Writing Center." *Teaching English in the Two-Year College,* 9, No. 2 (1983), 151–156.

Edwards, Suzanne. "Tutoring Your Tutors." In *Proceedings of the Southeastern Writing Center Conference: 1982.* Comp. Gary A. Olson. Tuscaloosa, Ala.: University of Alabama, 1982 (ERIC ED 214 164).

Eggers, Tilly. "The Problem of Change in Writing Centers." In *Proceedings of the Southeastern Writing Center Conference: 1981.* Comp. Gary A. Olson, Tuscaloosa, Ala.: University of Alabama, 1981 (ERIC ED 202 041).

———. "Reassessing the Writing Center: Helping Students See Themselves as Writers." *CEA Forum,* 12, No. 3 (Feb. 1982), 3–4.

———. "Things Fall Apart: The Center Will Hold." *Writing Center Journal,* 1, No. 2 (1981), 36–40.

Ellson, Douglas. "Tutoring." In *The Psychology of Teaching Methods.* Ed. N.L. Gage. Chicago: University of Chicago Press, 1976, 130–165.

Epes, Mary, Carolyn Kirkpatrick, and Michael G. Southwell. "The Autotutorial Writing Lab: Discovering Its Latent Power." In *Tutoring Writing: A Source-*

book for Writing Labs. Ed. Muriel Harris. Glenview, Ill.: Scott, Foresman and Co., 1982, 132–146.

———. "The COMP-LAB Project: An Experimental Basic Writing Course." *Journal of Basic Writing,* 2, No. 2 (1979), 19–37.

Fassler, Barbara. "The Red Pen Revisited: Teaching Composition Through Student Conferences." *College English,* 40 (1978), 186–190.

Fiore, Kay and Nan Elsasser. "Strangers No More: A Liberatory Learning Curriculum." *College English,* 44 (Feb. 1982), 115–128.

Fischer, Lester A. and Donald M. Murray. "Perhaps the Professor Should Cut Class." *College English,* 35 (1973), 169–173.

Fishman, Judith. "On Tutors, the Writing Lab, and Writing." In *Tutoring Writing: A Sourcebook for Writing Labs.* Ed. Muriel Harris. Glenview, Ill.: Scott, Foresman and Co., 1982, 86–93.

———. "The Tutor as Messenger." *Writing Center Journal,* 1, No. 2 (1981), 7–12.

Flower, Linda. "Writer-Based Prose: A Cognitive Basis for Problems in Writing." *College English,* 41 (Sept. 1979), 19–37.

Flynn, Thom. "Beginning a Skills-Development Center in a Small School." In *Tutoring Writing: A Sourcebook for Writing Labs.* Ed. Muriel Harris. Glenview, Ill.: Scott, Foresman and Co., 1982, 170–178.

Fowler, Carl. "The Writing Center: Stepchild or Rightful Heir?" In *Proceedings of the Southeastern Writing Center Conference: 1981.* Comp. Gary A. Olson. Tuscaloosa, Ala.: University of Alabama, 1981 (ERIC ED 202 041).

Franke, Thomas L. "A Case for Professional Writing Tutors." *Teaching English in the Two-Year College,* 9, No. 2 (1983), 149–150.

Freedman, Aviva. "Research and the Writing Center." In *New Directions for College Learning Assistance: Improving Writing Skills.* Eds. Thom Hawkins and Phyllis Brooks. San Francisco: Jossey-Bass, 1981, 83–93.

———. "A Theoretic Context for the Writing Lab." In *Tutoring Writing: A Sourcebook for Writing Labs.* Ed. Muriel Harris. Glenview, Ill.: Scott, Foresman and Co., 1982, 2–12.

Freedman, Sarah Warshaver and Ellen Nold. "On Budz & Grabar's 'Tutorial vs. Classroom' Study." *College English,* 38 (1976), 427–429.

Gallo, Donald. "Birthing a Writing Lab." *Writing Lab Newsletter,* 3 (March 1977), 1–3.

Garrett, Marvin P. "Toward a Delicate Balance: The Importance of Role Playing and Peer Criticism in Peer-Tutor Training." In *Tutoring Writing: A Sourcebook for Writing Labs.* Ed. Muriel Harris. Glenview, Ill.: Scott, Foresman and Co., 1982, 94–100.

Garrison, Roger H. "One-to-one: Tutorial Instruction in Freshman Composition." *New Directions for Community Colleges,* 2 (Spring 1974), 55–84.

Gibson, Walker. "The Writing Teacher as a Dumb Reader." *College Composition and Communication,* 30 (1979), 192–195.

Glassman, Susan. "Tutor Training on a Shoestring." In *Tutoring Writing: A Sourcebook for Writing Labs.* Ed. Muriel Harris. Glenview, Ill.: Scott, Foresman and Co., 1982, 123–139.

Goldenberg, Myrna. "The Evolution of a Writing Center." *Writing Lab Newsletter,* 4 (Sept. 1979), 2–4.

Grattan, Mary C. and Susan P. Robbins. "Content Area Models: A Key to Student Writing Improvement in Writing Center Programs." *Teaching English in the Two-Year College,* 9, No. 2 (1983), 117–121.

Griffin, Thomas. "One Point of View: The Expanding Future of Developmental Education." *Journal of Developmental and Remedial Education,* 5, No. 1 (1981).

Gutschow, Deanna. "Stopping the March Through Georgia." In *On Righting Writing.* Ed. Ouida H. Clapp. Urbana, Ill.: NCTE, 1975, 96–100.

Haas, Teri. "The Unskilled Writer and the Formula Essay: Composing by Rules." *Writing Center Journal,* 3, No. 2 (Spring/Summer 1983), 11–21.

Hairston, Maxine. "The Winds of Change: Thomas Kuhn and the Revolution in the Teaching of Writing." *College Composition and Communication,* 33 (Feb. 1982), 76–88.

Harris, Muriel. "A Grab-Bag of Diagnostic Techniques." *Teaching English in the Two-Year College,* 9, No. 2 (1983), 111–115.

——. "Growing Pains: The Coming of Age of Writing Centers." *Writing Center Journal,* 2, No. 1 (1982), 1–8.

——. "Individualized Diagnosis: Searching for Causes, not Symptoms of Writing Deficiencies." In *Tutoring Writing: A Sourcebook for Writing Labs.* Ed. Muriel Harris. Glenview, Ill.: Scott, Foresman and Co., 1982, 53–65.

——. "Process and Product: Dominant Models for Writing Centers." In *New Directions for Learning Assistance: Improving Writing Skills.* Eds. Thom Hawkins and Phyllis Brooks. San Francisco: Jossey-Bass, 1981, 1–8.

——. "The Roles of Tutor Plays: Effective Tutoring Techniques." *English Journal,* 69 (Dec. 1980), 62–65.

——. "Teaching the Basics of Language: Structuring the Supplementary Writing Lab." *Arizona English Bulletin,* 19 (Feb. 1977), 26–29.

——. and Kathleen Blake Yancey. "Beyond Freshman Composition: Other Uses of the Writing Lab." *Writing Center Journal,* 1, No. 1 (1980), 43–49.

Hartwell, Patrick. "A Writing Laboratory Model." In *Basic Writing: Essays for Teachers, Researchers, and Administrators.* Eds. Lawrence N. Kasden and Daniel R. Hoeber. Urbana, Ill.: NCTE, 1980, 63–73.

Hawkins, Thom. "Dealing with Criticism." *Writing Lab Newsletter,* 4 (Oct. 1979), 2–4.

——. "Intimacy and Audience: The Relationship Between Revision and the Social Dimension of Peer Tutoring." In *Tutoring Writing: A Sourcebook for Writing Labs.* Ed. Muriel Harris. Glenview, Ill.: Scott, Foresman and Co., 1982, 27–31.

——. "Training Peer Tutors in the Art of Teaching." *College English,* 40 (1978), 440–449.

Hayhoe, George. "Beyond the Basics: Expanded Uses of Writing Labs." In *Tutoring Writing: A Sourcebook for Writing Labs.* Ed. Muriel Harris. Glenview, Ill.: Scott, Foresman and Co., 1982, 246–253.

Hayward, Malcom. "Assessing Attitudes Towards the Writing Center." *Writing Center Journal,* 3, No. 2, (Spring/Summer 1983), 1–10.

Hiatt, Mary. "Students at Bay: The Myth of the Conference." *College Composition and Communication,* 26 (1975), 38–41.

Hill, James. "The Writing Lab: An Anecdote." *Writing Lab Newsletter,* 2 (March 1978), 3.

Hodges, Karen. "Writing Instruction in a (non)Academic University Center." *Writing Lab Newsletter,* 8, No. 2, (October 1983), 6-8.

Holmes, Leigh Howard. "Three Sources for Writing Lab Tutors." *Writing Lab Newsletter,* 3 (Dec. 1978), 3.

Hunt, Doug. "Diagnosis for the Writing Lab." In *Tutoring Writing: A Sourcebook for Writing Labs.* Ed. Muriel Harris. Glenview, Ill.: Scott, Foresman and Co., 1982, 66-73.

———. "A Five-Minute Diagnostic for Writing Labs." *Writing Lab Newsletter,* 3 (Nov. 1978), 3.

Hunter, Boylan R. "Program Evaluation: Issues, Needs, and Realities." In *Assessment of Learning Assistance Services.* Ed. Carol C. Walvekar. San Francisco: Jossey-Bass, 1981.

Jacobs, Suzanne E. and Adela B. Karliner. "Helping Writers to Think: The Effect of Speech Roles in Individual Conferences on the Quality of Thought in Student Writing." *College English,* 38 (1977), 489-505.

James, Deborah and Diane Langston. "Person to Person: A Selected List of Readings of Conferencing and Tutorials for Writing Centers." *CEA Forum,* 12, No. 3 (1982), 15-17.

Jolly, Peggy. "Funding a Writing Center." In *Proceedings of the Southeastern Writing Center Conference: 1981.* Comp. Gary A. Olson. Tuscaloosa, Ala.: University of Alabama, 1981 (ERIC ED 202 041).

Jonz, Jon and Jeanette Harris. "Decisions, Records, and the Writing Lab." In *Tutoring Writing: A Sourcebook for Writing Labs.* Ed. Muriel Harris. Glenview, Ill.: Scott, Foresman and Co., 1982, 216-226.

Kail, Harvey and Kay Allen. "Conducting Research in the Writing Lab." In *Tutoring Writing: A Sourcebook for Writing Labs.* Ed. Muriel Harris. Glenview, Ill.: Scott, Foresman and Co., 1982, 233-245.

———. "Evaluating Our Own Peer Tutoring Programs: A Few Leading Questions." *Writing Lab Newsletter,* 7, No. 10 (June 1983), 2-4.

Karliner, Adela B. and Suzanne E. Jacobs. "Helping Writers to Think: The Effect of Speech Roles in Individualized Conferences on the Quality of Thought in Student Writing." *College English,* 38 (Jan. 1977), 489-505.

Katz, Molly. "A Blueprint for Writing." *Change,* 8 (Nov. 1976), 46-47.

Kelly, Lou. "One-on-One, Iowa City Style: Fifty Years of Individualized Writing Instruction." *Writing Center Journal,* 1, No. 1 (1980), 4-19.

King, David B. and Evelyn Cotter. "An Experiment in Writing Instruction." *English Quarterly,* 3 (Summer 1970), 51-56.

Kinkead, Joyce and Jan Ugan. "A Report on the 1983 CCCC Special Session for Writing Lab Directors." *Writing Lab Newsletter,* 7, No. 10 (June 1983), 5-6.

Kleiman, Susan and G. Douglas Meyers. "Senior Citizens and Junior Writers: A Center for Exchange." *Writing Center Journal,* 2, No. 1 (1982), 57-60.

Knapp, John V. "Contract/Conference Evaluations of Freshman Composition." *College English,* 37 (1976), 647-653.

Koring, Heidi. "The Lab Library: What Goes Where?" *Writing Lab Newsletter,* 3, No. 3 (November 1983), 9-10.

Lamb, Mary. "Evaluation Procedures for Writing Centers: Defining Ourselves Through Accountability." In *New Directions for College Learning Assistance: Improving Writing Skills.* Eds. Thom Hawkins and Phyllis Brooks. San Francisco: Jossey-Bass, 1981, 69–83.

Lamb, M. E. "Just Getting the Words Down on Paper: Results from the Five-Minute Writing Practice." *Writing Center Journal,* 2, No. 2 (1982), 1–6.

Lancaster, Marilyn. "Priorities and Goals for the Performance-Based Basic Writer." In *Proceedings of the Southeastern Writing Center Conference: 1982.* Comp. Gary A. Olson. Tuscaloosa, Ala.: University of Alabama, 1982 (ERIC ED 214 164).

Leeson, Lee Ann. "All of the Answers or Some of the Questions? Teacher As Learner in the Writing Center." *Writing Center Journal,* 2, No. 2 (1982), 18–23.

LeMoine, Jane. "Overcoming Resistance to the Writing Center." In *Proceedings of the Southeastern Writing Center Conference: 1981.* Comp. Gary A. Olson. Tuscaloosa, Ala.: University of Alabama, 1981 (ERIC ED 202 041).

Lichtenstein, Gary. "Super Tutor." *Writing Lab Newsletter,* 3, No. 1 (September 1983), 9–10.

Linden, Myra J. "Dear Editor: I'd Just Like to Say That . . . : A Letter to the Editor BW Assignment." *Writing Lab Newsletter,* 3, No. 2 (October 1983), 9–10.

Lopez, Toni. "Co-ordinating the Writing Lab with the Composition Program." *Writing Lab Newsletter,* 4 (Sept. 1979), 4–7.

Lorch, Sue. "Must Tutors Really Be Nice?" *Teaching English in the Two-Year College,* 9, No. 2 (1983), 145–148.

Loschky, Lynne. "The State of Peer Tutor Training: What We Are Presently Doing." *Writing Lab Newsletter,* 3, No. 1 (September 1983), 1–6.

Luban, Nina, Ann Matsuhashi, and Thomas Reigstad. "One-to-One to Write: Establishing an Individual-Conference Writing Place." *English Journal,* 67 (Nov. 1978), 30–35.

Lunsford, Andrea A. "The Content of Basic Writers' Essays." *College Composition and Communication,* 31 (Oct. 1980), 279–290.

———. "Preparing for a Writing Workshop: Some Crucial Considerations." In *Tutoring Writing: A Sourcebook for Writing Labs.* Ed. Muriel Harris. Glenview, Ill.: Scott, Foresman and Co., 1982, 164–169.

Martin, Francis. "Close Encounters of an Ancient Kind: Readings on the Tutorial Classroom and the Writing Conference." *Writing Center Journal,* 2, No. 2 (1982), 7–17.

MacDonald, Andrew. "Peer Tutoring and the Problem of Rhetorical Superiority." *Freshman English News,* 7, No. 3 (Winter 1979), 13–15.

McCracken, Nancy. "Evaluation/Accountability for the Writing Lab." *Writing Lab Newsletter,* 3 (Feb. 1979), 1–2.

McFarland, Betty. "The Non-Credit Writing Laboratory." *Teaching English in the Two Year College,* 1 (Spring 1975), 153–154.

McMurray, David A. "Writing Contests and Writing Labs." *Writing Lab Newsletter,* 3, No. 1 (September 1983), 11–12.

Miller, William V. "Now and Later at Ball State." *Writing Lab Newsletter,* 6 (Feb. 1982), 1.

Mills, Helen. "Diagnosing Writing Problems and Identifying Learning Disabilities in the Writing Lab." In *Tutoring Writing: A Sourcebook for Writing Labs.* Ed. Muriel Harris. Glenview, Ill.: Scott, Foresman and Co., 1982, 74–83.

Mitchell, Gertrude. "Welcome Back, Writing." *American Education,* 12 (Oct. 1976), 15–20.

Moreland, Kim. "The Benefits of Tutorial Work for Tutors." In *Proceedings of the Southeastern Writing Center Conference: 1982.* Comp. Gary A. Olson. Tuscaloosa, Ala.: University of Alabama, 1982 (ERIC ED 214 164).

Mulraine, Lloyd. "An Innovative Staffing Program for Writing Centers." In *Proceedings of the Southeastern Writing Center Conference: 1982.* Comp. Gary A. Olson. Tuscaloosa, Ala.: University of Alabama, 1982, (ERIC ED 214 164).

Murphy, Marguerite. "Publicity and Success." *Writing Lab Newsletter,* 4 (Nov. 1979), 1–2.

Murray, Donald M. "The Listening Eye: Reflections on the Writing Conference." *College English,* 41 (1979), 13–18.

Nash, Thomas. "Hamlet, Polonius, and the Writing Center." *Writing Center Journal,* 1, No. 1 (1980), 34–40.

———. "Review of *Tutoring Writing.*" *Writing Center Journal,* 2, No. 2 (1982), 36–39.

———. "Writing Centers: Overcoming an Identity Crisis." In *Proceedings of the Southeastern Writing Center Conference: 1981.* Comp. Gary A. Olson. Tuscaloosa, Ala.: University of Alabama, 1981 (ERIC ED 202 041).

Nesanovich, Stella and Eva Mills. "Helping the Reluctant Student." In *Proceedings of the Southeastern Writing Center Conference: 1982.* Comp. Gary A. Olson. Tuscaloosa, Ala.: University of Alabama, 1982 (ERIC ED 214 164).

Neuleib, Janice. "Evaluating a Writing Lab." In *Tutoring Writing: A Sourcebook for Writing Labs.* Ed. Muriel Harris. Glenview, Ill.: Scott, Foresman and Co., 1982, 227–232.

———. "Proving We Did It." *Writing Lab Newsletter,* 4 (March 1980), 2–4.

Nigliazzo, Marc. "Audiovisual Instruction in a Writing Laboratory." In *Tutoring Writing: A Sourcebook for Writing Labs.* Ed. Muriel Harris. Glenview, Ill.: Scott, Foresman and Co., 1982, 147–152.

North, Stephen. "Review of *Improving Writing Skills.*" *Writing Center Journal,* 2, No. 2 (1982), 43–45.

———. "Us 'N Howie: The Shape of Our Ignorance." In *Proceedings of the Southeastern Writing Center Conference: 1981.* Comp. Gary A. Olson. Tuscaloosa, Ala.: University of Alabama, 1981 (ERIC ED 202 041).

———. "Writing Center Diagnosis: The Composing Profile." In *Tutoring Writing: A Sourcebook for Writing Labs.* Ed. Muriel Harris. Glenview, Ill.: Scott, Foresman and Co., 1982, 42–52.

———. "Writing Lab Staffs: Four Labor Pools." *Writing Lab Newsletter,* 2 (June 1978), 2–5.

Norton, Don and Kristine Hansen. "The Potential of Computer-Assisted Instruction in Writing Labs." In *Tutoring Writing: A Sourcebook for Writing Labs.* Ed. Muriel Harris. Glenview, Ill.: Scott, Foresman and Co., 1982, 153–162.

Odell, Lee. "Teachers of Composition and Needed Research in Discourse Theory." *College Composition and Communication,* 30 (Feb. 1979), 39–45.

Olson, Gary A. "Attitudinal Problems and the Writing Center." *Liberal Education,* 67, No. 4 (1981), 310–318.

———. "Averting Negative Attitudes in the Students Referred to the Writing Center." *Teaching English in the Two-Year College,* 9, 2 (1983), 105–109.

———. "Beyond Evaluation: The Teacher's Response to Student Papers." *Teaching English in the Two-Year College,* 8, No. 2 (1982), 121–124.

———. "Cliches: Error Recognition Or Subjective Reality?" *College English,* 44 (Feb. 1982), 190–194.

———. "Establishing a Writing Center in the Junior or Community College." *Community College Review,* 9, No. 2 (1981), 19–26.

———. "Intention and Writing About Literature." *Teaching English in the Two-Year College,* 9, No. 1 (1982), 35–38.

———. "Research, the Humanistic Tradition, and the Modern Writing Center." *CEA Forum,* 12, No. 3 (Feb. 1982), 8–10.

———. "The Role of the Writing Center in Writing Across the Curriculum." *Crosscut,* 2, No.1 (1981), 1–2.

———. "Unity and the Future of Writing Centers." *Writing Lab Newsletter,* 5, No. 12 (1981), 5–7.

———. "Writing Center Atmosphere: An Experiment." *Writing Lab Newsletter,* 5, No. 1 (1980), 6–7.

——— and Jane Bowman Smith, "Creating a Writing Center in the High School." *Journal of Teaching Writing,* 3, No. 1 (1984).

——— and John Alton. "Heuristics: Out of the Pulpit and into the Writing Center." *Writing Center Journal,* 2, No. 1 (1982), 48–56.

Opitz, Jane. "Saint John's Writing Workshop: A Summary of the First Semester Report." *Writing Lab Newsletter,* 2 (May 1978), 2–3.

Otterbein, Leo E. "A Writing Laboratory." *Improving College and University Teaching,* 21 (Autumn 1973), 296–298.

Petite, Joseph. "Tape Recorders and Tutoring." *Teaching English in the Two-Year College,* 9, No. 2 (1983), 123–125.

Podis, Leonard A. "Training Peer Tutors for the Writing Lab." *College Composition and Communication,* 31 (Feb. 1980), 70–75.

Rabianski, Nancyanne. "Accommodating the IQ and Learning Style of a Student Writer." *Writing Center Journal,* 1, No. 2 (1981), 13–25.

Reigstad, Thomas. "The Writing Conference: An Ethnographic Model for Discovering Patterns of Teacher-Student Interaction." *Writing Center Journal,* 2, No. 1 (1982), 9–20.

Rippey, Donald. "I Never Get No Respect . . . Or Support Either." *Journal of Developmental and Remedial Education,* 4, No. 1 (1980), 12–13.

Rochelle, Larry. "The 'Just Pretend' Room: The Writing Center." *Clearing House,* 52 (Nov. 1978), 115–118.

Roderick, John. "Problems in Tutoring." In *Tutoring Writing: A Sourcebook for Writing Labs.* Ed. Muriel Harris. Glenview, Ill.: Scott, Foresman and Co., 1982, 32–39.

Rothman, Donald L. "Tutoring in Writing: Our Literacy Problem." *College English,* 39 (Dec. 1977), 484–490.

Rudisill, Vivian and Max L. Jabs. "Multimedia for Reading and Writing." *Community and Junior College Journal,* 47 (May 1977), 16–18.

Samuels, Shelly. "Using Videotapes for Tutor Training." *Writing Lab Newsletter,* 3, No. 3 (November 1983), 5–7.

Sbaratta, Philip. "Teaching Composition in the Portable Writing Laboratory." *College Composition and Communication,* 27 (May 1976), 202–204.

Scanlan, Richard. "A Computer-Assisted Instruction Course in Vocabulary Building through Latin and Greek Roots." *Foreign Language Annals,* 9 (Dec. 1976), 579–583.

Sherwood, Phyllis. "What Should Tutors Know?" In *Tutoring Writing: A Sourcebook for Writing Labs.* Ed. Muriel Harris. Glenview, Ill.: Scott, Foresman and Co., 1982, 101–104.

Silver, Marcia. "Using Peer Critiques to Train Peer Tutors." *College English,* 40 (1978), 433–436.

Simard, Rodney. "The Graduate Student-Tutor in the Writing Center." *CEA Forum,* 12, No. 3 (Feb. 1982), 14–15.

Skerl, Jennie. "Training Writing Lab Tutors." *Writing Program Administration,* 3 (Spring 1980), 15–18.

———. "A Writing Center for Engineering Students." *Engineering Education,* 70 (April 1980), 752–755.

Smith, Michael C. "Records, Statistics, and Reports: The Writing Center Justifies Itself." In *Proceedings of the Southeastern Writing Center Conference: 1981.* Comp. Gary A. Olson. Tuscaloosa, Ala.: University of Alabama, 1981 (ERIC ED 202 041).

Solinger, Rickie. "A Peer-Tutoring Program: The Director's Role." *Journal of Developmental and Remedial Education,* 2 (Fall 1978), 12–24.

Sorenson, Sharon. "The High-School Writing Lab: Its Feasibility and Function." In *Tutoring Writing: A Sourcebook for Writing Labs.* Ed. Muriel Harris. Glenview, Ill.: Scott, Foresman and Co., 1982, 186–195.

Spear, Karen. "After They Pass the Grammar Tests, Then What?" In *Proceedings of the Southeastern Writing Center Conference: 1981.* Comp. Gary A. Olson. Tuscaloosa, Ala.: University of Alabama, 1981 (ERIC ED 202 041).

———. "Building Cognitive Skills for Basic Writers." In *Proceedings of the Southeastern Writing Center Conference: 1982.* Comp. Gary A. Olson. Tuscaloosa, Ala.: University of Alabama, 1982 (ERIC ED 214 164).

———. "Toward a Comprehensive Language Curriculum." *Writing Center Journal,* 2, No. 1 (1982), 35–47.

Spigelmire, Lynne. "Use of a Modified Heuristic Device to Teach Peer Critiquing to Basic Writers." *CEA Forum,* 10, No. 3 (1980), 10–12.

Stallard, Charles K. "An Analysis of the Writing Behavior of Good Student Writers." *Research in the Teaching of English,* 8 (Fall 1974), 206–218.

Steiner, Karen. "A Selected Bibliography of Individualized Approaches to College Composition." *College Composition and Communication,* 28 (Oct. 1977), 232–234.

Steward, Joyce. "To Like to Have Written: Learning the Laboratory Way." *ADE Bulletin,* 6 (Sept. 1975), 32–43.

Stull, William. "The Hartford Sentence-Combining Laboratory: From Theory to Program." *Writing Center Journal,* 1, No. 1 (1980), 20–33.

Sullivan, Sally. "From Thought to Word: Learning to Trust Images." In *Proceedings of the Southeastern Writing Center Conference: 1982.* Comp. Gary A. Olson. Tuscaloosa, Ala.: University of Alabama, 1982 (ERIC ED 214 164).

Sutton, Doris G. and Daniel S. Arnold. "The Effects of Two Methods of Compensatory Freshman English." *Research in the Teaching of English,* 8 (Fall 1974), 241–249.

Thaiss, Christopher and Carolyn Kurylo. "Working with the ESL Student: Learning Patience, Making Progress." *Writing Center Journal,* 1, No. 2 (1981), 41–46.

Trevathan, Debby. "The Selection and Training of Peer Tutors." *Writing Lab Newsletter,* 3, No. 2 (October 1982), 1–5.

Vandett, Nancy. "So You Want to be a Developmental Educator?" *Journal of Developmental and Remedial Education,* 4, No. 3 (1981), 20–32.

Veit, Richard. "Are Machines the Answer?" *Writing Lab Newsletter,* 4 (Dec. 1979), 1–2.

Waldrep, Thomas D. "Redefining the Writing Center: Helping Clients Alter Their Composing Processes." *CEA Forum,* 12, No. 3 (Feb. 1982), 1.

Walsh, Stephen. "Institutional Support: A President's View." *Journal of Developmental and Remedial Education,* 3, No. 1 (1979), 22–23.

Welch, George W. "Organizing a Reading and Writing Lab in which Students Teach." *College Composition and Communication,* 25 (Dec. 1974), 437–439.

Wess, Robert. "Making Connections: The Writing Lab at PSU." *Writing Lab Newsletter,* 6, No. 7 (March 1980), 4–5.

Williams, Joseph M. "The Phenomenology of Error." *College Composition and Communication,* 32 (1981), 152–168.

Wolcott, Willa. "Writing in the Writing Center: Providing Practice and Instruction." In *Proceedings of the Southeastern Writing Center Conference: 1982.* Comp. Gary A. Olson. Tuscaloosa, Ala.: University of Alabama, 1982 (ERIC ED 214 164).

Zaniello, Fran. "Using Video-Tapes to Train Writing Lab Tutors." *Writing Lab Newsletter,* 3 (June 1979), 2–3.

Contributors

Linda Bannister-Wills is a writing specialist and Assistant Professor of English at Loyola Marymount University in Los Angeles. She has directed writing centers at the University of Central Arkansas and the University of Michigan–Flint. Bannister-Wills has published several articles about writing centers.

Lil Brannon is Assistant Professor of English Education and Director of the Writing Center at New York University. She is coauthor of *Writers Writing* and coeditor of the *Writing Center Journal.* She directed the Writing Center at the University of North Carolina at Wilmington before coming to New York University.

Kenneth A. Bruffee is Professor of English at Brooklyn College in New York. Among his many professional activities, he directed the Brooklyn College Summer Institute in Training Peer Tutors, and edited *WPA,* the journal of the Council of Writing Program Administrators. He has published many articles on innovations in university education, a writing textbook, and a book on modern fiction.

Loretta Cobb is Director of the Writing Center and an administrator with Special Services at the University of Montevallo in Alabama. She has published essays on writing centers in *Teaching English in the Two-Year College, Writing Center Journal,* and the *Writing Lab Newsletter.*

Bené Scanlon Cox is Assistant Professor of English and former Codirector of the Writing Center at Middle Tennessee State University. She has presented several papers on collaborative learning at the Conference on College Composition and Communication and other conferences.

Mary K. Croft is Associate Professor of English and Director of the Writing Laboratory at the University of Wisconsin at Stevens Point. She is coauthor with Joyce S. Steward of *The Writing Laboratory: Organization, Management, and Methods* and has written articles for *English Journal* and the *Wisconsin English Journal.*

Elaine Kilgore Elledge is Assistant Professor of Education and Director of Special Services at the University of Montevallo in Alabama, where she coordinates the Developmental Education Program. She has directed developmental studies programs at various institutions and is an active consultant on educational programs.

245

Bertie E. Fearing is Associate Professor of English at East Carolina University. She is coeditor of *Teaching English in the Two-Year College* and Associate Editor of *Technical Communication*. She has published widely, including essays in *ADE Bulletin, CEA Forum,* and the *Institute of Electronic and Electrical Engineers*.

Alexander Friedlander taught English at the University of Alabama, where he was Assistant Director of the Writing Center and where he helped establish an institute for speakers of foreign languages. He is currently a doctoral candidate at Carnegie-Mellon University.

Jeanette Harris is Assistant Professor of English and Director of the Writing Center at Texas Tech University. Currently, she serves as Vice President of the NCTE National Writing Centers Assembly. She has published articles in the *Journal of Basic Writing,* the *Journal of Developmental and Remedial Education, Rhetoric Review,* and *Writing Programs Administration*. She also has contributed chapters to two books: *Tutoring Writing: A Sourcebook for Writing Labs* and *Sentence Combining and the Teaching of Writing*.

Patrick Hartwell is Professor of English at Indiana University of Pennsylvania, where he teaches in the doctoral program in rhetoric and linguistics. He is coauthor with Robert H. Bentley of *Open to Language: A New College Rhetoric* and has published articles on writing centers, composition, and other topics in a number of journals.

Thom Hawkins is a writing specialist and Co-coordinator of the Writing Center at the University of California at Berkeley. He has been writing for a decade on writing centers and peer tutoring in *College English* and other journals. He is author of *Benjamin: Reading and Beyond* and *Group Inquiry Techniques for Teaching Writing*. He coedited with Phyllis Brooks the anthology *New Directions for Learning Assistance: Improving Writing Skills*.

Peggy Jolly is Associate Professor of English and Director of Freshman English at the University of Alabama in Birmingham. She is president of the Alabama Council of Teachers of English and has published articles in *Exercise Exchange* and *Journal of Developmental and Remedial Education* and contributed to *Tutoring Writing: A Sourcebook for Writing Labs*.

C. H. Knoblauch is Associate Professor of English at the State University of New York, Albany. He is coauthor of *The Writing Process: Discovery and Control* and has completed a new book on eighteenth-century theories of the composing process.

Thomas Nash is Assistant Professor of English and Codirector of the Secondary Education Program in English at Southern Oregon State College. Previously he directed writing centers at Auburn University and Central Michigan University. Nash is the past editor of *The Writing Teacher in Alabama* and has published articles in the *Writing Center Journal, Modern Drama,* and several folklore journals.

Stephen M. North is Assistant Professor of English, Director of the Writing Center, and Coordinator of Freshman English at the State University of New York, Albany. He is coeditor of the *Writing Center Journal* and has published essays in *College Composition and Communication, Freshman English News,* and *Writing Program Administration.*

Gary A. Olson is Assistant Professor of English and Director of the Center for Writing at the University of North Carolina, Wilmington, where he also directs the developmental writing program. He formerly directed writing centers at the University of Alabama and Indiana University of Pennsylvania. He is the founding president of the Southeastern Writing Center Association, associate editor of *Technical Communication,* and has published extensively.

Rodney Simard is Lecturer in English and Communication at California State College, Bakersfield. He is assistant editor of *The Variorum Edition of the Poetry of John Donne* and has published articles in numerous journals.

C. Michael Smith is Associate Professor of English and Chairman of the English and Drama Department at Winthrop College in South Carolina. He is the former Director of the Writing Center at Winthrop. He has published articles in *Writing Instructor, Modern Fiction Studies,* and other periodicals.

W. Keats Sparrow is Professor of English and Adjunct Professor of Marketing at East Carolina University. He is editor emeritus of *Teaching English in the Two-Year College* and of the *Victorians Institute Journal.* His text, *The Practical Craft,* won the 1982 NCTE award for the best collection of essays in technical and scientific writing.

Karen I. Spear is Associate Dean of Liberal Education and Assistant Professor of English at the University of Utah. She has published essays on cognitive development and other subjects in *College Composition and Communication, Liberal Education, Teaching English in the Two-Year College* and other journals.

John Warnock is Associate Professor of English and Law at the University of Wyoming. With Tilly Warnock, he originated the Wyoming Writing Project in 1978. He has directed freshman English and the Writing Center at the University of Wyoming and has published extensively on the subject of rhetoric and the writing process.

Tilly Warnock is Assistant Professor of English and Director of the Writing Center at the University of Wyoming. She directs the Wyoming Statewide Humanities Leadership Project, a federally funded project for school administrators and teachers. She has published journal articles on writing centers, composition, literary theory, Kenneth Burke, and James Joyce.